W9-CEB-462

About the Author

LOIS DIETERLY IS an elementary-school teacher in Pennsylvania and, until recently, baked vegan desserts for a local restaurant. She has been a vegetarian for the last decade and a vegan for four of these years. Dieterly lives with her family outside Reading, Pennsylvania.

Sinfully VEGAN

LOIS DIETERLY

Over 140 Decadent Desserts
to Satisfy Every Vegan's
Sweet Tooth

MARLOWE & COMPANY • NEW YORK

SINFULLY VEGAN: *Over 140 Decadent Desserts to Satisfy Every Vegan's Sweet Tooth*

Copyright © 2003 by Lois Dieterly

Published by
Marlowe & Company
An Imprint of Avalon Publishing Group, Incorporated
245 W. 17th Street * 11th Floor
New York, NY 10011

AVALON
publishing group incorporated

All rights reserved. No part of this book may be reproduced in whole or in part without written permission from the publisher, except by reviewers who may quote brief excerpts in connection with a review in a newspaper, magazine, or electronic publication; nor may any part of this book be reproduced, stored in a retrieval system, or transmitted in any form or by any means electronic, mechanical, photocopying, recording, or other, without written permission from the publisher.

Library of Congress Cataloging-in-Publication Data
Dieterly, Lois, 1959–
Sinfully vegan : over 140 decadent desserts to satisfy every vegan's sweet tooth / Lois Dieterly.
p. cm.
Includes index.
ISBN 1-56924-476-6 (alk. paper)
1. Desserts. 2. Vegan cookery. I. Title.
TX773.D54 2003
641.8'6—dc22 2003061428

ISBN-13: 978-1-56924-476-0

9 8 7

Designed by Pauline Neuwirth, Neuwirth and Associates, Inc.

Printed in the United States of America

$\mathcal{D}$EDICATION

THIS BOOK IS dedicated to the memory of my mother who instilled in me the love of cooking at an early age, and my husband and children for supporting me and taking up the slack when I was buried in work on this project.

CONTENTS

INTRODUCTION 3

Why Vegan Desserts are Healthy *and* Delicious *4*, A Guide to Deciphering Fats *6*, How Much Fat Is Too Much Fat? *7*, Nutritional Comparisons *8*, How to Veganize Your Own Recipes *9*, Buying Vegan Ingredients *10*, Stocking Your Vegan Pantry *11*, Sources for Vegan Ingredients *14*, Suggested Kitchen Equipment *16*, Peaceful Vegans *17*, Gone Vegan? You're Not Alone *18*

COOKIES AND BROWNIES 21

Vanilla Spritz Cookies *22*, Snappy Ginger Cookies *23*, Home-Style Chocolate Chip Cookies *24*, Little Oaties *25*, Mom's Warm Peanut Butter Cookies *26*, Snickerdoodles *27*, Chocolate-Coconut Crisps *28*, I Can't Believe They're Not Sinful Brownies *29*, Death by Chocolate Brownies *30*, Swirly Berry Brownies *31*, Heavenly Brownie Torte *32*, Peanut Butter Twist Brownies *34*

CAKES AND QUICK BREADS 35

Lemon Loaf *36*, Cherry, Cherry Not Contrary Cake *38*, Chocolate Raspberry Celebration Loaf *40*, Mocha Madness Cake *42*, Nuts about Chocolate Cake *43*, Just Loafing Around *44*, Mocha Goober Cake *45*, Chocolate-Covered Gold *46*, Mellow Yellow Cake *47*, Citrus Orange Cake *48*, Toasted Coconut Pecan Cake *50*, Tropical Mango Cake *52*, You Can't Catch Me I'm the Gingerbread . . . Cake *53*, Hold the Wheat Carrot Cake *54*, Bold Banana Cake *55*, Applesauce Applause Cake *56*, Orange Creamsicle Cake *57*, Tropical Fruit Cake *58*, Granny's Cranberry Cake *59*, Chocolate-Covered Mint *60*, My Grandmother's Crumb Cake *61*, Oops, I Dropped My Cake *62*, Banana Split Cake *63*, Long on Flavor Shortcake *64*, Lemon Times Two Cake *65*, Cinn-sational Apple Cake *66*, "P" Is for Pumpkin Cake *67*, Richer than Fort Knox Cake *68*, White on White Tropical Cake *70*, German Chocolate Cake *71*, Peanut Butter Surprise *72*, Double Chocolate Delight *74*, Mint Madness *75*, Cherry Vanilla Dream *76*, Triple Cherry Treat *77*, Ten-Carat Gold Cake *78*, Orange You Glad It Has Chocolate Chips Cake *79*, Raised Sugar Cake *80*, Coconut-Covered Delight *81*, Peanut Butter Kandy Kake *82*, Rootin' Tootin' Raisin Spice Cake *84*, Cherry + Chocolate = Delicious Cake *85*, Going Nuts for Banana Bread *86*, Fruit 'n' Nut Bread *87*

BOSTON CREAM PIES 89

Chocolate Glaze Topping *90*, Chocolate Raspberry Boston Cream Pie *91*, Traditional Boston Cream Pie *92*, Peanut Butter Boston Cream Pie *94*, Triple-Chocolate Boston Cream Pie *96*, Chocolate Caramel Boston Cream Pie *98*, Chocolate Peanut Butter Boston Cream Pie *100*

PIES AND TARTS 101

Wetzel's Pretzel Pie *102*, I Love Chocolate Cream Pie *104*, Mom's Apple Crisp *105*, All-American Apple Crumb Pie *106*, Award-Winning Peach Crumb Pie *107*, Rave Review Raisin Crumb Pie *108*, Festive Apple Cranberry Pie *109*, Washington's Cherry Crumb Pie *110*, Newfangled Mince Pie *111*, Fall Harvest Pie *112*, State Fair Pear Pie *113*, Confetti Fruit Pie *114*, Beats Singin' the Blues Pie *115*, Pumpkin Pie *116*, Funny Cake *117*, Island Breezes Cream Pie *118*, Peppermint Patty Cream Pie *119*, A Hint of Mint Cream Pie *120*, You Got Your Chocolate in My Peanut Butter Cream Pie *121*, Black and White Cream Pie *122*, Monkey's Choice Cream Pie *123*, That's One Nutty Banana! *124*, Midnight Monkey Cream Pie *126*, Berry Chip Cream Pie *127*,

Pucker-Up Cream Pie *128*, Clouds of Strawberry Pie *129*, Strawberry Surprise Cream Pie *130*, Piña Colada Cream Pie *131*, Patriotic Cream Pie *132*, The Queen of Tarts *133*, Tangy Tasty Tart *135*, Fruity Artistry *136*, A Taste of the Tropics *137*, I'm Nuts for Peanut Butter Tart *138*, Just Peekin' Pie *140*, Apple Dumplings *141*, Tantalizing Truffle Pie *142*

CHEESECAKES   *143*

Caramel Apple Streusel Cheesecake *144*, New York–Style Cheesecake *146*, Three Cheers for Cherry Cheesecake *148*, Swirled Raspberry Cheesecake *149*, I Dream of Lemon Cream Cheesecake *150*, Minty Chip Chocolate Cheesecake *152*, Pumpkin Pie Cheesecake *154*, Inside-Out Peanut Butter Cup Cheesecake *156*, Peanut Butter Cup Cheesecake *158*, Coconut Dream Cheesecake *159*, Tropical Chocolate Chip Cheesecake *160*, Peanut Butter Chocolate Chip Cheesecake *161*, Black Forest Cheesecake *162*, Chocolate-Covered Cherry Cheesecake *164*, Chocolate Tuxedo Cheesecake *166*

PUDDINGS   *167*

Chocolate Lover's Pudding *169*, Guiltless Pudding *170*, Peanut Butter and No Jelly Pudding *171*, Bahama Mama Pudding *172*, The Berry Best Pudding *173*, Creamy Rice Pudding *174*, Orange Chocolate Chip Pudding *175*, Tangy Lemon Pudding *176*, Strawberry Fields Pudding *177*

DONUTS AND CANDY   *179*

Fasnachts *180*, Jelly-Filled Donuts *182*, Boston Cream–Filled Donuts *184*, Peanut Butter Balls *186*, Coconut Cream Eggs *187*, Melt in Your Mouth Fudge *188*, Raisin and Peanut Clusters *189*, Chocolate Coconut Nests *190*

BEVERAGES AND SMOOTHIES   *191*

Ain't No Chocolate Here Smoothie *192*, Orange Creamsicle Smoothie *193*, Bananas in Pajamas Smoothie *194*, Green (I Swear to God It's Good!) Smoothie *195*, Berry Delicious Smoothie *196*, Pink Passion Smoothie *196*, Caribbean Cruise Smoothie *197*, Red Baron Smoothie *197*, Rich Hot Cocoa (Single Serving) *198*, Rich Hot Cocoa (Four Servings) *198*

FROSTINGS, TOPPINGS, AND CRUSTS   *199*

Cherry Filling *201*, Cherry Topping *201*, Whipped Cherry Topping *202*,

Whipped Chocolate Frosting *202*, Chocolate Cream Cheese Frosting *203*, Vegan Chocolate Syrup *203*, Vanilla Tofu Whipped Topping *204*, Vanilla Glaze *204*, Pumpkin Whipped Topping *205*, Standard Chocolate Frosting *205*, Coffee Frosting *206*, Creamy Peanut Butter Frosting *206*, Fluffy Orange Frosting *207*, Light Raspberry Frosting *207*, Whipped Lemon Frosting *208*, Toasted Coconut Pecan Frosting *208*, Whipped Coconut Cream Frosting *209*, Coconut Cream Cheese Frosting *209*, Mega-Coconut Cream Cheese Frosting *210*, Cream Cheese Frosting *210*, Soy Cream Cheese Glaze *211*, Maple Cocoa Frosting *211*, Whipped Cream Cheese Frosting *212*, Chocolate Decorative Topping *212*, German Chocolate Coconut-Pecan Frosting *213*, Fluffy Mint Frosting *213*, Fudge Ice Cream Topping *214*, Caramel Ice Cream Topping *215*, Standard Vegan Single Pie Crust *216*, Standard Vegan Double Pie Crust *217*, Tart Crust *218*

Metric Conversions   *219*
Acknowledgments   *221*
Index   *223*

Sinfully VEGAN

$\mathscr{I}$NTRODUCTION

"Nothing will benefit human health and increase chances for survival of life on Earth as much as the evolution to a vegetarian diet"

—ALBERT EINSTEIN

I DECIDED TO become vegan about ten years ago. It was not a quick transformation—it took me about two years to complete. I have always had a sweet tooth, and the one thing that I missed was good desserts. Other than that, I loved being vegan. I loved the new foods that I was eating—kale and tahini with hot pepper sauce, TVP stroganoff (stroganoff made with chunks of textured vegetable protein to replace the meat), and veggie stir-fries replaced heavy meals like chicken with dumplings and roast beef and mashed potatoes. I was much happier. Except for the desserts. All the vegan desserts that I tried were either tasteless or dry. And all of them were very expensive. Was I destined to live out the rest of my life without indulging in a few decadent treats every once in a while?

I was born with a love of cooking, especially baking. My mother was a home economics teacher who allowed me to work side-by-side with her from the time I was very small. I was never satisfied using somebody else's recipe; I always liked to create my own. One of my first memories is making "chocolate pudding" with flour, cocoa, milk, and many other ingredients. I don't think anyone else appreciated my efforts, but I was pleased! By becoming vegan, I provided myself with a vast area in which to experiment. Since I could not find any decent vegan baked goods, I set out to create my own. I worked with recipes that I had enjoyed as a non-vegan first. I looked at creations in gourmet cookbooks and magazines and attempted to "veganize" them, and I created many of my own recipes from scratch. I found that I love to create new culinary masterpieces.

I also discovered that not only are vegan baked goods healthier for you, but they can taste delicious too! If you are like the majority of Americans, you made eating more healthfully or losing a few pounds one of your New Year's resolutions. But, as the year progresses, that resolution becomes harder and harder to keep. You see gooey candy and creamy chocolate on TV, smell buttery popcorn at movie theaters, salivate over the dessert cart at business lunches. So you're faced with either another failed resolution or a year of deprivation. Neither choice sounds appealing, but what are you to do? If only you could have your cake and eat it too. . . . Well, perhaps you can. *Sinfully Vegan* will show you how to make decadent cakes and treats that will satisfy your sweet tooth without blowing your diet or your resolution to eat more healthfully.

WHY VEGAN DESSERTS ARE HEALTHY *AND* DELICIOUS

OF COURSE CAKES and pies alone will never provide us with all the vitamins, minerals, and nutrients we need, but they can be made healthier so that indulging in a piece once in a while is not a sin. Traditional cake and icing recipes are rich in cholesterol and fat (eggs, milk, and butter) and refined sugar. You probably already know that cholesterol is not good for your body. Too much of it clogs your arteries and makes it harder for your heart to pump blood to the rest of your body. Your body produces all of the cholesterol that you need on its own—you don't need to get it from an outside source. Therefore, if your resolution is to eat healthier, you should be trying to avoid cholesterol. To quote Dr. Charles Glueck, director of the University of Cincinnati Lipid Research Center, "For every one percent reduction in total cholesterol level, there is a two percent reduction of heart disease risk."

Fat is another nutritional bad boy, although it is highly misunderstood. All fat is *not* bad. Our bodies do need some fats, like omega-3 fatty acids found in fish and flax oils and monounsaturated fats found in olive and canola oil. It's the hydrogenated fats found in solid shortenings, which make pie crusts flaky and cakes fluffy, that you should avoid at all costs. Hydrogenated fats are fats to which more hydrogen has been artificially added. Our bodies don't know what to do with this "fake" fat, so it is deposited in our arteries. Most of the recipes in this book use monounsaturated fats—fats necessary (in small amounts) for healthy hair, skin, and hearts. If a vegan butter spread is required, a spread like Spectrum, which is non-hydrogenated, is suggested. The same goes for shortening. Spectrum also makes a good non-hydrogenated vegetable shortening. You must learn to be an avid label reader in order to eat more healthfully.

The eggs that are used to bind ingredients together in most traditional recipes are also a large source of dietary cholesterol. Each egg contains 215 milligram of cholesterol, and many traditional recipes, like carrot cake, for example, usually require several eggs. If a cake contains four eggs, that means it has 860 mg of cholesterol or about 108 mg per slice! Compare this to xanthan gum, a natural carbohydrate made from a tiny microorganism called *Xanthomonas campestris*. Xanthan gum works as a wonderful substitute for eggs. It contains no cholesterol, only 8 calories, and provides 9 grams of fiber, or 36 percent of the daily amount recommended by the USDA—all in a tiny 1-tablespoon serving! What a great ingredient! Flax powder is another substitute that can be used for eggs. I use 1 teaspoon of flax powder mixed with ¼ cup water for each egg called for in a recipe. If 4 teaspoons of flax powder is used to replace the four eggs in the above carrot cake example, you would have 0 grams cholesterol and less than 5 grams of total fat, none of which is saturated (the bad kind). So now you see how much sense it makes to replace eggs in recipes if you are trying to eat more healthfully.

The milk used in most traditional cake recipes is loaded with fat and cholesterol. Think of it this way: A newborn calf weighs approximately sixty pounds. In one year, eating only cow's milk, it will grow to weigh between 300 and 600 pounds. Now that's powerful stuff! Even one cup of reduced-fat 2-percent milk still has 120 calories and 5 grams of fat, 3 of those grams being saturated, as well as 20 milligrams of cholesterol. True, it has 30 percent of the recommended daily percentage of calcium that a person needs, but compare that to 1 cup of soy milk, which can be used as a milk substitute in all recipes. The soy milk has 100 calories per cup, 4 grams of fat, .5 grams of that being saturated, and no cholesterol! And it has 25 percent of the recommended daily percentage of calcium. In addition, many studies have shown allergies to milk and dairy products can cause many uncomfortable symptoms, including irritability, restlessness, hyperactivity, muscle pain, mental depression, abdominal pain, cramps or bloating, gas, diarrhea, bad breath, headaches, lack of energy, constipation, poor appetite, nasal stuffiness, runny nose, sinusitis, asthma, shortness of breath, rashes, eczema, and hives. Milk and dairy products have also been linked to diabetes in children, several types of cancer, benign breast conditions, acne, fibroids, chronic intestinal upset, and heart disease. Do you still want milk and dairy products in your dessert?

Butter is another high cholesterol ingredient—250 milligrams per 100 gram portion with 100 percent of its calories derived from fat. It can easily be replaced with applesauce, mashed bananas, canola oil, whipped tofu, or prune butter depending on the recipe. Besides the substitution of healthier ingredients for unhealthy ones, several of the cakes in this book already include fruits and vegetables as one of the ingredients. Bananas, a fruit high in niacin, are a main ingredient in the Bold Banana Cake (page 55) and carrots, high in vitamin A, are found in abundance in the Hold the Wheat Carrot Cake (page 54) and Ten-Carat Gold Cake (page 78). Zucchini can be found in some of the chocolate cake recipes such as Nuts about Chocolate Cake (page 43) and Cherry, Cherry Not Contrary Cake (page 38). What better way to "sneak" veggies to your kids than in a cake? They'll never know it! And, remember, all is fair when trying to eat healthier!

The desserts in this book should still be viewed as snack foods to be eaten in moderation; however, they are much healthier than their full-fat, cholesterol-laden counterparts. You will be pleasantly surprised by the delectable confections you can create with these recipes.

A GUIDE TO DECIPHERING FATS

ONE OF THE most confusing aspects of reading food labels and trying to eat more healthfully is trying to understand the differences between types of fats. All fats are not created equal. Fats have gotten a bad rap in the last few years as consumers have gone from eating a lot of fat, to eating no fat, and back to eating a lot of fat again. Somewhere in the middle is the key to eating healthfully, but how are you to know? To start, you must become familiar with the major types of fat. The fats defined below are listed in descending order of healthiness. You should try to eat as close to the top of the list as you can and avoid the fats at the bottom of the list. Not only is the type of fat that you eat important, but the amount of fat is critical as well. You will find a section on how to calculate the amount of fat that you should consume and information on where to find equations to calculate your own BMR (basal metabolic rate).

- **Unsaturated fats:** These are fats that help lower blood cholesterol if used in place of saturated fats. There are two types: **monounsaturated** and **polyunsaturated**. Most (but not all) liquid vegetable oils are unsaturated. The exceptions include coconut, palm, and palm kernel oils.
  - ➤ **Monounsaturated fats:** This is one of the two healthiest fats, the other being polyunsaturated fat. Examples include olive, canola, and peanut oil. It is known to reduce the levels of LDL (bad) cholesterol.
  - ➤ **Polyunsaturated fats:** These fats are also considered relatively healthy. Examples include safflower, sesame, corn, and soybean oil. There is a special group of polyunsaturated fats called omega-3 oils that have been thought to lower LDL (bad) cholesterol and elevate HDL (good) cholesterol. Omega-3 oils are found in cold-water fish such as mackerel and herring. They are also found in plant sources, the best of which is the flax seed. Heat appears to destroy the benefit of the oil extracted from flax seeds, so I have not used flax oil in any of the recipes in this book; however, flax oil makes a wonderful base for salad dressings, which do not have to be heated.
- **Saturated fats:** These are the biggest dietary cause of high LDL levels (bad cholesterol). When looking at a food label, pay very close attention to the percent of saturated fat and avoid or limit any foods that are high (over 20 percent

saturated fat is considered high). Saturated fats are found in animal products such as butter, cheese, whole milk, ice cream, cream, and fatty meats, none of which are found in the recipes in this book. Saturated fats are also found in some vegetable oils like coconut*, palm, and palm kernel oils. Most other vegetable oils contain unsaturated fat and are healthier.

- **Trans-fatty acids:** These fats are formed when vegetable oil is hardened, through either **full or partial hydrogenation.** They are synthetically created saturated fats. Trans-fatty acids raise LDL levels, and they can also lower HDL (good cholesterol) levels. They are difficult to eliminate from the body and are a low quality source of energy. Trans-fatty acids can be found in fried foods, commercial baked goods (donuts, cookies, crackers), processed foods, and margarines. They are listed on food labels as partially hydrogenated or hydrogenated oil.
- **Partially hydrogenated:** This term refers to oils that have become partially hardened but not completely solid. Foods made with partially hydrogenated oils contain high levels of trans-fatty acids (formed by the hydrogenation process), which are linked to heart disease. Most commercially produced cookies, crackers, snack foods, and some cereals contain partially hydrogenated oils.
- **Hydrogenated:** This term refers to oils that have become hardened (such as hard butter and margarine) through the addition of hydrogen molecules. Foods made with hydrogenated oils also contain high levels of trans-fatty acids. Again, most commercially prepared baked goods contain hydrogenated oils.

HOW MUCH FAT IS TOO MUCH?

YOUR IDEAL AMOUNT of fat intake is unique and depends on the amount of calories you consume. As a rule of thumb, no more than 30 percent of your total daily calories should come from fat, with less than 10 percent coming from saturated fat. For example, if you consume 1,200 calories a day, no more than 360 calories should come from fat and no more than 120 calories from saturated fat. If you consume 2,000 calories, you should consume no more than 600 calories of fat, no more than 200 of those coming from saturated fat. Perhaps an easier way to calculate this is by grams. Each fat gram is equal to 9 calories. Therefore, in the above 1,200 calorie per day example, 360 fat calories equals 40 grams of fat and 120 calories of saturated fat equals 13 grams. You will always find fat grams listed on nutrition labels. The following chart will help you determine the amount of fat you should consume.

*While coconut oil is a saturated fat, there are claims that it is a healthier fat that actually increases your BMR. It is also thought that coconut oil is a "low-fat" fat that is converted directly into energy—like a complex carbohydrate—when digested. To read more about these studies, go to www.tropicaltraditions.com/cnolowfat.htm.

Total calories per day	Total fat calories per day (30%)	Total fat per day (30%) (grams)	Total saturated fat calories per day (10%)	Total saturated fat per day (10%) (grams)
1,200	360	40	120	13
1,500	450	50	150	16
1,800	540	60	180	20
2,000	600	66	200	22

How many calories should you be eating per day? On average, men should consume between 1,600 and 1,800 calories and women should consume between 1,300 and 1,500 calories. Many factors—such as age, height, lean body mass, environmental temperature, and activity level—can affect these numbers. If you are interested in calculating your personal BMR, here are some Web sites available to help you:

- www.thinrich.com (Thinrich.com)
- www.foodandhealth.com/bmi.php (Food and Health Communications)

The key to eating healthfully is being informed. You only have one body—take care of it. Be aware of what you put into it. As the saying goes, "You are what you eat!"

NUTRITIONAL COMPARISONS

HOW DO THE recipes in this book stack up nutritionally? Let's compare them to traditional recipes and see. As you look at this chart, keep in mind that you do not need to (and should not) consume any cholesterol. As you can see, the vegan recipes all have 0 milligrams of cholesterol, and the regular recipes have quite a lot of cholesterol, varying from 24 milligrams per serving of Apple Crumb Pie (page 106) to 176 milligrams per serving of Caramel Apple Streusel Cheesecake (page 144). Look at it this way: A 1,500-calorie diet should not contain more than 16 grams of saturated fat per day. One serving of the regularly prepared Raised Sugar Cake (page 80) almost uses up that total allotment by itself with a whopping 13 grams! And the Caramel Apple Streusel Cheesecake is way over that amount for just one serving. But fortunately, the vegan version of the cheesecake comes in at only 4 grams of saturated fat per serving, thus allowing you to indulge in this treat once in a while without ruining your healthy diet!

Food	Calories per serving	Total Fat (g) per serving	Cholesterol (mg) per serving	Saturated fat (g) per serving
Raised Sugar Cake—Vegan	656	25	0	2
Raised Sugar Cake—Regular	745	32	81	13
Caramel Apple Streusel Cheesecake—Vegan	541	26	0	4
Caramel Apple Streusel Cheesecake—Regular	551	35	176	21
Brownies—Vegan	126	<1	0	<1
Brownies—Regular	141	7	40	3
Hot Cocoa—Vegan	136	5	0	<1
Hot Cocoa—Regular	441	8	35	5
Apple Crumb Pie—Vegan	268	9	0	3
Apple Crumb Pie—Regular	440	20	24	9

= Vegan Recipes

HOW TO "VEGANIZE" YOUR OWN RECIPES

ONCE YOU HAVE become comfortable with making some of the recipes in this book, you may want to try to "veganize" some of your own favorite recipes. Here are some easy substitutions you can make to accomplish this.

You can replace any milk in a recipe with soy milk. You would use the same amount of soy milk as milk.

Butter can be replaced with a variety of ingredients such as applesauce, mashed bananas, canola oil, whipped tofu, or prune butter, depending on the recipe. The texture of the finished product will vary depending on which substitute you choose. You may want to experiment with several choices until you get the results you want. Another consideration when substituting butter is how healthy you want your cake to be. Applesauce, prune butter, tofu, or bananas will produce the healthiest dessert, but will be different in texture and taste. If you are making something chocolate, which has a strong flavor of its own, the taste of the applesauce, prune butter, or bananas might not make much of a difference. Using whipped tofu will not alter the flavor, but the texture will be different. If you want to stay close to the taste and texture of the original cake, you can substitute vegan butter spread—just remember to read the label and try to buy a brand that is non-hydrogenated.

Eggs are another ingredient that should be replaced. I use flax powder, xanthan gum, or commercial egg replacer depending on the recipe. I suggest using the xanthan gum in a non-wheat-based recipe because it also helps the product rise and replaces the gluten as well. In most wheat-based desserts, I mix 1 teaspoon of flax powder with ¼ cup water for every egg. If the dessert that I am making is light colored or a lighter cake such as My Grandmother's Crumb Cake recipe (page 61), I opt for a commercial egg replacer such as Ener-G. I use the same ratio as the flax powder—1 teaspoon of egg replacer and ¼ cup water for each egg. Whipped egg whites may be replaced in some recipes with commercial egg replacer. Use the directions on the back of the box for this. When making meringue, I have found that the pie must be eaten immediately or the meringue deflates. This type of meringue does not work for making crispy meringue cookies, and it is only marginally successful for angel food cakes.

BUYING VEGAN INGREDIENTS

THE QUALITY OF your finished product is directly related to the quality of the ingredients that you put into it. Be selective when choosing ingredients. I encourage you to always read ingredient labels to make sure you're choosing the healthiest products. You'll see that I mention several brand names throughout this book, but this does not in any way mean that these are the only products you should use. There are probably several other brands available that are equally healthy and would work just as well. These are just the brands that I use—I'm familiar with them and I like the results they produce, and they appear to be generally available at most supermarkets or health food stores. For example, I use Tofutti cream cheese for the cheesecakes. Unfortunately, it is hydrogenated, but it doesn't contain casein, a dairy derivative, and it has a creamy texture that is almost indistinguishable from regular cream cheese. If you choose to use another brand of cream cheese, be sure to test the texture and taste before you take the time and effort to make a cheesecake. If you do not like either the taste or texture of the cream cheese straight from the container, you will not like it in the cheesecake. I threw away several early attempts at desserts just because I didn't use the best vegan products to make them.

When buying soy milk, look for a brand that is made from non-genetically modified soybeans. Vanilla soy milk works well in many dessert recipes. If you can't find any vanilla soy milk, you can simply add a teaspoon of vanilla to each cup of plain soy milk.

I buy organic ingredients whenever possible. Not only do they taste better, but some studies indicate that they retain more of their natural nutrients than their chemically-produced counterparts. Be sure to buy only the freshest ingredients. I try to use fresh in-season fruit whenever possible. That means that I can't make the Tropical Fruit Cake (page 58) in the winter because strawberries are not available locally where I live until the summer. I can find fresh strawberries in the grocery store throughout the winter, but they are imported from foreign countries that may not have the same health codes the U.S. does and may be contaminated with bacteria such as salmonella and *E. coli*.

STOCKING YOUR VEGAN PANTRY

IN ORDER TO successfully make delicious vegan baked goods, you must be fully prepared, which means you should stock your pantry with several staples. If you have trouble finding an ingredient, check the Sources for Vegan Ingredients section on page 14. Most of these ingredients can be purchased in large grocery stores or health food stores. I have also included Internet sources to help you in case you live in an area that doesn't have a health food store within a reasonable distance. I can't stress strongly enough that your finished product will only be as good as the ingredients you put into it, so make sure that you take the time to select the proper ingredients. The ingredients listed below are common to many of the recipes in this book and it's a good idea to always keep them in good supply. They are also essential to a healthy vegan diet.

Agar (also called agar-agar): This substance can be found in a powder or flake form. It is made from red seaweed (although it is white in color when you buy it). It is the vegetarian form of gelatin and is used as a thickener.

Arrowroot flour: This flour is also known as arrowroot starch or simply arrowroot. It can be purchased in some grocery stores in the baking section or in most health food stores. It works as a thickener, has no taste of its own, and is easily digestible. Be careful not to boil arrowroot—continued heating tends to break down the arrowroot and diminish its thickening ability.

Barley flour: Barley is a hardy grain that was first cultivated in the Stone Age. Barley flour is made from ground pearl barley and is combined with a gluten-containing flour for use in baking. Therefore, it is low in gluten, but not gluten-free. It is easily digestible and wheat-free, and is a good source of dietary fiber.

Carob (also known as carob powder): A chocolate alternative made from the pod of the honey locust tree that grows in the Mediterranean region. The pod is dried, roasted, and pulverized. It is naturally sweeter than chocolate.

Coconut oil: Rich in lauric acid and primarily used to make pie crusts tender and flaky, coconut oil has no hydrogenated fat in it. It is naturally solid under 76°F. (Vegetable shortening is made from hydrogenated fat so that it is a solid at room temperatures.) I was not successful finding this product in any store, so I ordered it on the Internet. I have included the site where you can purchase it, and find more information about this product, in the Sources for Vegan Ingredients section on page 14.

Ener-G Egg Replacer: Commercial egg replacer. Main ingredients are potato starch, tapioca flour, and leavening.

Flax powder: This powder is made from ground flax seeds and is one of the only plant sources of omega-3 fatty acids. Flax powder has 540 milligrams of omega-3 per serving and is also high in fiber and lignans. It is mixed with water to replace eggs in vegan recipes. The ratio is ¼ cup water to 1 teaspoon flax powder. I recommend using Nutri Flax by Arrowhead Mills.

Garbanzo bean flour (also known as chickpea flour): An ancient grain that was first grown in Mesopotamia. It is a gluten-free flour.

Lignans: Potential anti-cancer substances found in higher-order plants. Flaxseeds are high in lignans.

Rice flour: Can be used to thicken soups and stews and to provide an alternative to wheat flour in cakes and biscuits.

Sea salt: Higher in trace minerals than table salt and additive-free.

Soy butter spread: Used to replace butter in vegan baking recipes when you want to retain the same texture as the original recipe. Be sure to read the labels on the butter spreads before buying them. Most margarines are vegan; however, not all are healthy. Choose one that is made with a healthy oil such as canola and does not contain any hydrogenated or partially hydrogenated fats. I prefer to use Spectrum or Soy Garden brands.

Soy cream cheese: Cream cheese made with soy milk instead of cow's milk. There are many brands of soy cream cheese on the market, so be sure to read the labels. Many contain casein, a dairy-derived ingredient that should be avoided. Also, be sure to test the soy cream cheese that you choose for flavor and texture before you use it. It should be pleasing in taste and similar in texture to Philadelphia Cream Cheese, or you may not be happy with the results of the recipe that you are making. I like to use Tofutti Brands soy cream cheese, but it does contain partially hydrogenated fats—something that I usually avoid at all costs. However, the end product is delicious, and I believe cheesecake should be treated as a special treat even if it's vegan. Despite my use of a hydrogenated soy cream cheese product, you will find that my recipes for vegan cheesecakes are still much healthier than their full-fat counterparts.

Soy milk: There are many kinds of soy milk on the market today, many of them available at local grocery stores. You'll probably need to experiment to find the type that you like the best. Again, read labels. Be sure to purchase a brand that is made with non-genetically engineered soybeans. Brands such as Edensoy are nuttier in taste and have a slightly brownish tint to them. They work well in all these recipes, but you may want a soy milk that more closely resembles cow's milk. Silk brand soy milk and 8th Continent soy milk are both white like cow's milk. If you want a sweeter end product, use vanilla soy milk. If you have plain soy milk and the recipe calls for vanilla soy milk, simply add 1 teaspoon vanilla for every cup of soy milk. If you are allergic to soy, or do not care for it, you may substitute any non-dairy milk product. Almond milk is an excellent choice. Rice milk is slightly thinner and may change the texture of the finished product.

Spelt flour: A flour that is more quickly and easily digested than most grains because of its high water solubility. It is considered a high energy grain because it has more protein, fiber, fat, iron, zinc, copper, and vitamins B1 and B2 than wheat.

Springform pan: This is a round, straight-sided baking pan that has sides that can be unclamped and removed. It works well for making cheesecakes, Boston cream pies, and other types of cakes that you do not want to flip out of a pan.

Stevia: An extraordinarily sweet herb (200–300 times sweeter than sugar) used as a sugar substitute.

Sucanat: Sucanat stands for "**su**gar **ca**ne **nat**ural." It is a sweetener made from dried, granulated cane sugar. The mineral salts and vitamins naturally present in sugar cane are preserved because only the water and fiber are removed in the processing of this product. It is coarsely granular, dark in color like brown sugar, and tastes a little like molasses.

Tahini: Paste made from ground sesame seeds.

Textured Vegetable Protein (TVP): A food product made from soybeans that makes an excellent meat substitute. It has a long shelf life if stored properly and is an excellent source of protein and fiber.

Tofu: Tofu is a vegan staple. If you have not discovered this wonder food, it's about time that you do! There are two different types of tofu. Japanese-style tofu, or silken tofu, is usually sold in aseptic boxes on store shelves. It can be found in most grocery stores. It has a creamy texture when processed in a food processor and is best suited for the recipes in this book. It works well to make puddings, cream sauces, frostings, and as an egg replacer in baking. The other type of tofu is Chinese-style. It is usually packed in tubs of water and has a spongier texture. It is much better suited for stir-fries, where the tofu needs to hold its shape. If you try to use this type of tofu for making puddings, cream sauces, or frostings you will probably be disappointed with the results. The texture will be grainy rather than smooth. Also remember to read labels and be sure to buy tofu made with non-genetically modified soybeans.

Vegetable shortening: You probably have a can of vegetable shortening sitting in your pantry right now. To ensure a healthier vegan product, don't use it until you read the label. Chances are that it is made with hydrogenated fats. Spectrum is the only brand of shortening I've been able to find that's made with non-hydrogenated fat. For many years I did not make recipes with shortening until I found Spectrum.

Xanthan gum: Xanthan gum is made from a tiny microorganism called *Xanthomonas campestris*. It can be used to replace gluten in wheat-free recipes (gluten is what helps the baked good rise), and it can also be added to recipes as a stabilizer. It can be found in the baking section of some grocery stores. If you can't find xanthan gum and do not wish to purchase it over the Internet, you may substitute powdered pectin (equal substitution for xanthan gum). The taste and texture will vary slightly, but the end product will still be good.

SOURCES FOR VEGAN INGREDIENTS

Coconut oil
Mt. Banahaw Health Products, Corp.
PO Box 0144
4031 College Laguna
Philippines
Telephone: 866.311.2626
Web site: www.coconut-info.com

Flax powder or ground flax seeds

Barlean's Organic Oils, LLC
4936 Lake Terrell Rd.
Ferndale, Washington 98248
Telephone: 800.445.3529
Web site: www.barleans.com

If you simply can't find this product, you may substitute 1 teaspoon baking powder for the flax flour.

Rice flour

True Foods Market
1289 West 635 South
Orem, UT 84058
Telephone: 877.274.5914
Web site: www.truefoodsmarket.com

This flour can usually be found in most health food stores. If you can't find it in a store near you, substitute 1 cup white flour for every ⅞ cup rice flour called for in the recipe.

Ener-G Egg Replacer

Ener-G Foods, Inc.
5960 First Avenue South
PO Box 84487
Seattle, WA 98124-5787
Telephone: 800.331.5222
Web site: www.ener-g.com

Garbanzo bean flour

True Foods Market
1289 West 635 South
Orem, UT 84058
Telephone: 877.274.5914
Web site: www.truefoodsmarket.com

This flour can usually be found in most health food stores. If you can't find it in a store near you, substitute white flour in the amount of 1 cup white flour for every ⅞ cups garbanzo bean flour called for in the recipe.

Sucanat
Wholesome Sweeteners
8016 Highway 90A
Sugar Land, TX 77478
Web site: www.wholesomesweeteners.com

Tofutti Cream Cheese
Tofutti Brands, Inc.
50 Jackson Drive
Cranford, NJ 07016
Telephone: 908.272.2400
Fax: 908.272.9492
Web site: www.tofutti.com

Most health food stores carry Tofutti Cream Cheese.

Xanthan gum
True Foods Market
1289 West 635 South
Orem, UT 84058
Telephone: 877.274.5914
Web site: www.truefoodsmarket.com

Xanthan gum can be found in most health food stores. It's rather pricey, but most recipes only call for about 1 teaspoon, so it lasts for a long time.

SUGGESTED KITCHEN EQUIPMENT

Food processor: I encourage you to invest in a good food processor (if you don't already have one) to process the silken tofu into a smooth, creamy consistency. Small food processors (1-cup capacity) are nice for pureeing small amounts of tofu or chopping nuts for a garnish, but a larger (3-quart capacity) food processor is necessary for the cheesecakes and frostings.

Electric mixer: You can use one to mix some of the recipes if you like. I mix all my cakes by hand.

Handheld blender or stick blender: This is a cheaper alternative to the food processor and can be used to cream the tofu in these recipes. It will take longer to cream the tofu, and you must stand and hold it the entire time rather than allowing the food processor to do it on its own, but the end result will be the same. It can be purchased in most kitchen supply stores.

Parchment paper: Useful because it keeps food from coming in direct contact with the baking pan, thus prevents sticking. I use it to line pans, roll out crusts, and place donuts on to rise.

Pie weights: These are clay balls or metal balls strung together that are placed in a pie crust while it bakes to prevent it from shrinking or bubbling up. You can find them in most kitchen supply stores.

PEACEFUL VEGANS

Eating vegetables and tofu will keep you in peace.
—Chinese folk saying

"Spare Me" Says the Animal
When a small animal is killed
and trembling, It wants to say "Spare Me" but who is hearing!
I beg all of the mankind who wants peace
try to have great compassion and stop killing!
—MENCIUS C. 372–289 B.C.
Chinese philosopher

For as long as man continues to be the ruthless destroyer
of lower living beings, he will never know health or peace.
For as long as men massacre animals, they will kill each other.
Indeed, he who sows the seeds of murder
and pain cannot reap joy and love.
—PYTHAGORAS
6th century B.C.
Greek philosopher and mathematician

Many people strongly believe that by becoming vegan you become more aware of other living things around you. You develop empathy for living creatures, no matter how small. If this is true, would this make a more peaceful world in which to live? Would we be as quick to solve differences with war—the senseless killing of human beings—if we did not even condone the senseless killing of animals for food? What do you think?

GONE VEGAN? YOU'RE NOT ALONE

YOU MIGHT BE surprised to know the vast number of past and present famous vegans. For example, respected American pediatrician Benjamin Spock was raised as a vegetarian until the age of twelve. This is all the more interesting because he was born in 1903, long before being a vegetarian was the "in" thing to do. He grew to be 6′4″ tall on this diet and even earned a spot on the Olympic rowing crew that won a gold medal in the 1924 Olympic Games. Not too shabby! At some point during young adulthood, Dr. Spock began to eat a SAD (**S**tandard **A**merican **D**iet) diet composed of typical high-fat fare. He continued this dietary regimen until he had a mild stroke at the age of eighty-eight, at which point he returned to vegetarianism. He eventually became vegan and lived to the ripe old age of ninety-five. Below is a list of some of the more well-known vegans. This list includes singers, entertainers, politicians, Olympic medal winners, triathletes, producers, humanitarians, athletes, and authors. You are in great company!

Alicia Silverstone	Actress
Amy Ray	Musician
Brendan Brazier	Ironman triathlete
Bryan Adams	Musician
Carl Lewis	Olympic track star
Carol Givner	Author
Crystal Ballroom	Musicians
Daniel Johns	Musician
Dave Davies	Singer
Dave Goodman	Producer
Dennis Kucinich	U.S. Congressman
Dr. Benjamin Spock	Medical doctor
Dr. John Harvey Kellogg	Doctor
Earth Crisis	Musicians
Ed Begley Jr.	Actor
Ed Templeton	Pro skateboarder
Elizabeth Berkeley	Actress
Fiona Apple	Singer
Fugazi	Band
Geoff Rowley	Pro skateboarder

Grace Slick	Singer
Heather Small	Musician
Howard Lyman	Author
Jamie Thomas	Pro skateboarder
Jarrett Lennon	Actor
Jo Stevens	Real World (San Francisco)
Joanne Rose	Model
Joaquin Phoenix	Actor
John Feldmann	Musician
John Power	Singer
John Robbins	Writer
Julia Stiles	Actress
kd lang	Musician
Kaia	Real World (Hawaii)
Katherine Monbiot	Arm wrestler
Keenan Ivory Wayans	Actor
Kerrie Saunders	Ph.D., author
Kevin Nealon	Saturday Night Live actor
Kim Andrew	Singer
Linda Blair	Actress
Lindsay Wagner	Actress
Lisa Edelstein	Actress
Lucy Stephens	Triathlete
Martina Navratilova	Tennis player
Michelle Malone	Singer
Moby	Singer
Mohandas Gandhi	Humanitarian
Moses Itkonen	Pro skateboarder
Mutt Lange	Producer
Niels Tijssen	Dutch actor
Pat Reeves	Power lifter
Peter Brock	Race car driver
Peter Max	Artist
Reed Mangels	Ph.D., writer
Rikki Rockett	Musician
River Phoenix	Actor
Russell Simmons	Rapper/designer
Ruth Heidrich	Three-time ironman
Sabrina LeBeauf	Actress
Sally Eastall	Marathon runner

Sara Gilbert	Actress
Sergei Trudnowski	Pro skateboarder
Shania Twain	Singer
Spice Williams	Actress
Stephanie Powers	Actress
Steve Brill	Author
Summer Phoenix	Actress
Sunny Harris	Market analyst
Terence Stamp	Actor
Tom Lenk	Actor
Tom Scholz	Musician
Vesanto Melina	Writer
Weird Al Yankovic	Comedian/singer
Woody Harrelson	Actor

COOKIES AND BROWNIES

VANILLA SPRITZ COOKIES

THIS RECIPE IS easy to use in a cookie press and makes dainty and delicious vanilla cookies. I like to include them in my cookie tray assortment during the holiday season.

1 cup soft vegan butter (such as Spectrum)
½ cup vegetable shortening (preferably non-hydrogenated, such as Spectrum)
1 cup granulated sugar
1 teaspoon egg replacer (such as Ener-G)
¼ cup water
4 tablespoons soy milk, or any non-dairy milk of your choice
1 teaspoon vanilla
4 cups unbleached flour
1 teaspoon baking powder

. . . .

MAKES ABOUT 6 DOZEN COOKIES
PREPARATION TIME: 15 minutes
BAKING TIME: 8 minutes per tray

. . . .

- Preheat oven to 400°F.
- Cream butter, shortening, and sugar together in a medium bowl. In a small cup, mix egg replacer and ¼ cup water. Add egg replacer mixture, soy milk, and vanilla to butter mixture and stir to combine. Mix flour and baking powder in a bowl and add slowly to butter mixture.
- Batter will be stiff and should form a ball in the bowl. (If batter is too sticky, add a little flour. If mixture is too dry, add more soy milk.) Do **not** chill dough. Place dough in cookie press and press out cookies onto cookie sheet lined with parchment paper. If you do not have a cookie press, chill the dough for about 1 hour, then roll it between two pieces of wax paper until it is ¼-inch thick. Cut it into shapes using cookie cutters. You can use the rim of a drinking glass as an alternative to a cookie cutter. The amount of cookies that this recipe makes will vary depending on the size of the cookie cutter that you use. Cookies made using a cookie press are generally small, so count on fewer cookies if you roll them out and cut them into shapes.
- Bake for 8 minutes. Cool on wire rack.

Variation: Try melting vegan chocolate chips and dip each cookie halfway in the chocolate for black and white cookies. Or, add 2 teaspoons lemon or orange extract for lemon or orange spritz cookies. These fruit-flavored cookies are also delicious dipped in chocolate.

PER SERVING: 64 calories, 3g fat (<1g saturated), 8g carbohydrate, <1g dietary fiber, <1g protein, 0mg cholesterol, 16mg sodium, 9mg potassium. Calories from fat: 44 percent.

SNAPPY GINGER COOKIES

THESE COOKIES REMIND me of the ones I used to buy at the grocery store around Halloween—crispy and spicy. They taste great dunked in cold soy milk or hot coffee.

1 cup vegetable shortening (non-hydrogenated, such as Spectrum)
1 cup brown sugar
1 teaspoon flax powder
¼ cup water
1 cup molasses
2 tablespoons vinegar
2½ cups unbleached white flour
2½ cups whole wheat flour
1½ teaspoons baking soda
½ teaspoon salt
3 tablespoons fresh ginger or 3 teaspoons ground ginger (optional)
1 teaspoon ground cinnamon
1 teaspoon ground cloves

. . . .

MAKES ABOUT 5 DOZEN COOKIES
PREPARATION TIME: 15 minutes
BAKING TIME: 6 minutes
per tray

. . . .

- Preheat oven to 375°F.
- Cream shortening and sugar together in a large bowl. In a cup, combine flax powder and ¼ cup water. Add flax mixture, molasses, fresh ginger, and vinegar to shortening and sugar mixture. Beat until combined.
- Sift together dry ingredients, including spices, in another bowl. Add to shortening/sugar mixture and stir to combine. Roll dough ¼-inch thick between two pieces of wax paper. Remove the top piece of wax paper and cut cookies into shapes. You may use decorative cookie cutters or a plain circle. If you do not have cookie cutters you may use the top edge of an 8-ounce drinking glass to cut the cookies. The number of cookies that you make will vary depending on the size of the cookie cutter(s) that you use. I based the number of cookies in this recipe on 2-inch round cookies.
- Place on cookie sheet that is lined with parchment paper (or greased). Bake for 5 to 6 minutes. Cool slightly, remove to wire rack and cool completely.

(If dough is hard to work with, refrigerate until it is stiffer—about 2 hours.)

PER SERVING: 90 calories, 4g fat (1g saturated), 14g carbohydrate, <1g dietary fiber, 1g protein, 0mg cholesterol, 35mg sodium, 118mg potassium. Calories from fat: 34 percent.

HOME-STYLE CHOCOLATE CHIP COOKIES

THESE COOKIES ARE a real favorite at my house and disappear fast! But they're so easy to make that I don't mind.

2½ cups maple syrup
1 cup canola oil
2 cups vegan chocolate chips
7 cups barley flour
2 teaspoons vanilla

. . . .

MAKES ABOUT 4 DOZEN COOKIES
PREPARATION TIME: 10 minutes
BAKING TIME: 20 minutes
per tray

. . . .

- Preheat oven to 350°F.
- Combine maple syrup, canola oil, chocolate chips, and vanilla in a medium bowl. Add barley flour and stir to combine. Drop teaspoon-size amounts onto cookie sheet lined with parchment paper (or greased).
- Bake 20 minutes (or until cookies just begin to brown).
- Allow to cool for 5 minutes. Remove to wire rack and cool completely.

Variation: Try substituting 2 teaspoons peppermint extract for the 2 teaspoons vanilla for an interesting tasting mint chocolate chip cookie.

Hint: If you measure out the oil *before* the maple syrup, the maple syrup will come out of the measuring cup more easily.

PER SERVING: 254 calories, 9g fat (2g saturated), 42g carbohydrate, 2g dietary fiber, 14g sugar, 3g protein, 0mg cholesterol, 6mg sodium, 105mg potassium. Calories from fat: 31 percent.

LITTLE OATIES

SAME DELICIOUS TASTE as traditional oatmeal cookies, but much quicker and easier to make!

2½ cups maple syrup
½ cup brown sugar or Sucanat
¼ cup applesauce
1 cup canola oil
3 cups barley flour
6 cups uncooked oatmeal
2 teaspoons vanilla
1 teaspoon baking soda

. . . .

MAKES 3½ DOZEN
PREPARATION TIME: 10 minutes
BAKING TIME: 15 minutes
per tray

. . . .

- Preheat oven to 350°F.
- Combine maple syrup, canola oil, and vanilla and stir to combine. Add flour and oatmeal and mix. Drop in teaspoon-size amounts onto cookie sheet lined with parchment paper (or greased).
- Bake 15 minutes (or until cookies just begin to brown).
- Allow to cool for 5 minutes. Remove to wire rack and cool completely.

Variations: Try adding 1 cup chocolate chips for oatmeal chocolate chip cookies. Or replace 1 cup oatmeal with 1 cup unsweetened coconut and add 1 cup chocolate chips for a deliciously rich-tasting cookie.

Hint: If you measure out the oil *before* the maple syrup, the maple syrup will come out of the measuring cup more easily!

PER SERVING: 160 calories, 6g fat (<1g saturated), 26g carbohydrate, 1g dietary fiber, 12g sugar, 2g protein, 0mg cholesterol, 45mg sodium, 88mg potassium. Calories from fat: 31 percent.

Mom's Warm Peanut Butter Cookies

Y HUSBAND LOVES peanut butter cookies and he's always asking me to make them. Since I (like all moms) have a busy schedule, I created this recipe to be tasty, healthy, and very easy to make. It has only five ingredients—how's that for simple?

1 cup maple syrup
½ cup canola oil
1 cup natural peanut butter
2 teaspoons vanilla
2 cups unbleached flour

. . . .

MAKES ABOUT 4 DOZEN COOKIES
PREPARATION TIME: 10 minutes
BAKING TIME: 20 minutes
per tray

. . . .

- Preheat oven to 350°F.
- Combine maple syrup, canola oil, peanut butter, and vanilla in a medium bowl. Add flour and mix to combine. Form batter into teaspoon-size balls of dough with your hands.
- Put on a cookie sheet lined with parchment paper (or greased). Press the tines of a fork across the top of the cookie to make perpendicular imprints.
- Bake for 20 minutes. Allow to cool for 5 minutes. Place on wire rack and allow to cool completely.

Variations: Roll dough into balls. Make a hole in the center of the dough with your finger tip or knuckle, being careful not to press all the way through the cookie. Bake as directed above. When cookies are completely cool, fill hole with grape jelly for peanut butter and jelly cookies. Or you can melt vegan chocolate chips and fill the hole with the melted chocolate for chocolate peanut butter cookies. Chill before serving.

PER SERVING: 89 calories, 5g fat (<1g saturated), 10g carbohydrate, <1g dietary fiber, 4g sugar, 2g protein, 0mg cholesterol, 26mg sodium, 55mg potassium. Calories from fat: 49 percent.

SNICKERDOODLES

I GREW UP eating these delicious cookies with a funny name. They're crispy vanilla cookies rolled in cinnamon and sugar, then baked. Guaranteed not to last long!

½ cup vegan butter spread
*½ cup vegetable shortening
    (non-hydrogenated)*
1 cup granulated sweetener
¼ teaspoon salt
2 teaspoons vanilla
2 teaspoons flax powder
½ cup water
3 cups unbleached white flour
½ cup sugar
½ teaspoon cinnamon

. . . .

MAKES ABOUT 3 DOZEN COOKIES
PREPARATION TIME: 15 minutes
BAKING TIME: 20 minutes
per tray

. . . .

- Preheat oven to 375°F.
- Cream butter spread, shortening, and 1 cup sweetener together. Add vanilla and salt and stir to combine. In a small cup, mix water and flax powder, add to shortening mixture, and stir to combine. Add flour and mix well.
- In a small, wide bowl, mix ½ cup sugar and cinnamon. Form dough into 1-inch balls. Roll in cinnamon/sugar mixture. Place on baking sheet that has been coated with nonstick cooking spray or lined with parchment paper.
- Flatten balls with the floured bottom of a glass and bake for 20 minutes. Remove from oven immediately and cool on wire rack.

Variation: Try rolling cookies in plain sugar for vegan sugar cookies.

PER SERVING: 113 calories, 5g fat (1g saturated), 16g carbohydrate, <1g dietary fiber, 1g protein, 0mg cholesterol, 13mg sodium, 16mg potassium. Calories from fat: 37 percent.

CHOCOLATE-COCONUT CRISPS

HAD LEFTOVER chocolate cookie dough from the crust of a cheesecake I was making and wondered what it would taste like with coconut mixed in. I tried it and liked it, so I worked to adjust the recipe and *voila*—Chocolate-Coconut Crisps.

½ cup vegan butter spread
½ cup vegetable shortening
1 cup granulated sweetener
½ cup maple syrup
¼ teaspoon salt
2 teaspoons coconut extract
2 teaspoons flax powder
½ cup water
2½ cups unbleached white flour
½ cup cocoa
½ cup shredded unsweetened
coconut

. . . .
MAKES ABOUT 3 DOZEN COOKIES
PREPARATION TIME: 15 minutes
BAKING TIME: 20 minutes
per tray
. . . .

- Preheat oven to 375°F.
- Cream together butter spread, shortening, and 1 cup sweetener. Add coconut extract and salt and stir to combine. In a small cup, mix water and flax powder, add to shortening mixture, and stir to combine. Add flour and cocoa and mix well.
- Place coconut in a shallow bowl. Form dough into 1-inch balls and roll in coconut.
- Place on baking sheet that has been coated with nonstick cooking spray or lined with parchment paper. Flatten balls with the floured bottom of a glass.
- Bake for 20 minutes. Remove from oven immediately and cool on wire rack.

PER SERVING: 113 calories, 5g fat (2g saturated), 16g carbohydrate, <1g dietary fiber, 3g sugar, 1g protein, 0mg cholesterol, 14mg sodium, 43mg potassium. Calories from fat: 40 percent.

I Can't Believe They're
Not Sinful Brownies

THIS WAS ONE of the first recipes I ever "veganized." There are times when I simply must have chocolate! I can even eat the batter of these brownies before they are baked. That's an added bonus for vegan recipes—you don't have to worry about the health hazards of raw eggs in the batter, so you can sneak batter to your heart's content.

1⅓ cups granulated sweetener
¾ cup applesauce (preferably organic)
2 tablespoons water
2 teaspoons flax powder
½ cup water
2 teaspoons vanilla
1⅓ cups unbleached white flour
¾ cup cocoa
½ teaspoon baking powder
¼ teaspoon salt

. . . .

Makes 9 servings
Preparation time: 10 minutes
Baking time: 40–47 minutes
Freezes well

. . . .

PER SERVING: 225 calories, 1g fat (<1g saturated), 54g carbohydrate, 3g dietary fiber, 3g protein, 0mg cholesterol, 29mg sodium, 146mg potassium. Calories from fat: 4 percent.

- Preheat oven to 350°F. Coat an 8 × 8-inch square baking dish with nonstick cooking spray.
- Stir together granulated sweetener, applesauce, and 2 tablespoons water in a medium size bowl. In a small cup, mix flax powder with ½ cup water. Add to applesauce mixture and stir to combine. Add vanilla to this mixture.
- In another small bowl, combine flour, cocoa, baking powder, and salt. Add applesauce mixture to flour mixture. Stir just to combine and pour into prepared pan.
- Bake for 40 minutes for chewy brownies, 45–47 minutes for cake-like brownies.
- Allow to cool before serving.

Hint: Brownies are difficult to test for doneness. Using the toothpick-in-the-center method is not a reliable measure. I usually do the touch test. When you touch the top of the brownies, it should not leave an indentation. If it does, the batter is still soft. You may want to experiment with baking times, and when you have made brownies that are the exact doneness that you like, write that time on the recipe. Oven temperatures vary and everyone likes brownies baked to a different doneness. I like brownies gooey and moist. If you like them cake-like, you will have to adjust the baking time.

DEATH BY CHOCOLATE BROWNIES

WARNING: THESE BROWNIES are for the serious chocolate lover only! They are not quite as healthy as the I Can't Believe They're Not Sinful Brownies (page 29), but they are my favorite brownie recipe. I could live on these brownies!

1⅓ cups granulated sweetener
¾ cup applesauce (preferably organic)
2 tablespoons water
2 teaspoons flax powder
½ cup water
2 teaspoons vanilla
1⅓ cups unbleached white flour
¾ cup cocoa
½ teaspoon baking powder
¼ teaspoon salt
1 cup vegan chocolate chips

CHOCOLATE TOPPING:
1 cup powdered sugar
¼ cup canola oil
½ teaspoon vanilla
⅙ cup cocoa (use ⅓-cup measurer and only fill it half full)
3½ tablespoons arrowroot
½ cup water

. . . .

MAKES 16 SERVINGS
PREPARATION TIME:
  BROWNIES: 10 minutes
  TOPPING: 10 minutes
BAKING TIME: 40-47 minutes
FREEZES WELL

. . . .

PER SERVING: 223 calories, 8g fat (3g saturated), 40g carbohydrate, 3g dietary fiber, 3g protein, 0mg cholesterol, 18mg sodium, 107mg potassium. Calories from fat: 29 percent.

- Preheat oven to 350°F. Coat an 8 × 8-inch square baking dish with nonstick cooking spray.
- Stir together granulated sweetener, applesauce, and 2 tablespoons water in a medium-size bowl. In a small cup, mix flax powder with ½ cup water. Add to applesauce mixture and stir to combine. Add vanilla to this mixture.
- In another small bowl, combine flour, cocoa, baking powder, and salt. Add applesauce mixture to flour mixture. Stir just to combine. Add chocolate chips and stir to combine. Pour into prepared pan.
- Bake for 40 minutes for chewy brownies, 45–47 minutes for cake-like brownies (or until middle of brownie is set when you touch it, meaning you don't leave finger imprint but it's not too springy and cake-like).
- *To make chocolate topping:* While brownies are baking, place powdered sugar, canola oil, vanilla, cocoa, and arrowroot in small saucepan. Stir to combine, using a wire whisk for best results. Stir in water. Turn on heat and keep stirring until mixture starts to thicken, but do not boil.
- Pour hot topping over brownies and smooth out evenly. Allow to cool completely before serving.

Hint: When making the topping, I hold the pan over the heat. As I allow the topping to thicken, I don't have it sitting directly on the burner. This enables it to thicken more quickly, but still keeps it from coming to a boil. The thickening power of arrowroot is destroyed if it boils. The topping will thicken more as it cools, which is why it should be spread on the brownies immediately and then allowed to cool.

Swirly Berry Brownies

I CREATED THESE brownies to add a little variety to plain brownies. Sometimes I cut them up into bite-size pieces and put them on my cookie tray at holiday time.

1⅓ cups granulated sweetener
¾ cup applesauce (preferably organic)
2 tablespoons water
2 teaspoons flax powder
½ cup water
2 teaspoons vanilla
1⅓ cups unbleached white flour
¾ cup cocoa
½ teaspoon baking powder
¼ teaspoon salt
½ cup raspberry preserve

. . . .

MAKES 9 SERVINGS
PREPARATION TIME: 10 minutes
BAKING TIME: 45–50 minutes
FREEZES WELL

. . . .

- Preheat oven to 350°F. Coat an 8 × 8-inch square baking dish with nonstick cooking spray.
- Stir together granulated sweetener, applesauce, and 2 tablespoons water in a medium-size bowl. In a small cup, mix flax powder with ½ cup water. Add to applesauce mixture and stir to combine. Add vanilla to this mixture.
- In another small bowl, combine flour, cocoa, baking powder, and salt. Add applesauce mixture to flour mixture. Stir just to combine and pour into prepared pan. Drop spoonfuls of raspberry preserve on top of brownie batter. Using a knife, swirl raspberry into brownie batter. Do not mix in completely.
- Bake for 45 minutes for chewy brownies, 50 minutes for cake-like brownies.
- Allow to cool before serving.

PER SERVING: 280 calories, 2g fat (<1g saturated), 66g carbohydrate, 4g dietary fiber, 4g protein, 0mg cholesterol, 37mg sodium, 178mg potassium. Calories from fat: 6 percent.

HEAVENLY BROWNIE TORTE

I CREATED THIS dessert to dress up plain old brownies when I was baking for a restaurant. I saw one like it at an exclusive bakery that wasn't vegan. It looked so good that I just had to give it a shot.

1⅓ cups granulated sweetener
¾ cup applesauce (preferably
    organic)
2 tablespoons water
2 teaspoons flax powder
½ cup water
2 teaspoons vanilla
1⅓ cups unbleached white flour
¾ cup cocoa
½ teaspoon baking powder
¼ teaspoon salt
½ cup vegan chocolate chips

CARAMEL SAUCE:
(MAKE THE DAY BEFORE
IF POSSIBLE)
⅓ cup corn syrup
⅓ cup brown sugar
2 teaspoons vanilla
3½ tablespoons soy milk
¼ teaspoon salt

CHOCOLATE CANDY
TOPPING:
2 cups vegan chocolate chips
½ cup soy creamer
½ teaspoon vanilla
1 cup whole pecans

- Preheat oven to 350°F. Coat an 8 × 8-inch round baking dish with nonstick cooking spray. Line the bottom of the pan with parchment or wax paper.
- Stir together granulated sweetener, applesauce, and 2 tablespoons water in a medium-size bowl. In a small cup, mix flax powder with ½ cup water. Add to applesauce mixture and stir to combine. Add vanilla to this mixture.
- In another small bowl, combine flour, cocoa, baking powder, and salt. Add applesauce mixture to flour mixture. Stir just to combine. Add chocolate chips and stir to combine. Pour into prepared pan and bake for 40 minutes for chewy brownies, 45–47 minutes for cake-like brownies. Allow to cool for 10 minutes in pan. Remove from pan and cool on wire rack completely before assembling.
- *To make caramel sauce:* While brownies are baking, place corn syrup and brown sugar in small pan. Heat until boiling. Simmer until sugar reaches the soft ball stage or 240°F. Add vanilla, salt, and soy milk. Allow mixture to cool completely at room temperature. (Do not refrigerate before assembling torte—caramel will thicken as it cools.)
- *To assemble torte:* Place completely cooled brownie upside down on wire rack that is placed on a bowl that has a diameter larger than that of the brownie. Gently pour the caramel sauce over the brownie. Allow about a ½-inch space at the outer edge of the brownie where you do not spread caramel to keep it from dripping down the side of the brownie when you pour the chocolate on it. You may want to reserve a little caramel to drizzle on each serving

plate before placing the brownie on it. Place the pecans in an evenly spaced pattern around the top of the brownie on the caramel, spacing them close together so that all the caramel is covered. Refrigerate to harden caramel while you heat the chocolate.

- *To make chocolate candy topping:* Heat vanilla soy creamer in a small pan until hot, but not boiling. *Slowly* stir in vegan chocolate chips. Stir until chocolate chips are completely melted and mixture is smooth. While mixture is hot, *gently* pour over the brownie, nuts, and caramel, being careful not to dislodge the nuts or caramel. Allow excess chocolate to drip into bowl under brownie. When brownie is completely covered with chocolate, place bowl, wire rack, and torte in refrigerator until chocolate hardens, about 10 minutes. Remove from refrigerator and remove any hard drips of chocolate that formed when chocolate ran off torte through wire rack (a kitchen shears works well for this). Place torte on serving plate. When serving, drizzle reserved caramel on individual serving plate (optional) and place slice of torte on top.

Hint: If caramel is too hard, allow to set at room temperature for about 10 minutes before serving.

MAKES 12 SERVINGS
PREPARATION TIME:
  BROWNIE: 10 minutes
  CARAMEL: 10 minutes
  CHOCOLATE CANDY
  COATING: 10 minutes
  ASSEMBLY: 10 minutes
BAKING TIME: 40–47 minutes

PER SERVING: 493 calories, 19g fat (7g saturated), 85g carbohydrate, 6g dietary fiber, <1g sugar, 5g protein, 0mg cholesterol, 46mg sodium, 194mg potassium. Calories from fat: 31 percent.

PEANUT BUTTER TWIST BROWNIES

OR REESE'S PEANUT Butter Cup lovers everywhere: Brownies with peanut butter swirled in them. Be careful not to overbake these brownies, or they will be dry.

1⅓ cups granulated sweetener
¾ cup applesauce (preferably organic)
2 tablespoons water
2 teaspoons flax powder
½ cup water
2 teaspoons vanilla
1⅓ cups unbleached white flour
¾ cup cocoa
½ teaspoon baking powder
¼ teaspoon salt
½ cup vegan chocolate chips
½ cup natural peanut butter
½ cup maple syrup
3 ounces firm silken tofu

. . . .

MAKES 16 SERVINGS
PREPARATION TIME:
    BROWNIE: 10 minutes
    PEANUT BUTTER FILLING: 5 minutes
BAKING TIME: 45–50 minutes
FREEZES WELL

. . . .

- Preheat oven to 350°F. Coat an 8 × 8-inch square baking dish with nonstick cooking spray.
- Stir together granulated sweetener, applesauce, and 2 tablespoons water in a medium-size bowl. In a small cup, mix flax powder with ½ cup water. Add to applesauce mixture and stir to combine. Add vanilla to this mixture.
- In another small bowl, combine flour, cocoa, baking powder, and salt. Add applesauce mixture to flour mixture. Stir just to combine. Add chocolate chips and stir to combine. Pour into prepared pan.
- Place peanut butter, maple syrup, and tofu together in food processor. Process until smooth. Drop by spoonfuls onto brownie batter. With a knife, swirl peanut butter into brownie batter. (Be careful not to mix completely.)
- Bake for 45 minutes for chewy brownies, 50 minutes for cake-like brownies.
- Allow to cool before serving.

PER SERVING: 235 calories, 7g fat (2g saturated), 42g carbohydrate, 3g dietary fiber, 6g sugar, 5g protein, 0mg cholesterol, 56mg sodium, 187mg potassium. Calories from fat: 24 percent.

CAKES AND QUICK BREADS

LEMON LOAF

*T*HIS IS SIMPLY a delectable lemon pound cake. The name *pound* cake comes from a time when each ingredient in the recipe weighed a pound! How times have changed.

2 cups unbleached white flour
1 teaspoon baking powder
½ teaspoon baking soda
½ cup maple syrup
⅓ cup soft margarine
4 teaspoons Ener-G Egg Replacer
¾ cup water
3½ teaspoons lemon extract
¾ cup vanilla soy milk, or other non-dairy milk of your choice

. . . .

MAKES 12 SERVINGS
PREPARATION TIME:
    CAKE: 15 minutes
    GLAZE: 5 minutes
    RASPBERRY SAUCE: 10 minutes
BAKING TIME: 1 hour
FREEZES WELL

. . . .

- Preheat over to 350°F. Lightly grease 8 × 3½ × 2½-inch loaf pan with nonstick cooking spray.
- In a separate bowl, combine flour, baking powder, and baking soda. Using an electric mixer, combine maple syrup, soy milk, and margarine.
- In small bowl, mix egg replacer with water. Add to maple syrup mixture along with lemon extract and mix. Slowly add flour to liquid mixture. Mix just until combined and pour batter into prepared pan.
- Bake for 1 hour or until toothpick inserted in center comes out clean. Cool completely before removing from pan.

Serving suggestions:
Top with lemon glaze or raspberry sauce.

CAKE
PER SERVING: 287 calories, 6g fat (1g saturated), 28g carbohydrate, <1g dietary fiber, 8g sugar, 30g protein, 0mg cholesterol, 542mg sodium, 448mg potassium. Calories from fat: 17 percent.

LEMON GLAZE:

¾ cup powdered sugar
2 tablespoons lemon juice (freshly squeezed will give the
   best flavor)

- Mix together. Pour over cake before slicing.

RASPBERRY SAUCE:

1 12-ounce package frozen raspberries
¼ cup water
⅓ cup granulated sweetener
1 tablespoon arrowroot
2 tablespoons water

- Bring first three ingredients to boil in medium
  saucepan. Dissolve arrowroot in 2 tablespoons of
  water and add to hot raspberry mixture. Heat just
  until thickened—do not boil. (Mixture will thicken
  more as it cools.) Allow to cool.
- Slice cake and place on serving plates. Spoon sauce
  over cake slices. Serve immediately.

Variation: Add ¾ cup poppy seeds to batter for
lemon poppy seed cake.

RASPBERRY SAUCE
PER SERVING: 19 calories, <.1g fat (0g
saturated), 5g carbohydrate, <1g
dietary fiber, <1g protein, 0mg
cholesterol, <1mg sodium, 6mg
potassium. Calories from fat: 0 percent.

LEMON GLAZE
PER SERVING: 31 calories, <1g fat (0g
saturated), 8g carbohydrate, <1g
dietary fiber, <1g protein, 0mg
cholesterol, <1mg sodium, 12mg
potassium. Calories from fat: 0 percent.

CHERRY, CHERRY NOT CONTRARY CAKE

*T*ENDER, MOIST CHOCOLATE cake filled with fresh cherry filling and topped with fluffy chocolate icing is sure to please your guests every time. And, they'll never guess the secret ingredient that makes it so moist—zucchini!

1 cup rice flour
1¼ cups garbanzo bean flour
2 teaspoons xanthan gum
½ cup cocoa
1 tablespoon baking powder
1½ teaspoons baking soda
¼ teaspoon salt
¼ cup organic applesauce
½ cup soft soy margarine
2 cups granulated sweetener
3 teaspoons flax powder or
   Ener-G Egg Replacer
1¼ cups water
2 teaspoons vanilla
2 cups shredded zucchini
8–10 fresh cherries with stems
   for garnish
Cherry Filling, page 201
Whipped Chocolate Frosting,
   page 202
Vegan Chocolate Syrup,
   page 203

- Preheat oven to 325°F. Coat 9-inch springform pan with nonstick cooking spray.
- Combine flours, xanthan gum, cocoa, baking powder, baking soda, salt in a bowl and then set aside. In another bowl, combine applesauce, margarine, and granulated sweetener and mix until fluffy and set aside. In small bowl, mix flax flour or Ener-G Egg Replacer with ¾ cup water. Add to applesauce mixture and stir to combine. Add vanilla, zucchini, and ½ cup water. Slowly add flour mixture to liquid ingredients and stir to combine. Pour batter into prepared pan.
- Bake at 325°F for 1½ hours or until toothpick inserted in center comes out clean. Allow to cool in oven for 30 minutes with oven turned off and door open. Remove from oven and allow to cool completely in pan.
- While cake is cooling, make Cherry Filling, page 201, and set aside. When cake is cool, remove collar of pan and cut cake in half horizontally to make two layers. Remove top layer and set aside. Put collar back on bottom of pan. Spread cherry filling over bottom layer of cake. Replace top of cake upside down (so that flat cut side is on top) on top of cherries and gently press down. Frost with Whipped Chocolate Frosting, page 202.

- Garnish with fresh pitted cherries placed around the outside of the cake if desired. For a fancier look, leave the stems on cherries, pit, melt ½ cup vegan chocolate chips, and dip bottom half of each cherry in chocolate. Allow chocolate to harden. (Place chocolate-covered cherries in refrigerator.) Drizzle Vegan Chocolate Syrup, page 203, on top of cake in lattice pattern and place chocolate cherries around outside edge of cake just before serving. The number of cherries that you will need will vary depending on size of cherries and how closely you space them. Eight to ten cherries is usually enough.

. . . .
MAKES 12 SERVINGS
PREPARATION TIME:
    CAKE: 20 minutes
    FILLING: 15 minutes
    FROSTING: 10 minutes
ASSEMBLY/FROSTING: 15 minutes
BAKING TIME: 1½ hours
COOL IN OVEN: 30 minutes
REFRIGERATE OVERNIGHT
. . . .

PER SERVING: 523 calories, 19g fat (6g saturated), 89g carbohydrate, 6g dietary fiber, 6g sugar, 9g protein, 0mg cholesterol, 914mg sodium, 450mg potassium. Calories from fat: 29 percent.

Chocolate Raspberry Celebration Loaf

IMPRESS YOUR FRIENDS with this luscious blend of chocolate and raspberry. It's easy to make and looks quite festive. Use your imagination to decorate it with a combination of fluffy chocolate icing, fresh raspberries, and mint leaves.

1½ cups unbleached white flour
⅓ cup cocoa
1 tablespoon baking powder
½ teaspoon vanilla
3 ounces firm silken tofu
¾ cup water or apple juice
¼ cup organic applesauce
¾ cup maple syrup
Standard Chocolate Frosting,
    page 205
½ cup fresh raspberries for garnish (optional)
8–10 fresh mint leaves for garnish (optional)

FILLING:
¾ cup raspberry jam

- Preheat oven to 350°F. Lightly grease 8 × 3½ × 2½-inch loaf pan with nonstick cooking spray.
- In a large bowl, combine flour, cocoa, and baking powder. Mix with a whisk to combine. In a food processor, puree tofu until smooth. Add vanilla and applesauce and blend. Add water (or apple juice) and maple syrup and blend. Slowly add liquid ingredients to flour mixture and mix with whisk until combined. Do not overmix. Pour batter into prepared pan.
- Bake for 45 minutes or until toothpick inserted in center comes out clean. While cake is baking, make Standard Chocolate Frosting. (If possible, it is best to make frosting the day before.)
- Cool cake for 10 minutes, then remove from pan and cool completely. When cool, cut rounded part off of top of cake with a sharp knife or wire cake cutter to make it almost flat. Cut cake in thirds lengthwise to make three layers. Place top layer upside down on serving plate. Spread with ⅓ cup of the raspberry jam. Top with the next layer. Spread with the rest of the jam. Place the last layer on top. This will be the smallest layer because the cake tapers to the top. Place this layer on upside down so that the top is completely flat.

- Frost cake top and sides with Standard Chocolate Frosting. Pipe chocolate icing around bottom edge of cake. If raspberries are in season, line fresh raspberries along long edges of cake only. Garnish with several fresh mint leaves. If vegan chocolate candy bars are available, use a potato peeler to make chocolate curls to place in middle of cake between the rows of raspberries.

Hint: If you don't have a loaf pan, you may bake this cake in an 8-inch square cake pan. Adjust baking time to about 35 minutes. When cake has cooled, cut the top rounded part off the cake and discard (or eat!). Cut cake in half vertically to make two rectangular pieces. With a sharp knife or wire cake cutter, cut each rectangle in half horizontally to make 4 thin layers. Alternate cake and raspberry filling. Frost top and sides and decorate.

MAKES **12** SERVINGS

PREPARATION TIME:

CAKE: 15 minutes

FROSTING: 10 minutes

BAKING TIME: 45 minutes

FROSTING AND ASSEMBLY: 10 minutes

DECORATION: 10 minutes

PER SERVING: 351 calories, 10g fat (4g saturated), 62g carbohydrate, 3g dietary fiber, 14g sugar, 9g protein, 0mg cholesterol, 19mg sodium, 327mg potassium. Calories from fat: 23 percent.

MOCHA MADNESS CAKE

COFFEE SHOPS SELLING lattes and mocha drinks are springing up all over the place proving that people adore coffee and chocolate! I developed this cake to mimic the taste of a chocolate cappuccino.

3 cups unbleached white flour
⅓ cup cocoa
2 tablespoons baking powder
1 teaspoon vanilla
6 ounces firm silken tofu
1½ cups water or apple juice
½ cup organic applesauce
1½ cups maple syrup
Coffee Frosting, page 206
½ cup vegan chocolate chips or chocolate-covered espresso beans for garnish (optional)

. . . .

MAKES 12 SERVINGS
PREPARATION TIME:
   CAKE: 15 minutes
   FROSTING: 10 minutes
FROSTING AND DECORATION:
5 minutes

. . . .

- Preheat oven to 350°F. Lightly grease 9 × 12-inch rectangular pan with nonstick cooking spray.
- In a large bowl, combine flour, cocoa, and baking powder. Mix with a whisk to combine. In a food processor, puree tofu until smooth. Add vanilla and applesauce and blend. Add water (or apple juice) and maple syrup and blend. Slowly add liquid ingredients to flour mixture and mix with whisk until combined. Do not overmix. Pour batter into prepared pan.
- Bake for 45 minutes or until toothpick inserted in center comes out clean. Prepare the Coffee Frosting while cake is baking. (If possible, it is best to make frosting the day before.)
- Remove cake from oven after 35–45 minutes or when a toothpick inserted in the center comes out clean. Allow to cool in pan. Frost, leaving cake in pan. Decorate with vegan chocolate chips or chocolate-covered espresso beans (if chocolate covering is vegan) if desired.

PER SERVING: 367 calories, 5g fat (1g saturated), 71g carbohydrate, 3g dietary fiber, 27g sugar, 12g protein, 0mg cholesterol, 13mg sodium, 483mg potassium. Calories from fat: 12 percent.

Nuts about Chocolate Cake

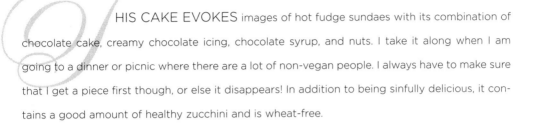

THIS CAKE EVOKES images of hot fudge sundaes with its combination of chocolate cake, creamy chocolate icing, chocolate syrup, and nuts. I take it along when I am going to a dinner or picnic where there are a lot of non-vegan people. I always have to make sure that I get a piece first though, or else it disappears! In addition to being sinfully delicious, it contains a good amount of healthy zucchini and is wheat-free.

1 cup rice flour
1¼ cups garbanzo bean flour
2 teaspoons xanthan gum
½ cup cocoa
1 tablespoon baking powder
1½ teaspoons baking soda
¼ teaspoon salt
¼ cup organic applesauce
½ cup soft soy margarine
2 cups granulated sweetener
3 teaspoons flax powder or
    Ener-G Egg Replacer
¾ cup water
2 teaspoons vanilla
2 cups shredded zucchini
½ cup water
¾ cup chopped pecans for gar-
    nish (optional)
Whipped Chocolate Frosting,
    page 203
Vegan Chocolate Syrup,
    page 203

. . . .
MAKES 12 SERVINGS
PREPARATION TIME:
    CAKE: 20 minutes
    SYRUP: 5 minutes
    FROSTING: 10 minutes
BAKING TIME: 1½ hours
COOL IN OVEN: 30 minutes
. . . .

- Preheat oven to 325°F. Coat 9-inch springform pan with nonstick cooking oil.
- Combine flours, xanthan gum, cocoa, baking powder, baking soda, and salt in a bowl and set aside. Combine applesauce, margarine, and granulated sweetener and mix until fluffy. Mix flax flour or Ener-G Egg Replacer with ¾ cup water in small bowl, add to applesauce mixture, and stir to combine. Add vanilla, zucchini, and ½ cup water. Slowly add flour mixture to liquid ingredients. Stir to combine. Pour batter into prepared pan.
- Bake at 325°F for 1½ hours or until toothpick inserted in center comes out clean. Allow to cool in oven for 30 minutes with oven turned off and door open. Allow to cool completely in pan. Prepare Whipped Chocolate Frosting.
- After cake is completely cooled, frost. Sprinkle with chopped nuts. Prepare Vegan Chocolate Syrup. Drizzle chocolate syrup over nuts (zigzag over cake).
- Refrigerate cake overnight before serving, if possible.

PER SERVING: 542 calories, 25g fat (6g saturated), 78g carbohydrate, 8g dietary fiber, 7g sugar, 11g protein, 0mg cholesterol, 210mg sodium, 409mg potassium. Calories from fat: 37 percent.

JUST LOAFING AROUND

THIS POUND CAKE tastes great plain, but can be used as a base for a variety of creations. It is scrumptious topped with fresh fruit—strawberries, raspberries, peaches, or cherries. Drizzle chocolate sauce over the fresh fruit mounded on this firm, yet moist cake and you have a truly memorable dessert. You could also serve it with a scoop of non-dairy frozen dessert such as Tofutti and Vegan Chocolate Syrup (page 203) for a wonderful taste experience.

2 cups unbleached white flour
1 teaspoon baking powder
½ teaspoon baking soda
½ cup brown sugar
½ cup maple syrup
⅓ cup soft margarine
4 teaspoons Ener-G Egg Replacer
½ cup water
2 tablespoons vanilla extract
¾ cup vanilla soy milk, or other non-dairy milk of your choice
Vanilla Glaze, page 204
Vegan Chocolate Syrup, page 203

. . . .

MAKES 12 SERVINGS
PREPARATION TIME:
   CAKE: 15 minutes
   GLAZE: 5 minutes
CHOCOLATE SAUCE: 10 minutes
BAKING TIME: 1 hour
FREEZES WELL

. . . .

PER SERVING (cake only): 178 calories, 7g fat (<1g saturated), 26g carbohydrate, <1g dietary fiber, 8g sugar, 3g protein, 0mg cholesterol, 94mg sodium, 74mg potassium. Calories from fat: 32 percent.

- Preheat over to 350°F. Lightly grease 8 × 3½ × 2½-inch loaf pan with nonstick cooking spray.
- In a large bowl, combine flour, baking powder, and baking soda. Using an electric mixer, add maple syrup, soy milk, and margarine and mix to combine.
- In small bowl, mix egg replacer with water. Add to maple syrup mixture along with vanilla extract and mix. Slowly add flour to liquid mixture and mix just until combined. Pour batter into prepared pan.
- Bake for 1 hour or until toothpick inserted in center comes out clean. Cool completely before removing from pan.

Serving suggestions: Top cake with Vanilla Glaze, page 204, or top each slice with a drizzle of Vegan Chocolate Syrup, page 203.

Variation: Add ¾ cup vegan chocolate chips to batter just before pouring into prepared pan to bake for a delicious chocolate chip pound cake.

Mocha Goober Cake

I GOT SO many requests for desserts made with chocolate and peanut butter when I was doing commercial baking that I created several variations on that theme, so that the desserts were always a bit different. This treat consists of dark chocolate cake smothered in creamy peanut butter frosting. Here's a helpful hint: The Creamy Peanut Butter Frosting tastes best if you prepare it the day before and allow it to set.

3 cups unbleached white flour
⅓ cup cocoa
2 tablespoons baking powder
1 teaspoon vanilla
6 ounces firm silken tofu
1½ cups water or apple juice
½ cup organic applesauce
1½ cups maple syrup
Creamy Peanut Butter
    Frosting, page 206
¼ cup vegan chocolate chips
    (ground) for garnish (optional)

. . . .

MAKES 12 SERVINGS
PREPARATION TIME:
   CAKE: 15 minutes
   FROSTING: 10 minutes
BAKING TIME: 45 minutes
FROSTING AND GARNISH: 5
minutes

. . . .

PER SERVING: 437 calories, 13g fat (3g saturated), 67g carbohydrate, 4g dietary fiber, 27g sugar, 16g protein, 0mg cholesterol, 88mg sodium, 582mg potassium. Calories from fat: 26 percent.

- Preheat oven to 350°F. Lightly grease 9 × 12-inch rectangular pan with nonstick cooking spray.
- In a large bowl, combine flour, cocoa, and baking powder. Mix with a whisk to combine. In a food processor, puree tofu until smooth. Add vanilla and applesauce and blend. Add water (or apple juice) and maple syrup and blend. Slowly add liquid ingredients to flour mixture and mix with whisk until combined. Do not overmix. Pour batter into prepared pan.
- Bake for 45 minutes or until toothpick inserted in center comes out clean. Allow to cool in pan. If you did not make the Creamy Peanut Butter Frosting the day before, prepare it while cake is baking.
- Frost, leaving cake in pan, and garnish with ground vegan chocolate chips if desired. (You may put chocolate chips in a food processor or blender and process until finely ground.)

CHOCOLATE-COVERED GOLD

*T*HIS CAKE IS a traditional American favorite. Its delicate vanilla flavor is the perfect compliment for the rich, creamy chocolate icing. It's a sure crowd pleaser.

1¼ cups maple syrup
¾ cup soy margarine
4½ cups flour
1½ tablespoons baking powder
¼ teaspoon salt
2½ cups soy milk, rice milk, or
 non-dairy milk of choice
1 tablespoon vanilla
Whipped Chocolate Frosting,
 page 202

. . . .

MAKES 12 SERVINGS
PREPARATION TIME:
 CAKE: 15 minutes
 ICING: 10 minutes
BAKING TIME: 30 minutes
FROSTING/GARNISH: 5 minutes
. . . .

- Preheat oven to 350°F. Coat a 9 × 13-inch cake pan with nonstick cooking spray.
- Allow margarine to soften to room temperature or soften in microwave. Do not melt. (If you cannot find soy margarine, any vegetable-based margarine will work.) Place margarine in bowl and cream. Slowly add maple syrup and beat until light and fluffy, then add vanilla and mix. In another bowl, combine flour, baking powder, and salt and mix to combine. Alternately add flour mixture and soy milk to maple/margarine and mix well.
- Pour into prepared pan and bake for approximately 30 minutes, or until toothpick inserted in center comes out clean. Allow to cool completely before frosting.
- While cake is baking, prepare Whipped Chocolate Frosting.
- Frost cake and garnish with ground vegan chocolate chips if desired. Refrigerate cake before serving and store in the refrigerator.

PER SERVING: 548 calories, 17g fat (6g saturated), 89g carbohydrate, 4g dietary fiber, 22g sugar, 13g protein, 0 mg cholesterol, 48mg sodium, 394mg potassium. Calories from fat: 25 percent.

Mellow Yellow Cake

I LIKE TO make fruity cakes in the summer. For this treat, I layered yellow cake with raspberry jam and topped it off with a light raspberry frosting.

1¼ cups maple syrup
¾ cup soy margarine
4½ cups flour
1½ tablespoon baking powder
1 teaspoon salt
2½ cups soy milk, rice milk, or non-dairy milk of choice
1 tablespoon vanilla
Light Raspberry Frosting, page 207

FILLING:
¾ cup raspberry jam

. . . .

MAKES 12 SERVINGS
PREPARATION TIME:
  CAKE: 15 minutes
  ICING: 10 minutes
BAKING TIME: 50 minutes
FROSTING/GARNISH: 5 minutes

. . . .

- Preheat oven to 350°F. Coat a 9 × 11-inch cake pan with nonstick cooking spray.
- Allow margarine to soften to room temperature or soften in microwave. Do not melt. (If you cannot find soy margarine, any vegetable-based margarine will work.) Place margarine in bowl and cream. Slowly add maple syrup and beat until light and fluffy. Add vanilla and mix. In another bowl, combine flour, baking powder, and salt and mix to combine. Alternately add flour mixture and soy milk to maple/margarine mixture and stir well.
- Pour into prepared pan and bake for approximately 50 minutes, or until toothpick inserted in center comes out clean. Allow to cool completely before frosting. While cake is baking, prepare the Light Raspberry Frosting.
- When cake is completely cooled, carefully invert cake on wire rack. With a long, sharp knife, cut cake in half lengthwise, making two layers. Return bottom layer to pan and top with raspberry jam. Place top layer on layer of jam.
- Mound frosting onto cake and decorate with fresh raspberries if desired. Store in the refrigerator.

PER SERVING: 486 calories, 9g fat (<1g saturated), 91g carbohydrate, 2g dietary fiber, 22g sugar, 12g protein, 0mg cholesterol, 211mg sodium, 415mg potassium. Calories from fat: 15 percent.

CITRUS ORANGE CAKE

I CREATED THIS cake to be completely different from the dark chocolate creations that I usually work with. This is a light vanilla cake covered with orange frosting. It makes a lovely spring or summer dessert garnished with fresh fruit!

1¼ cups maple syrup
¾ cup soy margarine
4½ cups flour
1½ tablespoons baking powder
¼ teaspoon salt
2½ cups soy milk, rice milk, or
  non-dairy milk of choice
1 tablespoon vanilla
Fluffy Orange Frosting,
  page 207

MAKES 12 SERVINGS
PREPARATION TIME:
  CAKE: 15 minutes
  ICING: 10 minutes
BAKING TIME: 50 minutes
FROSTING/GARNISH: 5 minutes

- Preheat oven to 350°F. Coat a 9 × 11-inch cake pan with nonstick cooking spray.
- Allow margarine to soften to room temperature or soften in microwave. Do not melt. (If you can't find soy margarine, any vegetable-based margarine will work, but try to find one that is non-hydrogenated.) Place margarine in bowl and cream. Slowly add maple syrup and beat until light and fluffy. Add vanilla and mix. In another bowl, combine flour, baking powder, and salt and mix to combine.
- Alternately add flour mixture and soy milk to maple/margarine. Mix well. Pour into prepared pan and bake for approximately 50 minutes, or until toothpick inserted in center comes out clean.
- Allow to cool completely before frosting. While cake is baking, prepare Fluffy Orange Frosting.
- Mound onto cake and swirl or make peaks in frosting. Decorate with fresh orange wedges or mandarin orange sections if desired. Chill before serving. Store in the refrigerator.

Variations:
- Substitute 2½ cups orange juice for the 2½ cups soy milk—this will make a delicious orange cake. You can also top this cake with Fluffy Orange Frosting for a tasty orange treat.
- Substitute orange juice for the soy milk in the cake recipe and frost with Fluffy Orange Frosting as in variation above. But bake in two 8-inch round cake

pans coated with nonstick cooking spray and lined with wax or parchment paper. Adjust baking time to 30–35 minutes. Cut each cake layer in half horizontally so that you have four layers. Spread each layer with ⅓ cup raspberry preserve and then frost. Since the soft frosting and preserves do not make a sturdy cake, you may want to insert a wooden skewer, which is available at most grocery stores or kitchen supply stores, into the middle of the cake. If you cut it so that the skewer cannot be seen, no one but you will know it's there.

YELLOW CAKE WITH ORANGE FROSTING
PER SERVING: 422 calories, 9g fat (<1g saturated), 74g carbohydrate, 2g dietary fiber, 22g sugar, 11g protein, 0mg cholesterol, 45mg sodium. Calories from fat: 17 percent.

ORANGE CAKE WITH ORANGE FROSTING
PER SERVING: 447 calories, 11g fat (<1g saturated), 78g carbohydrate, 1g dietary fiber, 22g sugar, 11g protein, 0mg cholesterol, 100mg sodium, 425mg potassium. Calories from fat: 20 percent.

ORANGE CAKE WITH ORANGE FROSTING AND RASPBERRY FILLING
PER SERVING: 607 calories, 23g fat (1g saturated), 96g carbohydrate, 2g dietary fiber, 22g sugar, 11g protein, 0mg cholesterol, 176mg sodium, 445mg potassium. Calories from fat: 30 percent.

TOASTED COCONUT PECAN CAKE

EVEN AS A child, I loved to cook. My favorite recipe was for a toasted coconut pecan cake—a yellow cake mix to which pecans were added, topped with a cream cheese icing mixed with coconut toasted in butter. I loved that cake. As I got older and started thinking about my health, I realized that I could make the same cake, only healthier. So here's the new and improved version. Because of the soy cream cheese frosting, pecans, and coconut, it is still higher in calories than the other cakes in this book. The coconut raises the amount of saturated fat as well. But, it contains *no* cholesterol. Sometimes we all have to splurge!

$1\frac{1}{4}$ cups maple syrup
$\frac{3}{4}$ cup soy margarine
$4\frac{1}{2}$ cups flour
$1\frac{1}{2}$ tablespoons baking powder
$\frac{1}{4}$ teaspoon salt
$2\frac{1}{2}$ cups soy milk, rice milk, or
   non-dairy milk of choice
1 tablespoon vanilla
1 cup toasted coconut (broil
   unsweetened coconut until
   golden brown)
1 cup chopped pecans
Toasted Coconut Pecan
   Frosting, page 208

- Preheat oven to 350°F. Coat three 8-inch cake pans with nonstick cooking spray. Line the bottom of each pan with parchment paper or wax paper.
- To toast coconut for cake and frosting, line cookie sheet with aluminum foil. Coat with nonstick cooking spray. Spread coconut in a thin layer on baking sheet and place under broiler. Stir as coconut begins to brown. Remove from oven immediately when golden brown and set aside.
- Allow margarine to soften to room temperature or soften in microwave. Do not melt. (If you cannot find soy margarine, any vegetable-based margarine will work.) Place margarine in bowl and cream. Slowly add maple syrup and beat until light and fluffy. Add vanilla and mix. Add toasted coconut and pecans.
- In another bowl, combine flour, baking powder, and salt and mix to combine. Alternately add flour mixture and soy milk to maple/margarine mixture and stir well. Pour into prepared pan and bake for approximately 30 minutes, or until toothpick inserted in center comes out clean. While cake is baking, prepare the Toasted Coconut Pecan Frosting.

- Cool cake 10 minutes in pans and then remove from pans. Allow to cool completely before frosting.
- Frost only tops of cake. Do not frost sides. Allow icing to ooze out from between layers.

. . . .

MAKES 12 SERVINGS
PREPARATION TIME:
    CAKE: 20 minutes
    ICING: 10 minutes
BAKING TIME: 30 minutes
FROSTING/GARNISH: 5 minutes

. . . .

PER SERVING: 830 calories, 60g fat (31g saturated)*, 69g carbohydrate, 4g dietary fiber, 22g sugar, 10g protein, 0mg cholesterol, 177mg sodium, 284mg potassium. Calories from fat: 53 percent.

* These figures are higher than the other recipes in this book because this cake uses both nuts and coconut. These foods are both healthy, but they're also quite high in fat, some of it saturated.

TROPICAL MANGO CAKE

*T*HIS CAKE GOT rave reviews from my taste testers! It tastes great made with mango juice, but if you can't find any at your local health food store or grocery store, any juice that sounds good to you may be substituted. Just be sure that it is 100 percent juice.

1¼ cups maple syrup
¾ cup soy margarine
4½ cups flour
1½ tablespoon baking powder
¼ teaspoon salt
2½ cups mango juice
1 teaspoon vanilla
Whipped Coconut Cream
  Frosting, page 209

....

MAKES 12 SERVINGS
PREPARATION TIME:
  CAKE: 15 minutes
  ICING: 10 minutes
BAKING TIME: 55 minutes
FROSTING/GARNISH: 5 minutes

....

- Preheat oven to 350°F. Coat a 9 × 11-inch cake pan with nonstick cooking spray.
- Allow margarine to soften to room temperature or soften in microwave. Do not melt. (If you cannot find soy margarine, any vegetable-based margarine will work.) Place margarine in bowl and cream. Slowly add maple syrup and beat until light and fluffy. Add vanilla and mix.
- In another bowl, combine flour, baking powder, and salt and mix to combine. Alternately add flour mixture and mango juice to maple/margarine mixture and stir well.
- Pour into prepared pan and bake for approximately 55 minutes, or until toothpick inserted in center comes out clean. Allow to cool completely before adding the Whipped Coconut Cream Frosting. Mound onto cake and swirl or make peaks in frosting.
- Sprinkle on reserved coconut.

PER SERVING: 507 calories, 21g fat (12g saturated), 71g carbohydrate, 1g dietary fiber, 22g sugar, 10g protein, 0mg cholesterol, 84mg sodium, 319mg potassium. Calories from fat: 35 percent.

You Can't Catch Me I'm the Gingerbread . . . Cake

ARM, SPICY GINGERBREAD cake is great to eat while wrapped in a fuzzy blanket snuggled in front of a fire with a cup of hot coffee or warm mulled apple cider. What could be better for the holidays?

¾ cup maple syrup
¾ cup molasses
⅓ cup canola oil
1 tablespoon vanilla
2 teaspoon ground ginger
1 teaspoon cinnamon
1 teaspoon ground nutmeg
¼ teaspoon ground cloves
¼ teaspoon allspice
4½ cups unbleached white flour
1½ tablespoons baking powder
¼ teaspoon salt
2½ cups soy milk, rice milk, or
    non-dairy milk of choice
Cream Cheese Frosting, page
    210, or Vanilla Glaze,
    page 204

. . . .
MAKES 12 SERVINGS
PREPARATION TIME:
    CAKE: 15 minutes
    ICING: 10 minutes
BAKING TIME: 30 minutes
FROSTING/GARNISH: 5 minutes
. . . .

- Preheat oven to 350°F. Coat a 9 × 11-inch cake pan or bundt pan with nonstick cooking spray.
- Combine maple syrup and molasses. Add maple syrup/molasses to oil. Add vanilla and mix. In another bowl, combine flour, baking powder, spices, and salt and mix well. Alternately add flour mixture and soy milk to maple/molasses and mix well. Pour into prepared pan and bake for approximately 30 minutes, or until toothpick inserted in center comes out clean.
- Allow to cool completely before frosting with either the Cream Cheese Frosting or the Vanilla Glaze.

Hint: I found that the Vanilla Glaze works well on bundt cake, and the Cream Cheese Frosting works will on 9 x 11-inch cake.

The bundt cake will take longer to bake—about 45 minutes. Check by sticking a cake tester into center of cake. When it comes out clean, cake is done.

PER SERVING (cake only): 406 calories, 14g fat (1g saturated), 65g carbohydrate, 2g dietary fiber, 12g sugar, 6g protein, 0mg cholesterol, 67mg sodium, 471mg potassium. Calories from fat: 29 percent.

PER SERVING: 540 calories, 21g fat (3g saturated), 78g carbohydrate, 2g dietary fiber, 14g sugar, 11g protein, 0mg cholesterol, 152mg sodium, 622mg potassium. Calories from fat: 26 percent.

HOLD THE WHEAT CARROT CAKE

MY HUSBAND LOVES carrot cake and I experimented with many carrot cake recipes trying to get just the right texture and taste. This recipe did the trick.

¾ cup garbanzo bean flour

1¼ cups rice flour

2 teaspoons xanthan gum

2 teaspoons baking soda

¼ teaspoon salt

2 teaspoons cinnamon

½ cup applesauce

1 cup canola oil

4 teaspoons flax powder

1 cup water

1¼ cups maple syrup

2 cups grated carrots (preferably
organic)

1 teaspoons vanilla

Cream Cheese Frosting,
page 210

. . . .

MAKES 12 SERVINGS

PREPARATION TIME:

CAKE: 20 minutes

ICING: 10 minutes

BAKING TIME: 80 minutes

FROSTING/GARNISH: 5 minutes

FREEZES WELL WITHOUT
FROSTING

. . . .

- Preheat oven to 325°F. Coat 9 × 13-inch pan, 9-inch round springform pan, or small bundt pan with non-stick cooking spray.
- Mix together bean flour, rice flour, xanthan gum, baking soda, salt, and cinnamon and set aside.
- Make a slurry* with the 1 cup water and 4 teaspoons flax powder and then add applesauce, oil, vanilla, and maple syrup.
- Add wet ingredients to dry ingredients and mix just until combined. Add carrots then pour into prepared pan. Bake at 325°F 75–80 minutes.
- Cool completely before frosting with the Cream Cheese Frosting.
- You may want to sprinkle ground nuts (walnuts or pecans) on top of the iced cake.
- Store in refrigerator.

Variation: You can also use the Soy Cream Cheese Glaze, page 211, instead of the Cream Cheese Frosting. Either way, this cake is delicious.

*A slurry is a thin mixture of liquid, usually water, mixed with a finely ground substance.

PER SERVING (cake only): 354 calories, 19g fat (1g saturated), 43g carbohydrate, 4g dietary fiber, 21g sugar, 3g protein, 0mg cholesterol, 233mg sodium, 184mg potassium. Calories from fat: 47 percent.

CAKE WITH CREAM CHEESE FROSTING
PER SERVING: 493 calories, 26g fat (3g saturated), 56g carbohydrate, 4g dietary fiber, 23g sugar, 8g protein, 0mg cholesterol, 318mg sodium, 340mg potassium. Calories from fat: 39 percent.

CREAM CHEESE GLAZE
PER SERVING: 133 calories, 7g fat (1g saturated), 13g carbohydrate, <.1g dietary fiber, 1g sugar, 5g protein, 0mg cholesterol, 85mg sodium, 152mg potassium. Calories from fat: 15 percent.

BOLD BANANA CAKE

Wheat Free

HIS IS A heavy, rich-tasting cake that works best as only one layer. You can either frost and serve it right from the pan, or remove it from the pan and frost and decorate it as a one-layer torte. I like to arrange vegan chocolate chips around the outside edge and along the bottom of the cake before serving. It gives it a professional look.

2½ cups oatmeal (ground into a fine flour in a blender or food processor)

2 teaspoons baking powder

1 teaspoon baking soda

1 teaspoon xanthan gum* (optional)

3 medium bananas, mashed with a fork (the riper, the sweeter)

½ cup maple syrup

½ cup unsweetened organic applesauce

3 teaspoons flax powder

¾ cup water

2 tablespoons whipped tofu

1 teaspoons vanilla

½ cup grain sweetened vegan chocolate chips (available at health food stores) plus another ½ cup chocolate chips if using them for a garnish

Maple Cocoa Frosting, page 211

• Preheat oven to 375°F. Coat 8-inch round cake pan or 8-inch springform pan with nonstick cooking spray.

• Mash bananas in medium bowl with fork. Add maple sugar, applesauce, whipped tofu, and vanilla. Make a slurry** with flax powder and ¾ cup water. Add flax/water to banana mixture.

• In another bowl, mix oat flour, baking powder, and baking soda. Add wet ingredients to dry ingredients and mix just to combine. Add chocolate chips and stir again, just to mix. Do not overmix. Pour batter into prepared pan

• Bake 30–35 minutes or until sides pull away from the edge of the pan and a toothpick inserted in the center comes out clean. Allow to cool completely before frosting with Maple Cocoa Frosting.

* Xanthan gum will produce a slightly softer filling, but will not give the mild flour taste that you may get if you use the flour.

** A slurry is a thin mixyture of liquid, usually water, combined with a finely ground substance.

. . . .

MAKES 10 SERVINGS

PREPARATION TIME:

   CAKE: 20 minutes

   ICING: 10 minutes

BAKING TIME: 30–35 minutes

FROSTING/GARNISH: 5 minutes

. . . .

PER SERVING: 216 calories, 5g fat (2g saturated), 46g carbohydrate, 6g dietary fiber, 20g sugar, 4g protein, 0mg cholesterol, 100mg sodium, 390mg potassium. Calories from fat: 17 percent.

APPLESAUCE APPLAUSE CAKE

*T*HIS MOIST APPLESAUCE cake tastes wonderful on a cool autumn day. Actually, it tastes great anytime! I like to make it as a two-layer cake iced with fluffy vanilla soy cream cheese icing and pipe a decorative edging of apple butter around the top edge and the bottom of the cake. I make sure that I buy the unsweetened, thick apple butter such as Bauman's to use for the edging.

3½ cups unbleached white flour
2 teaspoons baking soda
2 teaspoons cinnamon
¼ teaspoon sea salt
⅓ cup canola oil
1 cup unprocessed sugar such as Sucanat (or dark brown sugar)
2 teaspoons flax powder
2 cups unsweetened (preferably organic) applesauce
½ cup apple cider (apple juice or water)
Whipped Cream Cheese Frosting, page 212 (should be made the day before serving if possible)

. . . .
MAKES 12 SERVINGS
PREPARATION TIME:
   CAKE: 15 minutes
   ICING: 10 minutes
BAKING TIME: 30–35 minutes
FROSTING/GARNISH: 10 minutes
FREEZES WELL WITHOUT ICING
. . . .

PER SERVING: 421 calories, 20g fat (3g saturated), 54g carbohydrate, 2g dietary fiber, 6g sugar, 7g protein, 0mg cholesterol, 319mg sodium, 170mg potassium. Calories from fat: 29 percent.

- Preheat oven to 350°F. Coat two 8-inch round baking pans with nonstick cooking oil and line bottom of pans with waxed or parchment paper.
- In a large bowl, combine flour, baking soda, cinnamon, and salt and set aside. Using an electric mixer, beat oil and sweetener until combined in another bowl. Mix flax powder and apple cider (or apple juice or water) together in a small bowl, add to oil and sweetener, and mix until combined. Beat in applesauce. On low speed, add dry ingredients to oil/sweetener mixture and beat just until combined. Pour batter into prepared pans.
- Bake 30–35 minutes or until toothpick inserted in center comes out clean.
- If you have not made the frosting the day before, prepare the Whipped Cream Cheese Frosting while the cake is baking.
- Cool in pans for 10 minutes and remove from pans. Remove waxed or parchment paper from bottom of cakes. Cool completely on wire racks before frosting.

ORANGE CREAMSICLE CAKE

WHO CAN FORGET those delicious orange creamsicles that we ate as kids? This cake brings back memories of lazy summer days spent enjoying the combined flavors of orange and vanilla.

1¼ cups maple syrup
¾ cup soy margarine
4½ cups flour
1½ tablespoon baking powder
¼ teaspoon salt
2½ cups orange juice
1 tablespoon orange extract
Whipped Cream Cheese
    Frosting, page 212

. . . .

MAKES 12 SERVINGS
PREPARATION TIME:
    CAKE: 15 minutes
    ICING: 10 minutes
BAKING TIME: 55 minutes
FROSTING/GARNISH: 5 minutes
FREEZES WELL WITHOUT ICING
. . . .

- Preheat oven to 350°F. Coat an 8 × 11-inch cake pan with nonstick cooking spray.
- Allow margarine to soften to room temperature or soften in microwave. Do not melt. (If you cannot find soy margarine, any vegetable-based margarine will work.) Place margarine in bowl and cream. Slowly add maple syrup and beat until light and fluffy. Add orange extract and mix. In another bowl, combine flour, baking powder and salt and mix to combine. Alternately add flour mixture and orange juice to maple/margarine and mix well.
- Pour into prepared pan and bake for approximately 55 minutes, or until toothpick inserted in center comes out clean. Allow to cool completely before frosting.
- While cake is baking, prepare the Whipped Cream Cheese Frosting.

PER SERVING: 481 calories, 16g fat (2g saturated), 77g carbohydrate, 1g dietary fiber, 21g sugar, 8g protein, 0mg cholesterol, 216mg sodium, 300mg potassium. Calories from fat: 15 percent.

TROPICAL FRUIT CAKE

I USED TO love strawberry cake with coconut cream frosting before I became vegan. I wanted to be able to continue to enjoy that same taste, so I "veganized" it. This cake is a combination of strawberry cake, strawberry jam, and fluffy coconut cream cheese frosting.

1¼ *cups maple syrup*
¾ *cup soy margarine*
4½ *cups unbleached white flour*
1½ *tablespoons baking powder*
¼ *teaspoon salt*
2½ *cups soy milk, or other non-dairy milk of your choice*
1 *tablespoon vanilla*
10 *large strawberries*
Coconut Cream Cheese Frosting, page 209
½ *cup unsweetened coconut for garnish (optional)*

FILLING:
¾ *cup strawberry preserve*

. . . .

MAKES 12 SERVINGS
PREPARATION TIME:
   CAKE: 15 minutes
   FROSTING/GARNISH: 5 minutes
BAKING TIME: 30–35 minutes
FREEZES WELL WITHOUT FROSTING

. . . .

PER SERVING: 561 calories, 26g fat (10g saturated), 74g carbohydrate, 2g dietary fiber, 21g sugar, 10g protein, 0mg cholesterol, 223mg sodium, 289mg potassium. Calories from fat: 28 percent.

- Preheat oven to 350°F. Coat two 8-inch pans with nonstick cooking spray. Line the bottom of each pan with waxed or parchment paper.
- Allow margarine to soften to room temperature or soften in microwave. Do not melt. (If you cannot find soy margarine, any vegetable-based margarine will work.) In a bowl, slowly add maple syrup to margarine and beat until light and fluffy. Add strawberries and puree. Add vanilla and mix.
- In another bowl, combine flour, baking powder, and salt and mix to combine. Alternately add flour mixture and soy milk to strawberry mixture and mix well.
- Pour into prepared pans and bake for approximately 30 minutes, or until toothpick inserted in center comes out clean. Allow to cool completely before frosting.
- If you did not prepare the Coconut Cream Cheese Frosting the day before, prepare it while the cake is baking.
- *To assemble and frost:* With sharp knife or wire cake cutter, cut off rounded top of both cake layers. Then cut each layer in half lengthwise to form four thin layers. Place bottom layer on serving plate and spread with strawberry preserve. Place each layer on top, spreading each one with strawberry preserve. Place top layer on top of preserve upside down so that the side facing up is completely flat. Frost top and sides of cake with Coconut Cream Cheese Frosting. Sprinkle coconut over top and sides of cake and refrigerate.

GRANNY'S CRANBERRY CAKE

HOCOLATE AND CRANBERRY teamed together make an interesting duo. This cake is a great way to usher in the Christmas season, and it provides a way to use up some of those Thanksgiving leftovers—you can use your leftover cranberry relish as the filling.

3 cups unbleached white flour
⅓ cup cocoa
2 tablespoon baking powder
1 teaspoon vanilla
6 ounces firm silken tofu
1½ cups water or apple juice
½ cup organic applesauce
1½ cups maple syrup
Whipped Cream Cheese
    Frosting, page 212
1 cup fresh cranberries as gar-
    nish (optional)
Fresh mint leaves as garnish
    (optional)

FILLING:
¾ cup cranberry relish (check the
    label to make sure it is vegan)

. . . .
MAKES 12 SERVINGS
PREPARATION TIME:
    CAKE: 15 minutes
    FROSTING: 10 minutes
BAKING TIME: 35 minutes
. . . .

PER SERVING: 395 calories, 7g fat (2g saturated), 77g carbohydrate, 3g dietary fiber, 26g sugar, 9g protein, 0mg cholesterol, 136mg sodium, 356mg potassium. Calories from fat: 7 percent.

- Preheat oven to 350°F. Lightly grease two 8-inch cake pans with nonstick cooking spray. Line the bottom of each pan with wax or parchment paper.
- In a large bowl, combine flour, cocoa, and baking powder. Mix with a whisk to combine. In a food processor, puree tofu until smooth. Add vanilla and applesauce and blend. Add water (or apple juice) and maple syrup and blend. Slowly add liquid ingredients to flour mixture. Mix with whisk until combined. Do not overmix. Pour batter into prepared pan.
- Bake for 35 minutes of until toothpick inserted in center comes out clean. After baking, remove cake from oven. Allow to cool for 10 minutes in pans. Remove from pans and place on wire rack. Remove wax paper or parchment paper and allow to cool completely. If you have not prepared the Whipped Cream Cheese Frosting the day before, prepare it while cake is baking.
- *To assemble and decorate:* When cake is completely cool, level off top of cake layers with long, sharp knife or wire cake cutter. Cut each layer in half horizontally to form four thin layers. Place bottom layer onto serving plate. Top with ¼ cup cranberry relish. Place next layer on top and another ¼ cup of relish. Repeat. Frost top and sides of cake with Whipped Cream Cheese Frosting and decorate with fresh cranberries and mint leaves if desired.

CHOCOLATE-COVERED MINT

ave you ever dipped a candy cane in your hot chocolate? As a child, being a creative young chocoholic, I did just that and found that chocolate and mint flavors were natural companions.

2¼ cups unbleached white flour
1¾ cups granulated sweetener
¾ cup cocoa
1½ teaspoons baking powder
1¼ teaspoons baking soda
¼ teaspoon sea salt
3 teaspoons peppermint extract
2 cups soymilk (or non-dairy
    milk of your choice)
¼ cup soy mayonnaise (such as
    Nayonaise)
½ cup applesauce
Whipped Chocolate Frosting,
    page 202

. . . .
MAKES 12 SERVINGS
PREPARATION TIME:
    CAKE: 15 minutes
    FROSTING: 10 minutes
BAKING TIME: 45 minutes
FROSTING/GARNISH: 5 minutes
. . . .

- Preheat oven to 375°F. Coat a 9 × 12-inch baking pan with nonstick cooking spray.
- In a medium bowl, combine flour, sweetener, cocoa, baking powder, baking soda, and salt. In another bowl, combine soymilk, peppermint extract, soy mayonnaise, and applesauce. Slowly pour liquid mixture into dry mixture and stir to combine. Pour into prepared pan.
- Bake for 45 minutes or until toothpick inserted in center comes out clean. Remove from oven and allow to cool completely.
- If you did not prepare the Whipped Chocolate Frosting the day before, prepare it while cake is baking. Mound onto completely cooled cake and garnish with mini candy canes if desired. (Be sure to check ingredients on label to be sure they are vegan if you intend to eat them.)
- Refrigerate before serving.

PER SERVING: 391 calories, 13g fat (6g saturated), 64g carbohydrate, 5g dietary fiber, 1g sugar, 11g protein, 0mg cholesterol, 188mg sodium, 363mg potassium. Calories from fat: 27 percent.

MY GRANDMOTHER'S CRUMB CAKE

*T*HIS RECIPE HAS been handed down through my family for generations, and I was able to veganize it without sacrificing any of the good taste. My kids absolutely love it and ask me to make it all the time. It doesn't last long! We usually eat it for breakfast, but it is equally good for dessert (or even a snack).

1½ cups granulated sugar
2 cups unbleached white flour
½ cup vegetable shortening
  (preferably non-hydrogenated
  like Spectrum)
2 teaspoons baking powder
1 teaspoon vanilla
1 teaspoon Ener-G Egg
  Replacer
¼ cup water
¾ cup vanilla flavor soy milk,
  or other non-dairy milk of
  your choice

. . . .

MAKES 9 SERVINGS
PREPARATION TIME: 15 minutes
BAKING TIME: 45 minutes
. . . .

- Preheat oven to 350°F. Coat an 8 × 8-inch square baking pan with nonstick cooking spray.
- In a bowl, combine sugar, flour, and baking powder. Cut shortening into flour mixture with 2 knives until the shortening is smaller than pea-sized. Remove 1 cup of dry mix and set aside.
- In a measuring cup, mix egg replacer with ¼ cup water and add vanilla. Fill the cup the rest of the way with soy milk until it measures 1 cup (approximately ¾ cup of soy milk). Add liquid to dry ingredients and mix just until combined.
- Pour batter into prepared pan and sprinkle with reserved dry mix. Bake for 45 minutes or until toothpick inserted in center comes out clean.
- Allow to cool completely before serving.

Variations: Add 1 cup fresh peaches, blueberries, or cherries to batter before pouring in pan and adding crumbs. Bake as directed.

PER SERVING: 336 calories, 12g fat (5g saturated), 55g carbohydrate, 1g dietary fiber 3g protein, 0mg cholesterol, 84mg sodium, 61 mg potassium. Calories from fat: 29 percent.

Oops, I Dropped My Cake

*T*HIS TENDER CAKE dripping with pineapple and sugar is guaranteed to disappear in a snap!

TOPPING:

1 can (15½ ounces) crushed
    pineapple
1 cup packed brown sugar
¼ cup canola oil

BATTER:

1½ cups granulated sugar
2 cups unbleached white flour
½ cup vegetable shortening
    (preferably non-hydrogenated
    like Spectrum)
2 teaspoons baking powder
1 teaspoon vanilla
1 teaspoon Ener-G Egg
    Replacer
¼ cup water
1¼ cups pineapple juice
4 bing cherries, pitted and cut
    in half, if in season

. . . .

MAKES 12 SERVINGS
PREPARATION TIME: 15 minutes
BAKING TIME: 55 minutes
FREEZES WELL

. . . .

- Preheat oven to 375°F. Coat a 9-inch round baking pan with nonstick cooking spray.
- *To make topping:* Drain pineapple and reserve the juice. (If it does not measure 1¼ cups, add water to make up the difference.) In a small bowl, combine topping ingredients and mix. Pour topping into prepared pan. If using fresh cherries, arrange halves at equal distances around pan. Push them through topping so they are on the bottom of the pan, which will eventually be the top of the cake.
- *To make batter:* In a bowl, combine sugar, flour, and baking powder. Cut shortening into flour mixture with two knives until the shortening is smaller than pea-sized.
- In a small bowl, mix egg replacer with water. Add 1¼ cups reserved pineapple juice to egg replacer mixture and then add vanilla. Pour liquid ingredients into dry ingredients and mix just until combined. Spoon batter into prepared pan onto topping mixture.
- Bake for 55 minutes or until toothpick inserted in center comes out clean.
- Invert cake onto serving plate immediately upon removing from oven. Allow to cool completely before serving.

Hint: This cake tends to drip sticky pineapple juice so it is a good idea to place a sheet of aluminum foil on the bottom oven rack to make your clean-up easier.

PER SERVING: 308 calories, 13g fat (4g saturated), 50g carbohydrate, <1g dietary fiber, <1g protein, 0mg cholesterol, 66mg sodium, 127mg potassium. Calories from fat: 36 percent.

BANANA SPLIT CAKE

Wheat Free

HIS CAKE TAKES a bit more work because there are several parts to it, but it is definitely worth the extra time. It mimics the taste of a banana split—who can resist that?

2½ cups oatmeal (ground into a fine flour in a blender or food processor)

2 teaspoons baking powder

1 teaspoon baking soda

1 teaspoon xanthan gum* (optional)

3 medium bananas, mashed with a fork (the riper, the sweeter)

½ cup maple syrup

½ cup unsweetened pineapple

3 teaspoons flax powder

¾ cup pineapple juice

2 tablespoons whipped tofu

½ banana for garnish (optional)

Vanilla Tofu Whipped Topping, page 204

Cherry Topping, page 201

Vegan Chocolate Syrup, page 203

MAKES 10 SERVINGS

PREPARATION TIME:

CAKE: 15 MINUTES

CHERRY TOPPING: 10 minutes

WHIPPED TOPPING: 10 minutes

CHOCOLATE SYRUP: 5 minutes

BAKING TIME: 40 MINUTES

- Preheat oven to 375°F degrees. Coat 8-inch round cake pan or 8-inch springform pan with nonstick cooking spray.
- Mash bananas in medium-size bowl with fork. Add maple sugar, pineapple, whipped tofu, and vanilla. Make a slurry** with flax powder and ¾ cup pineapple juice. Add flax slurry to banana mixture.
- In another bowl, mix oat flour, baking powder, and baking soda. Add wet ingredients to dry ingredients and mix just to combine. Pour batter into prepared pan.
- Bake 40 minutes (or until sides pull away from the edge of the pan and a toothpick inserted in the center comes out clean). Allow to cool completely.
- While cake is baking, make the Vanilla Tofu Whipped Topping, the Cherry Topping, and the Vegan Chocolate Syrup.
- *To assemble:* When cake is completely cool (and immediately before serving), use a spoon to drop Vanilla Tofu Whipped Topping around outside edge of cake. Spoon cooled Cherry Topping inside ring of whipped topping. Slice banana and stand a slice in each mound of whipped topping. Drizzle Vegan Chocolate Syrup over cake in a lattice pattern. Serve immediately.

* Xanthan gum will produce a slightly softer filing, but will not give the mild flour taste that you may get if you use the flour.

** A slurry is a thin mixture of liquid, usually water, combined with a finely ground substance.

PER SERVING: 223 calories, 3g fat (<1g saturated), 46g carbohydrate, 3g dietary fiber, 16g sugar, 5g protein, 0mg cholesterol, 225mg sodium, 441mg potassium. Calories from fat: 11 percent.

Long on Flavor Shortcake

HEN I BECAME vegan, I was faced with the challenge of finding shortcake to use for one of my favorite desserts—strawberry shortcake. None of the commercial shortcakes were vegan, and I never really like their spongy consistency. So I came up with this vegan version of strawberry shortcake, which is long on flavor and short on fat and cholesterol.

1½ cups granulated sugar
2 cups unbleached white flour
*½ cup vegetable shortening
    (preferably non-hydrogenated
    like Spectrum)*
2 teaspoons baking powder
1 teaspoon vanilla
*1 teaspoon Ener-G Egg
    Replacer*
¼ cup water
*¾ cup vanilla flavor soy milk,
    or other non-dairy milk of
    your choice*
*2 pints fresh strawberries
    (organic if possible)*
*9 fresh mint leaves for garnish
    (optional)*
*Vanilla Tofu Whipped Topping,
    page 204*

. . . .

MAKES 9 SERVINGS
PREPARATION TIME:
    CAKE: 15 minutes
    PREPARING STRAWBERRIES:
    15 minutes
    WHIPPED TOPPING:
    5 minutes
BAKING TIME: 45 minutes

. . . .

- Preheat oven to 350°F. Coat an 8 × 8-inch square baking pan with nonstick cooking spray.
- In a bowl, combine sugar, flour, and baking powder. Cut shortening into flour mixture with two knives until the shortening is smaller than pea-sized. Remove 1 cup of dry mix and set aside. In a measuring cup, mix egg replacer with ¼ cup water and add vanilla. Fill the cup the rest of the way with soy milk until it measures 1 cup (approximately ¾ cup of soymilk). Add liquid to dry ingredients and mix just until combined. Pour batter into prepared pan. Sprinkle with reserved dry mix.
- Bake for 45 minutes or until toothpick inserted in center comes out clean. Allow to cool completely before serving. While cake is baking, prepare a double recipe of Vanilla Tofu Whipped Topping.
- Hull strawberries, place in a bowl, and crush with a fork. Refrigerate until ready to use.
- *To serve:* Place a spoonful of strawberry sauce onto serving plate. Top with slice of cake. Top with more strawberry sauce. Spoon on a dollop of Vanilla Tofu Whipped Topping. Drizzle a small amount of strawberry juice from the sauce over the whipped topping if desired. Garnish with a fresh mint leaf if desired. Serve immediately.

PER SERVING: 524 calories, 16g fat (6g saturated), 86g carbohydrate, 5g dietary fiber, 2g sugar, 12g protein, 0mg cholesterol, 94mg sodium, 631mg potassium. Calories from fat: 26 percent.

LEMON TIMES TWO CAKE

Y NOW, YOU'RE well aware of my love for chocolate (If it were up to me, everything would have chocolate in it!), but I always enjoy the tangy sweet flavor of lemon.

1¼ cups maple syrup
¾ cup soy margarine
4½ cups flour
1½ tablespoon baking powder
¼ teaspoon salt
2½ cups lemon juice
½ teaspoon lemon extract
½ fresh lemon, thinly sliced for garnish (optional)
Fresh mint leaves for garnish (optional)
Whipped Lemon Frosting, page 208

. . . .

MAKES 12 SERVINGS
PREPARATION TIME:
    CAKE: 15 minutes
    ICING: 10 minutes
BAKING TIME: 30 minutes
FROSTING/GARNISH: 5 minutes
. . . .

- Preheat oven to 350°F. Coat an 8 x 11-inch cake pan with nonstick cooking spray.
- Allow margarine to soften to room temperature or soften in microwave. Do not melt. (If you cannot find soy margarine, any vegetable-based margarine will work.) Slowly add maple syrup and beat until light and fluffy. Add lemon extract and mix. In another bowl, combine flour, baking powder, and salt and mix to combine. Alternately add flour mixture and lemon juice to maple/margarine mixture and mix well.
- Pour into prepared pan and bake for approximately 30 minutes, or until toothpick inserted in center comes out clean. Allow to cool completely before frosting.
- If you did not make the Whipped Lemon Frosting the day before, prepare while cake is baking. Mound onto cake and swirl or make peaks in frosting.
- *To garnish:* Make a cut starting at the middle of each lemon slice to the edge (radius of slice). Twist each lemon slice and arrange on cake top. Place a mint leaf with each lemon twist. Chill before serving. Store in the refrigerator.

PER SERVING: 429 calories, 11g fat (<1g saturated), 76g carbohydrate, 1g dietary fiber, 22g sugar, 10g protein, 0mg cholesterol, 100mg sodium, 383mg potassium. Calories from fat: 20 percent.

CINN-SATIONAL APPLE CAKE

CINNAMON STICKS IN apple cider were my inspiration for this cake. I make it in the fall when apples are abundant and at their best. The homey smell of cinnamon and apples wafts through the house as the cake bakes. This cake makes a wonderful dessert, but you can eat it for breakfast as well.

2 cups unbleached white flour
1½ cups whole wheat flour
2 teaspoons baking soda
2 teaspoons cinnamon
¼ teaspoon sea salt
⅓ cup canola oil
1 cup unprocessed sugar such as Sucanat (or dark brown sugar)
2 teaspoons flax powder
½ cup apple cider (apple juice or water)
⅓ cup applesauce
¾ cup vanilla soy milk
2 cups baking apples (such as Macintosh) cored, peeled, and grated

CINNAMON MAPLE GLAZE:
½ cup maple syrup
1 teaspoons cinnamon

....

MAKES 15 SERVINGS
PREPARATION TIME:
  CAKE: 15 minutes
  GLAZE: 5 minutes
BAKING TIME: 1 hour
FREEZES WELL
....

- Preheat oven to 350°F. Coat bundt pan with nonstick cooking spray.
- In a large bowl, combine flours, baking soda, cinnamon, and salt. Using an electric mixer, beat oil and sweetener until combined. Mix flax powder with apple cider (or apple juice or water) together in a small bowl. Add to oil and sweetener and mix until combined. Add applesauce and soy milk to oil mixture and stir to combine. On low speed, add dry ingredients to oil/sweetener mixture and beat just until combined. Stir in grated apples by hand.
- Pour batter into prepared pan. Bake 60 minutes or until toothpick inserted in center comes out clean. Cool in pan for 10 minutes. Remove from pan and cool completely on wire rack. Put cake on serving plate.
- *To make glaze:* In a small saucepan, heat maple syrup until it is hot, but not boiling. Add cinnamon and stir to combine. Pour warm glaze over cake and serve.

PER SERVING: 255 calories, 10g fat (<1g saturated), 38g carbohydrate, 3g dietary fiber, 11g sugar, 4g protein, 0mg cholesterol, 176mg sodium, 156mg potassium. Calories from fat: 35 percent.

"P" Is for Pumpkin Cake

*T*HIS IS A wonderful cake to make in the fall when pumpkins and chrysanthemums are everywhere, the air is crisp, and the leaves are turning red and gold. For those of you who do not live in a changing climate and have never experienced the splendid colors and tastes of fall in the northeast United States, you can still appreciate this cake. It's like pumpkin pie in cake form!

1½ cups unbleached white flour
1½ cups whole wheat flour
2 teaspoons ground cinnamon
2 teaspoons baking soda
½ teaspoon salt
2 cups maple syrup
1 can (15 ounces) pure pureed
    pumpkin
4 teaspoons flax powder
¾ cup water
½ cup canola oil
½ cup applesauce
Pumpkin Whipped Topping,
    page 209

. . . .

MAKES 15 SERVINGS
PREPARATION TIME:
    CAKE: 15 minutes
    FROSTING: 10 minutes
BAKING TIME: 80 minutes

. . . .

- Preheat oven to 350°F. Coat a bundt cake pan with nonstick cooking spray.
- Combine flours, cinnamon, baking soda, and salt in a large bowl. Combine maple syrup, pumpkin, oil, and applesauce in another bowl. In a small bowl, combine flax powder and water. Add to liquid ingredients and combine. Slowly add flour mixture to liquid ingredients. Mix only to combine.
- Pour batter into prepared pan. Bake for approximately 80 minutes, or until cake tester inserted in center comes out clean. Cool completely before serving.
- Make the Pumpkin Whipped Topping.
- *To serve:* Cut cake and place on serving plate. Top with a dollop of whipped topping and a sprinkle of cinnamon if desired.

PER SERVING: 367 calories, 10g fat (<1g saturated), 62g carbohydrate, 3g dietary fiber, 28g sugar, 7g protein, 0mg cholesterol, 285mg sodium, 371mg potassium. Calories from fat: 25 percent.

RICHER THAN FORT KNOX CAKE

HIS MOIST CHOCOLATE cake filled with chocolate pudding and coated with a thin chocolate candy covering is a chocolate lover's dream. If you feel ambitious and want to impress your friends, go ahead and take the extra time to garnish this cake to make it look truly spectacular.

2¼ cups unbleached white flour
1¾ cups granulated sweetener
¾ cup cocoa
1½ teaspoons baking powder
1¼ cups baking soda
½ teaspoon sea salt
1 teaspoon vanilla
2 cups soy milk, or non-dairy milk of your choice
¼ cup soy mayonnaise (such as Nayonaise)
½ cup applesauce
Chocolate Decorative Topping, page 212
15 fresh cranberries (or 5 long-stem cherries) for garnish (optional)
1 tablespoon granulated sugar for garnish (optional)
5 mint leaves for garnish (optional)
10 fresh orange sections or mandarin orange slices, patted dry, for garnish (optional)

- Prepare Chocolate Decorative Topping the day before you make this cake if you want to use it to garnish finished cake. Cake is delicious without it, but looks spectacular if fully garnished.
- Preheat oven to 375°F. Coat bundt pan with nonstick cooking spray.
- In a medium bowl, combine flour, sweetener, cocoa, baking powder, baking soda, and salt. In another bowl, combine soy milk, vanilla, mayonnaise, and applesauce. Slowly pour liquid mixture into dry mixture. Stir to combine.
- *To make filling:* Place tofu in food processor and blend until smooth and creamy. Add powdered sugar and vanilla and continue to blend. Add melted chocolate and blend to combine. Pour ½ of batter into prepared pan. Spoon filling over batter. Top with remaining batter being careful not to mix layers together. Bake for 50 minutes or edges pull away from sides of pan. Remove from oven and allow to cool completely.
- *To make candy coating:* When cake is cool, heat chocolate chips in microwave or double boiler until melted and smooth and creamy. Place cooled cake on wire rack that is placed on a bowl with a diameter that is larger than that of the cake, so that any extra chocolate sauce will drip into the bowl. Pour the chocolate topping over the cake to coat it completely. Refrigerate it until topping hardens into a chocolate shell. Remove from refrigerator and break off any hard points that have formed by the chocolate dripping through the wire rack so that the cake

will sit flat on serving plate. (A kitchen shears works well for this.)

- *To garnish:* Place Chocolate Decorative Topping in pastry bag fit with #2D decorating tip (large star). If you don't have a decorating bag, you can cut the corner off the bottom of a plastic bag and insert the decorating tip instead. Pipe five evenly spaced mounds of Chocolate Decorative Topping around top of cake. Dip cranberries in water and roll in sugar to coat them. Place three sugared cranberries on top of each mound of chocolate. Place 1 mint leaf with each set of cranberries. Arrange dried off orange slices in a fan shape in between mounds of chocolate. Serve immediately. (If not serving immediately, wait to add orange slices.)

PUDDING FILLING:

1 pound (16 ounces) firm
    silken tofu
1 cup powdered sugar
2 teaspoons vanilla
2 cups vegan chocolate chips,
    melted (use double boiler or
    microwave)

CANDY COATING:

2 cups vegan chocolate chips

. . . .

MAKES 15 SERVINGS
PREPARATION TIME:
    CAKE: 15 minutes
    FILLING: 10 minutes
    CANDY COATING: 10 minutes
    WHIPPED CHOCOLATE
    TOPPING: 15 minutes
BAKING TIME: 50 minutes
FROSTING/GARNISH:
15 minutes

. . . .

PER SERVING: 590 calories, 23g fat (11g saturated), 93g carbohydrate, 5g dietary fiber, 2g sugar, 12g protein, 0mg cholesterol, 212mg sodium, 363mg potassium. Calories from fat: 30 percent.

WHITE ON WHITE TROPICAL CAKE

I CALL THIS cake "white on white" because it truly is a vision in white—rich-tasting white coconut cake covered in white coconut frosting.

¾ cup vegetable shortening
   (preferably non-hydrogenated
   like Spectrum)
1½ cups granulated sugar
2 tablespoons water
1½ teaspoons coconut extract
2¼ cups unbleached white flour
3 teaspoons baking powder
¼ teaspoon sea salt
1 15-ounce can coconut milk
   (about 1½ cups)
½ cup Ener-G Egg Replacer
¾ cup water
2 teaspoons cream of tartar
¾ cup unsweetened shredded
   coconut
Coconut Cream Cheese
   Frosting, page 209

. . . .
MAKES 12 SERVINGS
PREPARATION TIME:
   CAKE: 20 minutes
   FROSTING: 10 minutes
BAKING TIME: 40 minutes
. . . .

PER SERVING: 627 calories, 38g fat
(26g saturated), 65g carbohydrate, 1g
dietary fiber, 1g sugar, 9g protein, 0mg
cholesterol, 129mg sodium, 432mg
potassium. Calories from fat: 53 percent.

- Preheat oven to 375°F. Coat a 9 × 12-inch baking pan with nonstick cooking oil.
- In a large bowl, combine shortening, sugar, water, and coconut extract. Cream until combined. In a smaller bowl, combine flour, baking powder, and salt. In a small electric mixer bowl, combine Ener-G Egg Replacer with water. Beat until soft peaks form. Add cream of tartar to whipped egg replacer and beat until combined.
- Pour coconut milk into shortening mixture, alternating with flour mixture. Stir to combine. Add coconut and stir just until combined. Gently fold in whipped egg replacer.
- Pour into prepared pan. Bake for 40 minutes or until a toothpick inserted in the center comes out clean. Allow to cool completely before frosting.
- If you did not make the Coconut Cream Cheese Frosting the day before, prepare while cake is baking. Mound onto cake after it has cooled completely. Refrigerate before serving.

German Chocolate Cake

GERMAN CHOCOLATE CAKE is a traditional favorite that I "veganized" so I did not have to live without it! If you've never tried it, you'll love its unusual blend of chocolate and cooked coconut-pecan frosting.

2¼ cups unbleached white flour
1¾ cups granulated sweetener
¾ cup cocoa
1½ teaspoons baking powder
1¼ teaspoons baking soda
½ teaspoon sea salt
1 teaspoon vanilla
2 cups soy milk, or non-dairy milk of your choice
¼ cup soy mayonnaise (such as Nayonaise)
½ cup applesauce
German Chocolate Coconut-Pecan Frosting, page 213

. . . .

MAKES 12 SERVINGS
PREPARATION TIME:
   CAKE: 10 minutes
   FROSTING: 15 minutes
BAKING TIME: 35 minutes

. . . .

- Preheat oven to 375°F. Coat three 8-inch cake pans with nonstick cooking spray. Line the bottom of each pan with wax or parchment paper.
- In a medium bowl, combine flour, sweetener, cocoa, baking powder, baking soda and salt. In another bowl, combine soy milk, vanilla, mayonnaise, and applesauce. Slowly pour liquid mixture into dry mixture and stir to combine.
- Pour into prepared pans and bake for 35 minutes or until toothpick inserted in center comes out clean. While cake is baking, prepare German Chocolate Coconut-Pecan Frosting.
- When cake is completely cool, frost only tops of layers and allow frosting to drip down between layers.

PER SERVING: 632 calories, 42g fat (26g saturated), 64g carbohydrate, 5g dietary fiber, <1g sugar, 6g protein, 0mg cholesterol, 209mg sodium, 296mg potassium. Calories from fat: 58 percent.

PEANUT BUTTER SURPRISE

REMEMBER THE TASTE of peanut butter TandyKakes? Perhaps these snack cakes are a regional treat. They are tiny snack cakes with yellow cake and peanut butter, covered with chocolate. Peanut Butter Surprise recreates this treat in a large, yummy vegan cake creation.

1½ cups granulated sweetener
¾ cup soy margarine
4½ cups flour
1½ tablespoons baking powder
¼ teaspoon salt
2¾ cups vanilla soy milk, or other non-dairy milk of your choice
1 tablespoon vanilla

FILLING AND WHIPPED GARNISH:
1 pound (16 ounces) firm silken tofu
1 cup powdered sugar
¾ cup creamy natural peanut butter
2 tablespoons unbleached white flour

CANDY COATING:
2 cups vegan chocolate chips

- Preheat oven to 375°F. Coat a bundt pan with non-stick cooking spray.
- Combine granulated sweetener and soy margarine in a medium bowl and cream until smooth. Add vanilla and blend. In another bowl, combine flour, baking powder, and salt. Alternately add flour mixture and soy milk to sugar/margarine mixture, stirring to combine. Pour half of the batter into prepared bundt pan.
- *To make peanut butter pudding filling and whipped garnish:* Place tofu in food processor and process until smooth, scraping down sides of processor bowl as necessary. Add peanut butter and blend. Add sugar and flour and blend. Spoon all but ½ cup of pudding filling onto batter in pan, being careful not to touch sides of pan. Do not mix batter with filling layers. Top with remaining batter. Refrigerate reserved ½ cup of peanut butter filling to use for garnish later on. Bake cake for 50 minutes or until edges pull away from sides of pan. Remove from oven and allow to cool completely. When cake is cool, prepare candy coating.
- *To make candy coating:* Heat chocolate chips in microwave or double boiler until they are smooth and creamy. Place cooled cake on wire rack that is placed on a bowl with a diameter that is larger than that of the cake, so that any extra chocolate sauce will drip into the bowl. Pour the chocolate topping over the cake to coat it completely and refrigerate it

until topping hardens into a chocolate shell. Remove from refrigerator and break off any hard points that have formed by the chocolate dripping through the wire rack, so that the cake will sit flat on serving plate (a kitchen shears works well for this). Place cake on serving plate.

- *To garnish:* Place reserved peanut butter filling in pastry bag fit with #2D decorating tip (large star). If you don't have a decorating bag, you may cut the corner off the bottom of a plastic bag and insert the decorating tip in the corner of the bag instead. Pipe five evenly spaced mounds of reserved peanut butter filling around top of cake. If desired, grind ½ cup vegan chocolate chips in food processor, blender, or coffee grinder until fine. Sprinkle onto mounds of peanut butter filling. Refrigerate until serving.

MAKES 15 SERVINGS
PREPARATION TIME:
 CAKE: 15 minutes
 FILLING: 10 minutes
 CANDY COATING: 10 minutes
BAKING TIME: 50 minutes
FROSTING/GARNISH: 10 minutes

PER SERVING: 561 calories, 24g fat (6g saturated), 79g carbohydrate, 4g dietary fiber, 1g sugar, 14g protein, 0mg cholesterol, 117mg sodium, 354mg potassium. Calories from fat: 35 percent.

DOUBLE CHOCOLATE DELIGHT

HIS IS THE cake that launched my vegan baking career. It's a rich chocolate cake covered in creamy chocolate cream cheese frosting. This is a favorite at my house and the ultimate chocolate lovers treat.

2¼ cups unbleached white flour
1¾ cups granulated sweetener
¾ cup cocoa
1½ teaspoons baking powder
1¼ teaspoons baking soda
½ teaspoon sea salt
1 teaspoon vanilla
2 cups soy milk, or non-dairy milk of your choice
¼ cup soy mayonnaise (such as Nayonaise)
½ cup applesauce
Chocolate Cream Cheese Frosting, page 203

. . . .

MAKES 12 SERVINGS
PREPARATION TIME:
   CAKE: 10 minutes
   FROSTING: 15 minutes
BAKING TIME: 35 minutes
ASSEMBLY AND GARNISH: 15 minutes

. . . .

- Preheat oven to 375°F. Coat two 8-inch cake pans with nonstick cooking spray. Line the bottom of each pan with wax or parchment paper.
- In a medium bowl, combine flour, sweetener, cocoa, baking powder, baking soda, and salt. In another bowl, combine soy milk, vanilla, mayonnaise, and applesauce. Slowly pour liquid mixture into dry mixture and stir to combine.
- Pour into prepared pans and bake for 35 minutes or until toothpick inserted in center comes out clean. Allow cake to cool completely before frosting.
- If you did not prepare the Chocolate Cream Cheese Frosting the day before, prepare it while the cake is baking.
- *To assemble cake:* Cut the rounded top off of each layer. Using a sharp knife or wire cake cutter, cut cake layers in half horizontally to form four thin layers. Place bottom layer on serving plate. Ice top and place another layer on. Continue until you reach the top layer. Place top layer on upside down so that the bottom of that layer is the top of the cake. This makes the top of the cake completely flat and easier to frost and decorate. Frost top and sides of the cake.
- Grind ½ cup vegan chocolate chips in food processor, blender, or coffee grinder. Sprinkle them on top of cake. If desired, pipe remaining frosting around bottom and top edges of cake using decorator tip and bag. Refrigerate until ready to serve.

PER SERVING: 686 calories, 23 fat (8g saturated), 115g carbohydrate, 5g dietary fiber, 2g sugar, 13g protein, 0mg cholesterol, 340mg sodium, 405mg potassium. Calories from fat: 19 percent.

Mint Madness

Chocolate and mint are so good together that I created several combinations. In this one, I have taken a chocolate cake that is made even richer with the addition of chocolate chips and topped it off with a fluffy mint frosting.

2¼ cups unbleached white flour
1¾ cups granulated sweetener
¾ cup cocoa
1½ teaspoons baking powder
1¼ teaspoons baking soda
½ teaspoon sea salt
3 teaspoons peppermint extract
2 cups soy milk, or non-dairy milk of your choice
¼ cup soy mayonnaise (such as Nayonaise)
½ cup applesauce
½ cup vegan chocolate chips
Fluffy Mint Frosting, page 213

. . . .

MAKES 12 SERVINGS
PREPARATION TIME:
    CAKE: 15 minutes
    FROSTING: 10 minutes
BAKING TIME: 45 minutes
. . . .

- Preheat oven to 375°F. Coat a 9 × 12-inch baking pan with nonstick cooking spray.
- In a medium bowl, combine flour, sweetener, cocoa, baking powder, baking soda and salt. In another bowl, combine soy milk, peppermint extract, mayonnaise, and applesauce. Slowly pour liquid mixture into dry mixture and stir to combine. Stir in chocolate chips.
- Pour into prepared pan. Bake for 45 minutes or until toothpick inserted in center comes out clean. Remove from oven and allow to cool completely.
- Either the day before or while cake is baking, prepare Fluffy Mint Frosting. Mound frosting onto cooled cake. If desired, grind vegan chocolate chips in food processor, blender, or coffee grinder until fine and sprinkle over the top of the cake. Refrigerate.

PER SERVING: 349 calories, 9g fat (2g saturated), 60g carbohydrate, 4g dietary fiber, 1g sugar, 10g protein, 0mg cholesterol, 216mg sodium, 378mg potassium. Calories from fat: 22 percent.

CHERRY VANILLA DREAM

I WAS WAITING IN line at the grocery store and saw this gorgeous cherry cake on the cover of a magazine. It looked so good that I knew I'd have to try to make a cake like it. I went home and came up with cherry cake with cherry filling in the middle topped with cream cheese frosting.

1½ cups granulated sweetener
¾ cup soy margarine
4½ cups flour
1½ tablespoons baking powder
¼ teaspoon salt
2½ cups vanilla soy milk, or other non-dairy milk of your choice
1 tablespoon cherry extract
½ cup fresh cherries (pitted and chopped)
Whipped Cream Cheese Frosting, page 212
6–8 whole fresh cherries for garnish (optional)

FILLING:
¾ cup cherry preserve or Cherry Topping, page 201

. . . .

MAKES 12 SERVINGS
PREPARATION TIME:
    CAKE: 15 minutes
    FROSTING: 10 minutes
BAKING TIME: 30–35 minutes
FROSTING/GARNISH: 5 minutes

. . . .

PER SERVING: 492 calories, 17g fat (2g saturated), 77g carbohydrate, 2g dietary fiber, <1g sugar, 9g protein, 0mg cholesterol, 209mg sodium, 215mg potassium. Calories from fat: 19 percent.

- Preheat oven to 375°F. Coat two 8-inch pans with nonstick cooking spray. Line the bottom of each pan with waxed or parchment paper.
- Allow margarine to soften to room temperature or soften in microwave. Do not melt. (If you cannot find soy margarine, any vegetable-based margarine will work.) In a bowl, slowly add granulated sweetener to margarine and beat until light and fluffy. Add cherry extract and mix. In another bowl, combine flour, baking powder, and salt and mix to combine.
- Alternately add flour mixture and soy milk to sugar/margarine mixture and mix well. Stir in chopped cherries. Pour into prepared pans and bake 30–35 minutes, or until toothpick inserted in center comes out clean.
- Allow to cool completely before frosting. While cake is baking, prepare Whipped Cream Cheese Frosting.
- *To assemble and frost:* Cut off rounded top of both cake layers. Place bottom layer on serving plate and spread with cherry preserve. Place top layer on top of preserve upside down so that top is completely flat. Frost top and sides of cake with cream cheese frosting. Garnish with several fresh cherries if desired. Refrigerate before serving.

Variation: If you desire, you can make this as a more informal cake. You can still put cherry preserve in the center of the cake, but allow it to ooze out and dribble down the sides of the cake. Mound the cream cheese frosting on the top of the cake and also allow it to dribble down the side. Do not frost the sides of the cake. Garnish with cherries.

TRIPLE CHERRY TREAT

*T*HIS IS BASICALLY a cherry cake with just a hint of chocolate. It is a one-layer cake as opposed to the two-layer Cherry Vanilla Dream Cake. It is the same cherry cake as the Cherry Vanilla Dream, but it is smothered with fluffy Whipped Cherry Topping, *Cherry Filling*, and then drizzled with Vegan Chocolate Syrup.

1½ cups granulated sweetener
¾ cup soy margarine
4½ cups flour
1½ tablespoons baking powder
¼ teaspoon salt
2½ cups vanilla soy milk, or other non-dairy milk of your choice
1 tablespoon cherry extract
½ cup fresh cherries (pitted and chopped)
Whipped Cherry Topping, page 202
Cherry Filling, page 201
Vegan Chocolate Syrup, page 203

. . . .

MAKES 12 SERVINGS
PREPARATION TIME:
    CAKE: 15 minutes
    CHERRY WHIP: 10 minutes
    CHERRY TOPPING: 10 minutes
    CHOCOLATE SYRUP: 5 minutes
BAKING TIME: 45 minutes
FROSTING/GARNISH: 10 minutes

. . . .

PER SERVING: 493 calories, 14g fat (1g saturated), 83g carbohydrate, 3g dietary fiber, 6g sugar, 12g protein, 0mg cholesterol, 113mg sodium, 447mg potassium. Calories from fat: 23 percent.

- Preheat oven to 350°F. Coat a 10-inch springform pan with nonstick cooking spray.
- Allow margarine to soften to room temperature or soften in microwave. Do not melt. (If you cannot find soy margarine, any vegetable-based margarine will work.) In a bowl, slowly add granulated sweetener to the margarine and beat until light and fluffy. Add cherry extract and mix. In another bowl, combine flour, baking powder, and salt. Mix to combine.
- Alternately add flour mixture and soy milk to sugar/margarine mixture. Mix well. Stir in chopped cherries. Pour into prepared pan and bake for approximately 45 minutes, or until toothpick inserted in center comes out clean.
- While cake is baking, prepare Whipped Cherry Topping. Refrigerate until ready to use. Next, make Cherry Filling.
- When cake is cool, remove collar of pan. Cut off rounded top of cake. Place cake back in pan upside down. Put collar back on bottom of pan. Mound Whipped Cherry Topping on top of cooled cake. Top with Cherry Filling. Drizzle with Vegan Chocolate Syrup. Refrigerate cake until ready to serve. Remove collar when cake is ready to be served. Store in the refrigerator with the collar on.

TEN-CARAT GOLD CAKE

Wheat Free

THIS CAKE IS a rich blend of coconut, cinnamon, and raisins that stays moist and tender because of the carrots. Here's a helpful hint: If you are into using a juicer that extracts juice and leaves the pulp of fruits and vegetables (such as the Champion), you may use the carrot pulp that is left over after juicing carrots for this cake. I like to freeze carrot pulp in 3-cup amounts so that when I am ready to make a carrot cake, I just have to get out one bag.

2¼ cups spelt flour
3 teaspoons baking powder
¾ teaspoon cinnamon
1 teaspoon xanthan gum*
   (optional—but it helps the
   cake rise by taking the place of
   gluten that is in wheat flour)
3 teaspoons flax powder
¾ cup water
1½ cups granulated sweetener
½ cup canola oil
1⅛ cups coconut milk
3 teaspoons vanilla
3 cups grated carrots (or
   carrot pulp)
¾ cup unsweetened shredded
   coconut
½ cup organic raisins
½ teaspoon coconut extract
2 tablespoons shredded unsweetened coconut for garnish
   (optional)
Whipped Cream Cheese
Frosting, page 212

MAKES 12 SERVINGS
PREPARATION TIME:
   CAKE: 15 minutes
   FROSTING: 10 minutes
BAKING TIME: 1 hour
FROSTING: 5 minutes

- Preheat oven to 350°F. Coat a 9-inch springform pan with nonstick cooking spray.
- In a large bowl, combine flour, baking powder, xanthan gum, and cinnamon. In a medium bowl, combine granulated sweetener, oil, coconut milk, vanilla, and carrots. In a cup, combine flax powder with water. Add to sugar mixture and mix to combine. Slowly add liquid mixture to flour mixture and stir just to combine. Stir in raisins and coconut.
- Pour into prepared pan and bake for 60 minutes or until toothpick inserted in center comes out clean. Allow to cool completely before frosting.
- Either the day before or while cake is baking, prepare Whipped Cream Cheese Frosting. When cake is completely cool, mound frosting onto cake. Sprinkle with coconut if desired. Refrigerate until serving. When ready to serve, remove the collar of the pan.

Variation: I wrote this recipe to be wheat-free for those people who cannot tolerate wheat flour; however, if you either can't find spelt flour, or choose not to use it, you may substitute unbleached white flour for the spelt flour, increase the coconut milk to 1¼ cups, and omit the xanthan gum.

* Xanthan gum will produce a slighly softer filling, but will not give the mild flour taste that you may get if you use the flour.

PER SERVING: 504 calories, 26g fat (11g saturated), 60g carbohydrate, 7g dietary fiber, 1g sugar, 9g protein, 0mg cholesterol, 193mg sodium, 430mg potassium. Calories from fat: 38 percent.

Orange You Glad It Has Chocolate Chips Cake

*T*HIS CAKE IS delightfully different with its unique blend of orange cake and dark chocolate chips. I like to make it when I need to bring dessert to a picnic for several reasons. First, it travels well because it does not have frosting. Second, it doesn't need refrigeration, so I don't have to worry about it sitting out on a picnic table for awhile. Finally, it's easy to make!

1¼ cups maple syrup
¾ cup soy margarine
4½ cups flour
1½ tablespoons baking powder
¼ teaspoon salt
2½ cups orange juice
1 tablespoon orange extract
2 cups vegan chocolate chips

ORANGE GLAZE:
¾ cup powdered sugar
2 tablespoons orange juice

. . . .

MAKES 15 SERVINGS
PREPARATION TIME:
  CAKE: 15 minutes
  ICING: 10 minutes
BAKING TIME: 55–60 minutes
FROSTING/GARNISH: 5 minutes
FREEZES WELL
. . . .

- Preheat oven to 350°F. Coat a bundt cake pan with nonstick cooking spray.
- Allow margarine to soften to room temperature or soften in microwave. Do not melt. (If you cannot find soy margarine, any vegetable-based margarine will work.) Place margarine in bowl and cream. Slowly add maple syrup and beat until light and fluffy. Add orange extract and mix. In another bowl combine flour, baking powder, and salt and mix to combine. Alternately add flour mixture and orange juice to maple/margarine. Mix well.
- Pour into prepared pan and bake 55–60 minutes, or until toothpick inserted in center comes out clean. Cool in pan 10 minutes. Remove from pan onto wire rack. Allow to cool completely before pouring on glaze.
- *To make glaze:* Combine powdered sugar and orange juice in a small food processor. Pour onto cake.
- Garnish with fresh orange wedges or mandarin orange slices and curls of vegan dark chocolate if desired.

PER SERVING: 412 calories, 14g fat (4g saturated), 71g carbohydrate, 2g dietary fiber, 16g sugar, 5g protein, 0mg cholesterol, 85mg sodium, 180mg potassium. Calories from fat: 27 percent.

Raised Sugar Cake

*T*HIS TENDER YEAST cake covered with sugar and butter makes for a delicious breakfast or dessert. You need to let the dough rise for a few hours, so I usually make it in the evening, let it rise overnight, and then finish the recipe the next morning. This recipe makes three cakes, so you can store two in the freezer for later use.

1 cup hot mashed potatoes, plain*
1 cup granulated sweetener
1/4 teaspoon salt
1 packet yeast dissolved in 1 cup lukewarm water
3/4 cup canola oil
2 teaspoons flax powder
1/2 cup water
4 cups unbleached white flour

Topping:

1/4 pound soy margarine (such as Spectrum, which is non-hydrogenated)
1 pound light brown sugar
Dash of cinnamon (optional)

. . . .

Makes 3 cakes, 12 servings each
Preparation time:
   Cake: 15 minutes
   Rising time: 6 hours
   Putting into pans: 10 minutes
Baking time: 25 minutes
Freezes well

. . . .

PER SERVING: 185 calories, 35g fat (1g saturated), 146g carbohydrate, 5g dietary fiber, 8g protein, 0mg cholesterol, 166mg sodium, 362mg potassium. Calories from fat: 33 percent.

- Put mashed potatoes in large bowl (if using instant potatoes, measure out enough flakes and water and soy milk to make 1 cup of mashed potatoes according to package directions). Add sweetener and salt to mashed potatoes and stir to combine. Add yeast (dissolved in 1 cup lukewarm water), oil, and flax powder (dissolved in 1/2 cup water), to mashed potato mixture. Add flour and stir until smooth. Cover bowl with towel and allow dough to rise for 5 hours in a warm place. (I usually allow the dough to rise overnight—just be sure to put it in a really big bowl so it doesn't fall out!)
- Coat three 9-inch round cake pans with nonstick cooking oil. Spoon dough into three pans dividing it evenly among them. Allow dough to rise for 1 hour or until puffy. Preheat oven to 350°F. Using the handle of a wooden spoon, poke holes about an inch apart in the dough. (Don't make the holes too deep or the sugar and margarine will go to the bottom of the cake.) Place small amount of soy margarine (1/4–1/2 teaspoon) in each hole and push it down with brown sugar. Sprinkle the rest of the sugar on top of the cakes. Sprinkle the top of the cakes lightly with cinnamon if desired.
- Bake for 25 minutes or until top of the cake is nicely browned. Allow to cool completely before serving.

*I usually cheat and use instant mashed potatoes. (Use the directions on the box of instant potatoes. With the brand that I use, I have to make 1 1/2 servings of potatoes to make 1 cup. I only add the potato flakes, water, and soy milk instead of milk—do not add butter.) If you're using real potatoes, 1-2 small potatoes will work well. Peel the potatoes, cut into small pieces and place in a little water in a small pan. Cover and boil until soft. Immediately mash them with an electric mixer. Do not use a hand masher or the cake will be lumpy and do not use a food processor or the potatoes will have the consistency of glue.

Coconut-Covered Delight

*T*HIS TRADITIONAL CHOCOLATE cake with coconut cream frosting reminds me of a Mounds candy bar.

3 cups unbleached white flour
1/3 cup cocoa
2 tablespoon baking powder
1 teaspoon vanilla
6 ounces firm silken tofu
1 1/2 cups water or apple juice
1/2 cup organic applesauce
1 1/2 cups maple syrup
*Mega-Coconut Cream Cheese
    Frosting, page 210*
*1 cup shredded unsweetened
    coconut for garnish (optional)*

. . . .

MAKES 12 SERVINGS
PREPARATION TIME:
   CAKE: 15 minutes
    FROSTING: 10 minutes
BAKING TIME: 35 minutes

- Preheat oven to 350°F. Lightly grease two 8-inch round cake pans with nonstick cooking spray. Line the bottom of each cake pan with wax or parchment paper.
- In a large bowl, combine flour, cocoa, and baking powder. Mix with a whisk to combine. In a food processor, puree tofu until smooth. Add vanilla and applesauce and blend. Add water (or apple juice) and maple syrup and blend. Slowly add liquid ingredients to flour mixture and mix with whisk until combined. Do not overmix.
- Pour batter into prepared pans. Bake for 35 minutes of until toothpick inserted in center comes out clean. If you did not make the Mega-Coconut Cream Frosting the day before, prepare it while cake is baking.
- Remove cakes from oven after 35–45 minutes or when a toothpick inserted in the center comes out clean. Allow to cool 10 minutes in pans. Remove from pans and cool completely. Cut rounded tops of cake layers off with sharp knife or wire cake cutter. Place bottom layer on serving plate. Cover with coconut frosting. Place top layer on upside down so that top is completely flat. Frost top and sides of cake.
- Sprinkle top and sides with shredded coconut. Refrigerate until serving.

PER SERVING: 485 calories, 16g fat (6g saturated), 77g carbohydrate, 3g dietary fiber, 26g sugar, 11g protein, 0mg cholesterol, 234mg sodium, 412mg potassium. Calories from fat: 12 percent.

PEANUT BUTTER KANDY KAKE

*F*OR THOSE OF you who are familiar with peanut butter TandyKakes, this cake tastes just like those yummy snack cakes. If you like this recipe, try the Peanut Butter Surprise, page 72, which is also reminiscent of this childhood favorite.

1¼ cups maple syrup
¾ cup soy margarine
4½ cups unbleached white flour
1½ tablespoons baking powder
1 teaspoon salt
2½ cups soy milk, rice milk, or
   non-dairy milk of choice
1 tablespoon vanilla

PEANUT BUTTER FILLING:
¾ cup smooth natural peanut
   butter
⅓ cup maple syrup
¾ cup soymilk

CHOCOLATE CANDY TOPPING:
2 cups vegan chocolate chips

- Preheat oven to 350°F. Coat a 10-inch springform pan or pie plate with nonstick cooking spray.
- Allow margarine to soften to room temperature or soften in microwave. Do not melt. (If you cannot find soy margarine, any vegetable-based margarine will work.) Place margarine in bowl and cream. Slowly add maple syrup and beat until light and fluffy. Add vanilla and mix. In another bowl, combine flour, baking powder, and salt and mix to combine. Alternately add flour mixture and soy milk to maple/margarine and mix well.
- Pour into prepared pan. Bake for 50 minutes or until toothpick inserted into cake comes out clean. Cool for 10 minutes in pan. Remove collar if using springform pan or invert cake onto wire rack to cool if using pie plate. Allow to cool completely before assembling. While cake is cooling, prepare peanut butter filling.
- *To make peanut butter filling:* Place all filling ingredients in food processor, process until smooth, and set aside. Cut off rounded top of cake. Cut cake in half horizontally with sharp knife or wire cake cutter. Place what was the top of the cake upside down on a wire rack that has been placed on a bowl with a diameter bigger than that of the cake. Cover the cake layer with peanut butter filling. Place the other layer of cake on the peanut butter with the flat side facing up.

• *To make chocolate candy topping:* Melt the chocolate chips in microwave or double boiler. Carefully pour the chocolate over the cake, making sure to cover the whole cake top and sides. Smooth out chocolate on top of cake so that it is not too thick. Refrigerate for 15 minutes to harden the chocolate. Remove from the refrigerator. Remove any pieces of chocolate that are hanging through the wire rack and place cake on serving plate (a good kitchen shears works well for this). Store in refrigerator.

MAKES 12 SERVINGS
PREPARATION TIME:
   CAKE: 10 minutes
   PEANUT BUTTER FILLING:
10 minutes
   CHOCOLATE: 10 minutes
ASSEMBLY: 10 minutes
BAKING TIME: 35 minutes

PER SERVING: 411 calories, 21g fat (7g saturated), 54g carbohydrate, 4g dietary fiber, 14g sugar, 9g protein, 0mg cholesterol, 130mg sodium, 236mg potassium. Calories from fat: 40 percent.

Rootin' Tootin' Raisin Spice Cake

THIS CAKE IS a great one to take to a special occasion. It tastes delicious and it travels well.

3½ cups unbleached white flour
2 teaspoons baking soda
2 teaspoons cinnamon
½ teaspoon sea salt
⅓ cup canola oil
1 cup unprocessed sugar such as Sucanat (or dark brown sugar)
2 teaspoons flax powder
2 cups unsweetened (preferably organic) applesauce (one 24-ounce jar)
½ cup apple cider (apple juice or water)
¾ cup organic raisins
½ cup chopped walnuts (optional)

. . . .

MAKES 15 SERVINGS
PREPARATION TIME:
   CAKE: 15 minutes
   BAKING TIME: 50 minutes
FREEZES WELL
. . . .

- Preheat oven to 350°F. Coat bundt pan with nonstick cooking spray.
- In a large bowl, combine flour, baking soda, cinnamon, and salt. Using an electric mixer, beat oil and sweetener until combined. Mix flax powder with apple cider (or apple juice or water) together in a small bowl. Add to oil and sweetener and mix until combined. Beat in applesauce. On low speed, add dry ingredients to oil/sweetener mixture and beat just until combined. Stir in raisins and nuts by hand.
- Pour batter into prepared pan. Bake 50 minutes or until toothpick inserted in center comes out clean. Cool in pan for 10 minutes. Remove from pan and cool completely on wire rack.
- If desired, dust with powdered sugar before serving.

PER SERVING: 276 calories, 13g fat (1g saturated), 38g carbohydrate, 3g dietary fiber, 4g sugar, 4g protein, 0mg cholesterol, 178mg sodium, 153mg potassium. Calories from fat: 41 percent.

Cherry + Chocolate = Delicious Cake

HIS DELICIOUS MOIST cherry cake dotted with chocolate chips and topped with tangy cherry topping and a drizzle of chocolate syrup was inspired by the cover of a magazine. All the desserts that I see while I'm waiting in line at the grocery store make me want to create them in a vegan version!

¾ cup granulated sweetener
½ cup soy margarine
2¼ cups flour
2½ teaspoons baking powder
¼ teaspoon salt
1¼ cups vanilla soy milk, or other non-dairy milk of your choice
2 teaspoons cherry extract
½ cup fresh cherries (pitted and chopped)
¾ cup vegan chocolate chips
Cherry Filling, page 201
Vegan Chocolate Syrup, page 203

. . . .

MAKES 12 SERVINGS
PREPARATION TIME:
   CAKE: 15 minutes
   TOPPING: 10 minutes
   CHOCOLATE SYRUP:
   5 minutes
BAKING TIME: 30–35 minutes

. . . .

- Preheat oven to 375°F. Coat an 8-inch springform pan with nonstick cooking spray.
- Allow margarine to soften to room temperature or soften in microwave. Do not melt. (If you cannot find soy margarine, any vegetable-based margarine will work.) In a bowl, slowly add granulated sweetener to margarine and beat until light and fluffy. Add cherry extract and mix. In another bowl, combine flour, baking powder, and salt and mix to combine.
- Alternately add flour mixture and soy milk to sugar/margarine mixture and stir well. Stir in chopped cherries and chocolate chips.
- Pour into prepared pans and bake 30–35 minutes, or until toothpick inserted in center comes out clean. Allow to cool completely before assembling. While cake is cooling, make Cherry Filling. When cake is cool, remove collar of pan. With a sharp knife, cut off the rounded top of the cake and discard (or eat!). Replace collar of pan. Gently pour cherry topping over cake.
- Refrigerate at least 2 hours before serving. When cherries are completely cool, drizzle Vegan Chocolate Syrup over cherries in a delicate lattice pattern.

PER SERVING: 291 calories, 10g fat (2g saturated), 50g carbohydrate, 3g dietary fiber, 4g sugar, 4g protein, 0mg cholesterol, 119mg sodium, 159mg potassium. Calories from fat: 28 percent.

GOING NUTS FOR BANANA BREAD

HIS MOIST BANANA bread is so good it can be eaten just as it is—without frosting. I like to wrap these mini loaves in foil, put festive pieces of fabric tied with twine or hemp around them, and give them as gifts at Christmastime. I add sprigs of silk greenery to make an eye-catching gift that is as attractive as it is delicious!

1 cup unbleached white flour
1 cup whole wheat flour
1 teaspoon baking soda
½ teaspoon salt
¾ cup maple syrup
1½ cups (about 3 medium)
  ripe bananas, mashed
2 teaspoons flax powder
½ cup water
¼ cup canola oil
¼ cup applesauce
¾ cup pecans, chopped

. . . .
MAKES 15 SERVINGS
PREPARATION TIME: 15 minutes
BAKING TIME: 75 minutes
FREEZES WELL
. . . .

- Preheat oven to 350°F. Lightly grease 8 × 3½ × 2½-inch loaf pan with nonstick cooking spray.
- In a medium bowl, combine white flour, wheat flour, baking soda, and salt. In another bowl, combine maple syrup with mashed banana. In a small cup, mix flax powder with ½ cup water, pour into maple/banana mixture and stir to combine. Add canola oil, applesauce, and pecans and mix. Pour banana mixture into flour mixture and stir only until combined.
- Pour into prepared pan. Bake at 350°F for about 75 minutes, or until toothpick inserted in center comes out clean. Remove from oven and allow to cool for 10 minutes in pan.
- Remove loaf from pan and allow to cool completely.

Variation: Use three 5 × 2½ × 2½-inch mini loaf pans and bake at 350°F for 45 minutes.

PER SERVING: 197 calories, 8g fat (<1g saturated), 30g carbohydrate, 3g dietary fiber, 10g sugar, 3g protein, 0mg cholesterol, 94mg sodium, 198mg potassium. Calories from fat: 37 percent.

FRUIT 'N' NUT BREAD

THIS BREAD IS so incredibly moist and delicious that even I t
believe that it's healthy. I like to make this bread to take along to pot luck suppers
And just like the Going Nuts for Banana Bread, page 86, this bread can be eaten for breakfast or
dessert and makes a great gift.

1½ cups unbleached white flour
1½ cups whole wheat flour
2 teaspoons ground cinnamon
2 teaspoons baking soda
¼ teaspoon salt
2 cups maple syrup
1 can (15 ounces) pure pureed
   pumpkin
4 teaspoons flax powder
¾ cup water
½ cup canola oil
½ cup applesauce
1 large baking apple (such as
   Macintosh) peeled, cored,
   and diced
1 cup dried cranberries

. . . .

MAKES 15 SERVINGS
PREPARATION TIME: 15 minutes
BAKING TIME: 85 minutes
FREEZES WELL

. . . .

- Preheat oven to 350°F. Coat a bundt pan with non-stick cooking spray.
- Combine flours, cinnamon, baking soda and salt in a large bowl. Combine maple syrup, pumpkin, oil, and applesauce in another bowl. In a small bowl, combine flax powder and water. Add to liquid ingredients and combine.
- Add diced apple and cranberries to liquids and stir. Slowly add flour mixture to liquid ingredients. Mix only to combine.
- Pour batter into prepared pan. Bake for approximately 85 minutes, or until cake tester inserted in center comes out clean. Cool in pan for 10 minutes.
- Remove from pan and cool completely on wire rack.

Variation: Use five 5 × 2½ × 2½-inch mini loaf pans and bake at 350°F for 60 minutes.

PER SERVING: 421 calories, 8g fat (<1g saturated), 85g carbohydrate, 7g dietary fiber, 27g sugar, 3g protein, 0mg cholesterol, 252mg sodium, 259mg potassium. Calories from fat: 17 percent.

BOSTON CREAM PIES

I DEVOTED AN entire section to Boston cream pies because there are just so many possibilities. I started out with the traditional vanilla cake, vanilla pudding, and chocolate icing, but then I started switching cake flavors and pudding flavors and came up with some really tasty treats. Each pie is topped off with the decadent chocolate icing you'd expect on a Boston cream pie, so I have included the recipe for Chocolate Glaze Topping here for easy reference. A helpful hint: You will be much happier with the results if you make it a day before you plan to serve it and refrigerate it overnight. This allows the tofu in the filling to set.

CHOCOLATE GLAZE TOPPING

1 cup powdered sugar
¼ cup canola oil
½ teaspoon vanilla
⅙ cup cocoa (use ⅓-cup measurer and only fill it half full)
3½ tablespoons arrowroot
½ cup water

- Place powdered sugar, canola oil, vanilla, cocoa, and arrowroot in small saucepan and stir to combine, using a wire whisk for best results. Stir in water.
- Turn on heat and bring *almost* to boil stirring constantly.
- Keep stirring until mixture starts to thicken, but do not boil. (I hold it above the heat to do this.)

CHOCOLATE RASPBERRY BOSTON CREAM PIE

THIS CREAMY PIE combines the slightly sweet, tangy taste of raspberries with wonderful dark chocolate.

1½ cups unbleached white flour
⅓ cup cocoa
1 tablespoon baking powder
1 teaspoon vanilla
3 ounces firm silken tofu
¾ cups water or apple juice
½ cup organic applesauce
¾ cups maple syrup
Chocolate Glaze Topping,
    page 90

FILLING:
1 pound (16 ounces) firm
    silken tofu
1 cup powdered sugar
¼ cup raspberry jam
¼ cup unbleached white flour or
    2 teaspoons xanthan gum*

MAKES 12 SERVINGS
PREPARATION TIME:
    CAKE: 15 minutes
    FILLING: 10 minutes
    GLAZE: 10 minutes
BAKING TIME: 35 minutes
ASSEMBLY: 10 minutes

PER SERVING: 290 calories, 6g fat (<1g saturated), 57g carbohydrate, 2g dietary fiber, 13g sugar, 4g protein, 0mg cholesterol, 38mg sodium, 179mg potassium. Calories from fat: 18 percent.

- Preheat oven to 350°F. Lightly grease an 8-inch round springform pan** with nonstick cooking spray.
- In a large bowl, combine flour, cocoa, and baking powder. Mix with a whisk to combine. In a food processor, puree tofu until smooth. Add vanilla and applesauce and blend. Add water (or apple juice) and maple syrup and blend. Slowly add liquid ingredients to flour mixture and mix with whisk until combined. Do not overmix. Pour batter into prepared pan.
- Bake for 35 minutes or until toothpick inserted in center comes out clean. After baking, remove cake from oven. Allow to cool for 10 minutes in pans. Remove from pan and place on wire rack. Set pan aside. (You will be replacing cake in pan.) Allow cake to cool completely.
- While cake is baking, make filling. Place all filling ingredients in food processor and process until smooth. Refrigerate until ready to use.
- When cake is completely cool, cut off rounded top with a sharp, long knife or cake wire. Then cut cake layer in half horizontally, making two smaller layers. Place the top layer back into the springform pan. (It will now form the bottom layer of the cake.) Pour filling over bottom layer and smooth out. Place bottom layer (which will now be the top) onto filling upside down so that the top of the cake has a straight, smooth surface. Press down *lightly*.
- When cake is assembled, make Chocolate Glaze Topping. Pour hot topping over cake and smooth out evenly. Refrigerate overnight before serving. (This allows topping to thicken and filling to set.) Remove collar of pan before serving. Store in refrigerator with collar on.

*Xanthan gum will produce a slightly softer filling, but will not give the mild flour taste that you get if you use the ¼ cup flour.
**If you do not have a springform pan, this cake works nicely in a 9-inch pie plate.

TRADITIONAL BOSTON CREAM PIE

*T*HIS WAS MY first official Boston cream pie recipe. It got such a great response that I began to create the same type of dessert in different flavor combinations.

1¼ cups maple syrup
¾ cup soy margarine
4½ cups unbleached white flour
1½ tablespoons baking powder
¼ teaspoon salt
2½ cups soy milk, rice milk, or
    non-dairy milk of choice
1 tablespoon vanilla
Chocolate Glaze Topping,
    page 90

VANILLA FILLING:
1 pound (16 ounces) firm
    silken tofu
1 cup powdered sugar
2 teaspoons vanilla
¼ cup unbleached white flour or
    2 teaspoons xanthan gum*

- Preheat oven to 350°F. Coat a 10-inch round spring-form pan** with nonstick cooking spray.
- Allow margarine to soften to room temperature or soften in microwave. Do not melt. (If you cannot find soy margarine, any vegetable-based margarine will work.) Place margarine in bowl and cream. Slowly add maple syrup and beat until light and fluffy. Add vanilla and mix. In another bowl, combine flour, baking powder, and salt and mix to combine. Alternately add flour mixture and soy milk to maple/margarine and mix well. Pour into prepared pan and bake for approximately 50 minutes, or until toothpick inserted in center comes out clean.
- Remove cake from oven and cool 10 minutes in pan. Remove collar of pan and flip cake onto wire rack to finish cooling. Put the collar back on and set aside. Allow to cool completely before filling and assembling.
- *To make filling:* While cake is baking, place tofu in food processor and whip until smooth, scraping down sides several times. Add sugar, flour, and vanilla and process. Refrigerate until ready to assemble cake.

*Xanthan gum will produce a slightly softer filling, but will not give the mild flour taste that you may get if you use the flour.

**If you do not have a springform pan, this cake works nicely in a 9-inch pie plate.

- *To assemble cake:* When completely cool, cut off rounded top of cake with a sharp, long knife or cake wire. Then cut cake layer in half horizontally making two smaller layers. Place the top layer back into the springform pan. This will now be the bottom of the cake. Pour filling over bottom layer and smooth out. Place bottom layer (which will now be the top) onto filling upside down so that the bottom of the cake will be on top, giving it a straight, smooth surface. Press down *lightly*.
- When cake is assembled, make Chocolate Glaze Topping. Pour hot topping over cake and smooth out evenly. Refrigerate overnight before serving. (This allows topping to thicken and filling to set.) Remove collar of pan before serving. Store in refrigerator with collar on.

. . . .

MAKES 12 SERVINGS
PREPARATION TIME:
   CAKE: 15 minutes
   FILLING: 10 minutes
   GLAZE: 10 minutes
BAKING TIME: 50 minutes
ASSEMBLY: 10 minutes

. . . .

PER SERVING: 537 calories, 17g fat (1g saturated), 86g carbohydrate, 2g dietary fiber, 22g sugar, 11g protein, 0mg cholesterol, 115mg sodium, 353mg potassium. Calories from fat: 27 percent.

PEANUT BUTTER
BOSTON CREAM PIE

*T*HIS COMBINATION OF gooey peanut butter cream and dark chocolate glaze nestled together with moist yellow cake is sure to get rave reviews from friends and family.

1¼ cups maple syrup
¾ cup soy margarine
4½ cups unbleached white flour
1½ tablespoons baking powder
¼ teaspoon salt
2½ cups soy milk, rice milk, or
   non-dairy milk of choice
1 tablespoon vanilla
Chocolate Glaze Topping,
   page 90

PEANUT BUTTER FILLING:
1 pound (16 ounces) firm
   silken tofu
1 cup powdered sugar
2 teaspoons vanilla
¾ cup smooth natural peanut
   butter
¼ cup unbleached white flour or
   2 teaspoons xanthan gum*

- Preheat oven to 350°F. Coat a 10-inch round springform pan** with nonstick cooking spray.
- Allow margarine to soften to room temperature or soften in microwave. Do not melt. (If you cannot find soy margarine, any vegetable-based margarine will work.) Place margarine in bowl and cream. Slowly add maple syrup and beat until light and fluffy. Add vanilla and mix. In another bowl, combine flour, baking powder, and salt and mix to combine. Alternately add flour mixture and soy milk to maple/margarine mixture and stir well. Pour into prepared pan and bake for approximately 50 minutes, or until toothpick inserted in center comes out clean.
- Remove cake from oven and cool 10 minutes in pan. Remove collar of pan and flip cake onto wire rack to finish cooling. You will be putting cake back in pan, so put the collar back on and set aside. Allow to cool completely before filling and assembling.
- *To make peanut butter filling:* Place tofu in food processor and whip until smooth, scraping down sides several times. Add sugar, flour, and vanilla and process. Add peanut butter, and process until smooth. Refrigerate until ready to assemble cake.

*Xanthan gum will produce a slightly softer filling, but will not give the mild flour taste that you get if you use the ¼ cup flour.

**If you do not have a springform pan, this cake works nicely in a 9-inch pie plate.

- *To assemble:* When cake is completely cool, cut off rounded top with a sharp, long knife or cake wire. Then cut cake layer in half horizontally, making two smaller layers. Place the top layer back into the springform pan—this is now the bottom of the cake. Pour filling over bottom layer and smooth out. Place bottom layer (which will now be the top) onto filling upside down so that the bottom of the cake will be facing up and providing a straight, smooth surface Press down *lightly.*

- When cake is assembled, make Chocolate Glaze Topping. Pour hot topping over cake and smooth out evenly. Refrigerate overnight before serving. (This allows topping to thicken and filling to set.) Remove collar of pan before serving. Store in refrigerator with collar on.

MAKES 12 SERVINGS
PREPARATION TIME:
  CAKE: 15 minutes
  FILLING: 10 minutes
  GLAZE: 10 minutes
BAKING TIME: 50 minutes
ASSEMBLY: 10 minutes

PER SERVING: 646 calories, 26g fat (3g saturated), 90g carbohydrate, 3g dietary fiber, 22g sugar, 16g protein, 0mg cholesterol, 205mg sodium, 523mg potassium. Calories from fat: 34 percent.

Triple-Chocolate Boston Cream Pie

*B*EWARE: THIS CREAM pie—made of moist chocolate cake with creamy chocolate filling and topped with a dark chocolate glaze—is for the serious chocolate lover only.

1½ cups unbleached white flour
⅓ cup cocoa
1 tablespoon baking powder
1 teaspoon vanilla
3 ounces firm silken tofu
¾ cup water or apple juice
½ cup organic applesauce
¾ cup maple syrup
Chocolate Glaze Topping,
*   page 90*

Filling:

1 pound (16 ounces) firm
*   silken tofu*
1 cup powdered sugar
2 cups vegan chocolate chips
¼ cup unbleached white flour or
*   2 teaspoons xanthan gum**

- Preheat oven to 350°F. Lightly grease an 8-inch round springform pan** with nonstick cooking spray.
- In a large bowl, combine flour, cocoa, and baking powder and mix with a whisk to combine. In a food processor, puree tofu until smooth. Add vanilla and applesauce and blend. Add water (or apple juice) and maple syrup and blend. Slowly add liquid ingredients to flour mixture and mix with whisk until combined. Do not overmix. Pour batter into prepared pan.
- Bake for 35 minutes or until toothpick inserted in center comes out clean. After baking, remove cake from oven. Allow to cool for 10 minutes in pans. Remove from pan and place on wire rack. Set pan aside. (You will be replacing cake back into pan.) Allow cake to cool completely.
- While cake is baking, make filling. Place all filling ingredients except chocolate chips in food processor and process until smooth. Melt chocolate chips in microwave or double boiler. Pour melted chips into processor and process until smooth. Refrigerate until ready to use.

*Xanthan gum will produce a slightly softer filling, but will not give the mild flour taste that you get if you use the ¼ cup flour.

**If you do not have a springform pan, this cake works nicely in a 9-inch pie plate.

- When cake is completely cool, cut off rounded top with a sharp, long knife or cake wire. Then cut cake layer in half horizontally, making two smaller layers. Place the top layer back into the springform pan to form the bottom of the cake. Pour filling over bottom layer and smooth out. Place bottom layer (which will now be the top) onto filling upside down so that the top of the cake has a straight, smooth surface. Press down *lightly*.
- When cake is assembled, make Chocolate Glaze Topping. Pour hot topping over cake and smooth out evenly. Refrigerate overnight before serving. (This allows topping to thicken and filling to set.) Remove collar of pan before serving. Store in refrigerator with collar on.

MAKES 12 SERVINGS
PREPARATION TIME:
CAKE: 15 minutes
FILLING: 10 minutes
GLAZE: 10 minutes
BAKING TIME: 35 minutes
ASSEMBLY: 10 minutes

PER SERVING: 466 calories, 17g fat (6g saturated), 74g carbohydrate, 4g dietary fiber, 14g sugar, 10g protein, 0mg cholesterol, 43mg sodium, 363mg potassium. Calories from fat: 31 percent.

CHOCOLATE CARAMEL BOSTON CREAM PIE

*T*HIS GOOEY COMBINATION of chocolate cake, vanilla filling, caramel sauce, nuts, and chocolate glaze topping is the perfect dessert when you're in the mood to splurge.

1½ cups unbleached white flour
⅓ cup cocoa
1 tablespoon baking powder
1 teaspoon vanilla
3 ounces firm silken tofu
¾ cups water or apple juice
½ cup organic applesauce
¾ cups maple syrup
Chocolate Glaze Topping, page 90
¾ cups chopped pecans for garnish

FILLING:

1 pound (16 ounces) firm silken tofu
1 cup powdered sugar
1 teaspoon vanilla
¼ cup unbleached white flour or 2 teaspoons xanthan gum*

CARAMEL SAUCE:

⅓ cup corn syrup
⅓ cup brown sugar
2 teaspoons vanilla
3 tablespoons vanilla soy milk
¼ teaspoon salt

- Preheat oven to 350°F. Lightly grease an 8-inch round springform pan** with nonstick cooking spray.
- In a large bowl, combine flour, cocoa, and baking powder and mix with a whisk to combine. In a food processor, puree tofu until smooth. Add vanilla and applesauce and blend. Add water (or apple juice) and maple syrup and blend. Slowly add liquid ingredients to flour mixture and mix with whisk until combined. Do not overmix. Pour batter into prepared pan.
- Bake for 35 minutes of until toothpick inserted in center comes out clean. After baking, remove cake from oven. Allow to cool for 10 minutes in pans. Remove from pan and place on wire rack. Set pan aside. (You will be replacing cake back into pan.) Allow cake to cool completely.
- *To make filling:* While cake is baking, place all filling ingredients in food processor and process until smooth. Refrigerate until ready to use.
- *To make caramel sauce:* Place sugars in small pan and bring to boil. Simmer until it gets to the soft ball stage or 240°F on a candy thermometer, if you have one. Stir in soy milk, vanilla, and salt. Remove from heat and allow to cool. (Mixture will thicken as it cools.)

*Xanthan gum will produce a slightly softer filling, but will not give the mild flour taste that you get if you use the ¼ cup flour.

**If you do not have a springform pan, this cake works nicely in a 9-inch pie plate.

- *To assemble:* When cake is completely cool, cut off rounded top with a sharp, long knife or cake wire. Then cut cake layer in half horizontally making two smaller layers. Place the top layer back into the springform pan to form the bottom layer of the cake. Pour filling over bottom layer and smooth out. Place bottom layer (which will now be the top layer) onto filling upside down so that the top of the cake will have a straight, smooth surface. Press down *lightly*.
- When cake is assembled, make Chocolate Glaze Topping. Pour hot topping over cake and smooth out evenly. Refrigerate for 10 minutes. Carefully drizzle caramel sauce over chocolate glaze and sprinkle nuts over top of cake. Refrigerate overnight before serving. (This allows topping to thicken and filling to set.) Remove collar of pan before serving, but store in refrigerator with collar on.

MAKES 12 SERVINGS
PREPARATION TIME:
    CAKE: 15 minutes
    FILLING: 10 minutes
    GLAZE: 10 minutes
    CARAMEL SAUCE: 10 minutes
BAKING TIME: 35 minutes
ASSEMBLY: 10 minutes

PER SERVING: 460 calories, 14g fat (2g saturated), 76g carbohydrate, 3g dietary fiber, 15g sugar, 10g protein, 0mg cholesterol, 60mg sodium, 431mg potassium. Calories from fat: 27 percent.

CHOCOLATE PEANUT BUTTER BOSTON CREAM PIE

*T*ENDER CHOCOLATE CAKE filled with creamy peanut butter makes this cake a tasty dessert at any time. It is topped off with a dark chocolate glaze.

1½ cups unbleached white flour
⅓ cup cocoa
1 tablespoon baking powder
1 teaspoon vanilla
3 ounces firm silken tofu
¾ cups water or apple juice
½ cup organic applesauce
¾ cups maple syrup
Chocolate Glaze Topping,
   page 90

FILLING:

1 pound (16 ounces) firm
   silken tofu
1 cup powdered sugar
¾ cup smooth natural peanut
   butter
¼ cup unbleached white flour or
   2 teaspoons xanthan gum*

. . . .

MAKES 12 SERVINGS
PREPARATION TIME:
   CAKE: 15 minutes
   FILLING: 10 minutes
   GLAZE: 10 minutes
BAKING TIME: 35 minutes
ASSEMBLY: 10 minutes

. . . .

PER SERVING: 427 calories, 17g fat (3g saturated), 59g carbohydrate, 3g dietary fiber, 14g sugar, 13g protein, 0mg cholesterol, 115mg sodium, 471mg potassium. Calories from fat: 34 percent.

- Preheat oven to 350°F. Lightly grease an 8-inch round springform pan** with nonstick cooking spray.
- In a large bowl, combine flour, cocoa, and baking powder and mix with a whisk to combine. In a food processor, puree tofu until smooth. Add vanilla and applesauce and blend. Add water (or apple juice) and maple syrup and blend. Slowly add liquid ingredients to flour mixture and mix with whisk until combined. Do not over mix. Pour batter into prepared pan.
- Bake for 35 minutes of until toothpick inserted in center comes out clean. Remove cake from oven and allow to cool for 10 minutes in pan. Remove from pan and place on wire rack. Set pan aside. (You will be replacing cake back into pan.) Allow cake to cool completely.
- While cake is baking, make filling. Place all filling ingredients in food processor and process until smooth. Refrigerate until ready to use.
- When cake is completely cool, cut off rounded top. With a sharp, long knife or cake wire, cut cake layer in half horizontally making two smaller layers. Place the top layer back into the springform pan to form the bottom of the cake. Pour filling over bottom layer and smooth out. Place bottom layer (which will now be the top layer) onto filling upside down so that the top of the cake will have a straight, smooth surface. Press down *lightly*.
- When cake is assembled, make Chocolate Glaze Topping. Pour hot topping over cake and smooth out evenly. Refrigerate overnight before serving. (This allows topping to thicken and filling to set). Remove collar of pan before serving. Store in refrigerator with collar on.

*Xanthan gum will produce a slightly softer filling, but will not give the mild flour taste that you get if you use the ¼ cup flour.
**If you do not have a springform pan, this cake works nicely in a 9-inch pie plate.

PIES AND TARTS

WETZEL'S PRETZEL PIE

*I*MPRESSIVE TO LOOK at and scrumptious to eat, this concoction of vanilla soy ice cream coupled with chocolate, nuts, and pretzels is truly a fabulous creation! It's like a sundae in a pie pan. I named it after my maiden name, which conveniently rhymes with pretzel.

SYRUP:
¾ cup cocoa
1¼ cups maple syrup
2 teaspoons vanilla

CRUST:
2 cups vegan chocolate chips
2 cups + at least 1 dozen regular twist-shaped pretzels. (Be sure to read ingredients so that the pretzels do not contain hydrogenated oils—I have found Snyder's pretzels work well.)

FILLING:
4 1-pint containers of non-dairy vanilla ice cream*
½ cup chopped peanuts

- Grease 8-inch springform pan with nonstick cooking spray.
- *To make the syrup:* In a small bowl, combine cocoa, maple syrup, and vanilla. Stir with a wire whisk until combined and set aside. In a microwave or double boiler, melt chocolate chips, set aside. Coarsely crush 2 cups pretzels and place in a small bowl. Pour ½ of melted chocolate over pretzels and toss to cover. Pour into bottom of prepared pan. Refrigerate until ready to fill.
- *To make crust:* Select whole, unbroken pretzels to use for the outside "crust" of the pie. The number of pretzels that you need will vary depending on the size of the pretzels (usually about 1 dozen). Take the pretzels and dip them ¾ of the way into the melted chocolate starting at the bottom. The two top loops of each pretzel will remain uncovered and will provide you with a clean place to pick them up. Place the chocolate covered pretzels on a wax paper covered cookie sheet. Be sure to make a few more than you think you will need in case you miscalculate or break some. If you have extras, you can use them whole for a garnish or just eat them! Place pretzels in the freezer to harden the chocolate while you work on the rest of the pie.

**I like to use Tofutti non-dairy frozen dessert for this pie. I find that its consistency works well—and it tastes delicious!

- Soften non-dairy ice cream. (I use the defrost function on my microwave to do this—the ice cream should be the consistency of soft serve ice cream, not runny.) Spread half of the non-dairy ice cream (about 2 containers) over the crushed pretzels in the bottom of the pan. Make syrup by combining all chocolate syrup ingredients in a small bowl and mixing until it is the consistency of commercial chocolate syrup. Drizzle half of the syrup over the ice cream. Sprinkle with ¼ cup nuts.
- Spread the rest of the ice cream over the topping. Make the top flat and smooth. Press chocolate-covered pretzels into the pie at the side of the pan so that when the collar of the pan is removed, the pretzels form the side crust. Part of the pretzel will be showing above the top of the pie, almost like a fence. Pour the rest of the syrup evenly on top. Sprinkle with the remaining nuts. Freeze at least 3 hours before serving. Remove the collar of the pan and allow to soften for 10 minutes before serving.

Hint: Running the serving knife under hot water before cutting makes the cutting of this pie easier.

MAKES 12 SERVINGS
PREPARATION TIME:
    FILLING: 5 minutes
    CRUST: 10 minutes
    SYRUP: 5 minutes

PER SERVING: 460 calories, 19g fat (5g saturated), 70g carbohydrate, 4g dietary fiber, 35g sugar, 7g protein, 0mg cholesterol, 530mg sodium. Calories from fat: 36 percent.

I LOVE CHOCOLATE CREAM PIE

*T*HIS CREAMY CHOCOLATE-filled pie laced with coconut nestled in a chocolate-coconut candy pie shell turns out best if you make it the day before serving so that the filling has a chance to set. It will maintain its shape better when you cut it into slices.

PIE SHELL:
2 cups vegan chocolate chips
½ cup vanilla soy creamer
1½ cups shredded unsweetened coconut

FILLING:
1 pound (16 ounces) firm silken tofu
1 cup powdered sugar
1 teaspoon coconut extract
2 cups vegan chocolate chips, melted (use double boiler or microwave)
1 cup shredded unsweetened coconut

. . . .

MAKES 16 SERVINGS
PREPARATION TIME:
    FILLING: 5 minutes
    SHELL: 10 minutes

. . . .

- Coat 9-inch pie plate with nonstick cooking spray. Heat soy creamer in small pan until hot, but not boiling. Add chocolate chips slowly and stir until melted, keeping heat on low. Stir in coconut. Pour into prepared pie plate and refrigerate until shell is hardened.
- While shell is in the refrigerator, prepare filling. Place tofu in food processor and process until smooth, scraping down sides of processor as necessary. Add sugar and coconut extract. Melt chocolate chips in microwave or double boiler. Pour melted chocolate into food processor and process until combined. Stir coconut in by hand.
- Pour into prepared pie shell. Sprinkle with coconut if desired.
- Refrigerate until ready to serve.

PER SERVING: 476 calories, 35g fat (28g saturated), 43g carbohydrate, 8g dietary fiber, <1g sugar, 6g protein, 0mg cholesterol, 43mg sodium. Calories from fat: 61 percent.

MOM'S APPLE CRISP

PPLE CRISP HAS all the good taste of apple pie without the crust. It's wonderful served warm with a scoop of cold non-dairy vanilla frozen dessert. The cold vanilla ice cream nicely complements the warm, spicy apples with the crunchy topping.

APPLES:

15 medium baking apples (I like a combination of Macintosh and a more firm apple such as Idared or Rome.)

¾ cup water

2 tablespoons arrowroot

3 teaspoons cinnamon

¼ teaspoon cardamom

½ teaspoon nutmeg

TOPPING:

½ cup whole wheat flour

½ cup Sucanat (or brown sugar)

½ cup ground walnuts

3 tablespoons canola oil

. . . .

MAKES 12 SERVINGS

PREPARATION TIME:

  PEELING, CORING, SLICING

  APPLES: 20 minutes

  APPLE FILLING: 10 minutes

  TOPPING: 5 minutes

BAKING TIME: 20 minutes

. . . .

PER SERVING: 280 calories, 7g fat (<1g saturated), 58 g carbohydrate, 9g dietary fiber, <.1g sugar, 2g protein, 0mg cholesterol, 4.5mg sodium. Calories from fat: 20 percent.

- Preheat oven to 350°F. Coat a 9 × 12-inch baking pan with nonstick cooking spray.
- Peel, core, and slice apples and place in a heavy cooking pot. Add ½ cup water to apples. Cover and cook until apples are soft, but not mushy. Add spices to apples and stir to combine. Remove from heat.
- Stir arrowroot into ¼ cup water. Stir arrowroot mixture into hot apples. Mixture will thicken from the heat of the apples—do not boil. Pour apples into prepared pan.
- *To prepare topping:* Place all topping ingredients in bowl and stir with a fork to combine. Sprinkle apples with topping.
- Bake for 20 minutes, or until crumbs begin to brown. Serve warm with a scoop of non-dairy vanilla ice cream if desired.

ALL-AMERICAN APPLE CRUMB PIE

S THERE ANYTHING that makes your house smell better than a warm apple pie baking in the oven? This pie is delicious alone or with a scoop of non-dairy vanilla frozen dessert on top.

Standard Vegan Single Pie
   Crust, page 216
10 medium baking apples (I like
   a combination of Macintosh
   and a more firm apple such as
   Idared or Rome.)
½ cup water
1 tablespoons arrowroot
1½ teaspoons cinnamon
½ teaspoon cardamom
¼ teaspoon nutmeg

CRUMB TOPPING:

½ cup unbleached white flour
½ cup granulated sweetener
2 tablespoons vegetable shortening (non-hydrogenated such
   as Spectrum)

. . . .

MAKES 10 SERVINGS
PREPARATION TIME:
   PEELING, CORING, SLICING
   APPLES: 15 minutes
   APPLE FILLING: 10 minutes
   TOPPING: 5 minutes
   CRUST: 10 minutes
BAKING TIME: 20 minutes

. . . .

PER SERVING: 268 calories, 9g fat (3g saturated), 47g carbohydrate, 6g dietary fiber, 2.6g protein, 0mg cholesterol, 7mg sodium. Calories from fat: 28 percent.

Note: This analysis was made using hydrogenated shortening, not non-hydrogenated. Non-hydrogenated is healthier.

- Preheat oven to 400°F. Coat an 8-inch pie plate with nonstick cooking spray.
- Prepare Standard Vegan Single Pie Crust. Weight pie crust with another empty pie plate filled with a little water or pie weights to keep the crust from bubbling or shrinking while it bakes. You can also line pie crust with aluminum foil and fill the foil with dry beans. Bake pie crust for 10 minutes or until edges begin to brown slightly.
- While crust is baking, make apple filling. Peel, core, and slice apples and place in a heavy cooking pot. Add ¼ cup water to apples. Cover and cook until apples are soft, but not mushy. Add spices to apples, stir to combine, and remove from heat.
- Stir arrowroot into ¼ cup water. Stir arrowroot mixture into hot apples. Mixture will thicken from the heat of the apples—do not boil. Pour apples into prepared crust when it is ready, making sure to remove pie weights before putting apple filling in crust.
- *To prepare topping:* Place all topping ingredients in bowl and cut shortening into flour with two knives until shortening pieces are no larger than a pea. Sprinkle apples with topping. Bake for 10 minutes, or until crumbs begin to brown. Serve warm with a scoop of non-dairy vanilla ice cream if desired.

AWARD-WINNING PEACH CRUMB PIE

*F*RESH PEACH PIE is a scrumptious summer treat. It's a three-step process, but you'll be glad that you made it when you smell the warm, spicy aroma filling your kitchen.

Standard Vegan Single Pie
 Crust, page 216
8–10 medium peaches (6 cups)
½ cup water
1 tablespoon arrowroot
1½ teaspoons cinnamon

CRUMB TOPPING:
½ cup unbleached white flour
½ cup granulated sweetener
2 tablespoons vegetable shortening (non-hydrogenated such
 as Spectrum)

. . . .

MAKES 10 SERVINGS
PREPARATION TIME:
 PEELING, PITTING, SLICING
 PEACHES: 15 minutes
 PEACH FILLING: 10 minutes
 TOPPING: 5 minutes
 CRUST: 10 minutes
BAKING TIME: 20 minutes

. . . .

- Preheat oven to 400°F. Coat an 8-inch pie plate with nonstick cooking spray.
- Prepare Standard Vegan Single Pie Crust. Weight pie crust with another empty pie plate filled with a little water or pie weights to keep the crust from bubbling or shrinking while it bakes. You can also line pie crust with aluminum foil and fill the foil with dry beans. Bake pie crust for 10 minutes or until edges begin to brown slightly.
- While crust is baking, make peach filling. Peel, pit, and slice peaches and place in a heavy cooking pot. Add ¼ cup water to peaches. Cover and cook until peaches are soft, but not mushy. Add cinnamon to peaches and stir to combine. Remove from heat.
- Stir arrowroot into ¼ cup water. Stir arrowroot mixture into hot peaches. Mixture will thicken from the heat of the peaches—do not boil. Pour peaches into prepared crust when it is ready, making sure to remove pie weights before putting peach filling in crust.
- *To make topping:* Place all topping ingredients in bowl and cut shortening into flour with 2 knives until shortening pieces are pea-sized. Sprinkle peaches with topping. Bake for 10 minutes, or until crumbs begin to brown. Serve warm with a scoop of non-dairy vanilla ice cream if desired.

PER SERVING: 246 calories, 8g fat (3g saturated), 42g carbohydrate, 5g dietary fiber, 3g protein, 0mg cholesterol, 16mg sodium. Calories from fat: 74 percent.

Note: This analysis was made using hydrogenated shortening, not non-hydrogenated. Non-hydrogenated is healthier.

RAVE REVIEW RAISIN CRUMB PIE

M Y FATHER TOLD me that back in his day raisin pie was called "funeral pie" because it was traditional to serve it at family gatherings after a funeral. Back then, fresh fruit wasn't always so readily available, and, since raisins are dried, they were something that most people had on hand all the time. If you're looking for something different, this is a good pie to try. Fresh raisin pie is almost impossible to get anymore, vegan or not.

Standard Vegan Single Pie Crust, page 216
3 cups raisins (preferably organic)
1¼ cups water
¾ teaspoon lemon juice
¾ cup maple syrup
3 tablespoons arrowroot

CRUMB TOPPING:
½ cup unbleached white flour
½ cup granulated sweetener
2 tablespoons vegetable shortening (non-hydrogenated such as Spectrum)

. . . .

MAKES 10 SERVINGS
PREPARATION TIME:
  FILLING: 10 minutes
  CRUST: 10 minutes
BAKING TIME: 20 minutes

. . . .

PER SERVING: 390 calories, 8g fat (3g saturated), 79g carbohydrate, 2g dietary fiber, 15g sugar, 4g protein, 0mg cholesterol, 15mg sodium, potassium 400mg. Calories from fat: 19 percent.

Note: This analysis was made using hydrogenated shortening, not non-hydrogenated. Non-hydrogenated is healthier.

- Preheat oven to 400°F. Coat an 8-inch pie plate with nonstick cooking spray.
- Prepare Standard Vegan Single Pie Crust. Weight pie crust with another empty pie plate filled with a little water or pie weights to keep the crust from bubbling or shrinking while it bakes. You can also line pie crust with aluminum foil and fill the foil with dry beans. Bake pie crust for 10 minutes or until edges begin to brown slightly.
- While crust is baking, make raisin filling. Place raisins, 1 cup water, and lemon juice in small pan. Bring to boil and simmer for 5 minutes. Add maple syrup, bring back to boil, and remove from heat.
- Stir arrowroot into ¼ cup water. Stir arrowroot mixture into hot raisins. Mixture will thicken from the heat of the peaches—do not boil. Pour raisins into prepared crust when it is ready, making sure to remove pie weights before putting raisin filling in crust.
- *To make topping:* Place all topping ingredients in a bowl and cut shortening into flour with 2 knives until shortening pieces are pea-sized. Sprinkle raisins with topping. Bake for 10 minutes, or until crumbs begin to brown. Serve warm with a scoop of non-dairy vanilla ice cream if desired.

FESTIVE APPLE CRANBERRY PIE

*T*HIS IS A slightly different twist on the traditional apple pie—it has a double crust surrounding cinnamon-spiced apples and tangy cranberries.

Standard Vegan Double Pie Crust, page 217

10 medium baking apples (I like a combination of Macintosh and a more firm apple such as Idared or Rome.)

¾ cup dried cranberries

½ cup water

1 tablespoons arrowroot

1½ teaspoons cinnamon

. . . .

MAKES 10 SERVINGS

PREPARATION TIME:

    PEELING, CORING, SLICING APPLES: 15 minutes

    APPLE FILLING: 10 minutes

    TOPPING: 5 minutes

    CRUST: 10 minutes

BAKING TIME: 30 minutes

. . . .

- Preheat oven to 400°F. Coat an 8-inch pie plate with nonstick cooking spray.
- Prepare Standard Vegan Double Pie Crust.
- Peel, core, and slice apples and place in a heavy cooking pot. Add cranberries, then add ¼ cup water to apples and cranberries. Cover and cook until apples are soft but not mushy and cranberries are plump but not bursting. Add cinnamon to apples/cranberries and stir to combine. Remove from heat.
- Stir arrowroot into ¼ cup water. Stir arrowroot mixture into hot apples/cranberries. Mixture will thicken from the heat of the apples—do not boil. Pour apple mixture into prepared crust.
- Remove top piece of wax paper from top crust that you rolled out earlier. Invert onto pie and remove other sheet of wax paper. Press edges down around edges of pie plate. Cut edges of dough off both upper and lower crusts to fit pie plate. Crimp together with your fingers. With a sharp knife, make decorative slits in top of crust. If desired, brush crust with soy milk and sprinkle with sugar.
- Bake for 30 minutes, or until crust begins to brown. Serve warm with a scoop of non-dairy vanilla ice cream if desired.

PER SERVING: 431 calories, 12g fat (<1g saturated), 78g carbohydrate, 7g dietary fiber, 3g protein, 0mg cholesterol, 14mg sodium. Calories from fat: 23 percent.

WASHINGTON'S CHERRY CRUMB PIE

THIS LUSCIOUS CHERRY crumb pie has all the flavor of the traditional favorite but less fat and calories.

Standard Vegan Single Pie Crust, page 216
4 cups fresh cherries (pitted and halved)
1 cup apple juice
2 tablespoons arrowroot
½ cup water

CRUMB TOPPING:

½ cup unbleached white flour
½ cup granulated sweetener
2 tablespoons vegetable shortening (non-hydrogenated such as Spectrum)

. . . .

MAKES 10 SERVINGS
PREPARATION TIME:
   PITTING AND PREPARING
   CHERRIES: 15 minutes
   CHERRY FILLING: 10 minutes
   TOPPING: 5 minutes
   CRUST: 10 minutes
BAKING TIME: 20 minutes

. . . .

PER SERVING: 235 calories, 8g fat (3g saturated), 38g carbohydrate, 2g dietary fiber, 3g protein, 0mg cholesterol, 14mg sodium, 130mg potassium. Calories from fat: 31 percent.

Note: This analysis was made using hydrogenated shortening, not non-hydrogenated. Non-hydrogenated is healthier.

- Preheat oven to 400°F. Coat an 8-inch pie plate with nonstick cooking spray.
- Prepare Standard Vegan Single Pie Crust. Weight pie crust with another empty pie plate filled with a little water or pie weights to keep the crust from bubbling or shrinking while it bakes. You can also line pie crust with aluminum foil and fill the foil with dry beans. Bake pie crust for 10 minutes or until edges begin to brown slightly.
- While crust is baking, make filling. Pit cherries and cut in half. Place in a heavy cooking pot. Add ¼ cup water to cherries. Cover and cook until cherries are soft, about 8 minutes, and remove from heat.
- Stir arrowroot into ¼ cup water. Stir arrowroot mixture into hot cherries. Mixture will thicken from the heat of the cherries—do not boil. Pour cherries into prepared crust when it is ready, making sure to remove pie weights before putting cherry filling in crust.
- *To prepare topping:* Place all topping ingredients in bowl and cut shortening into flour with two knives until shortening pieces are pea-sized. Sprinkle cherries with topping.
- Bake for 10 minutes, or until crumbs begin to brown. Serve warm with a scoop of non-dairy vanilla ice cream if desired.

Hint: You may want to place a piece of aluminum foil on the oven rack under this pie as the cherry juice tends to drip out.

NEWFANGLED MINCE PIE

F YOU LIKED the taste of mince pie, but thought that you'd never be able to have it again because you are now vegan, I have a compromise for you. This pie mimics the spicy flavor and "meaty" texture of the real thing. And because it's made with TVP (textured vegetable protein), it packs a healthy dose of protein without any added fat. For those of you who are not familiar with TVP, check the Stocking Your Vegan Pantry section on page 13 for a more complete description.

Standard Vegan Double Pie Crust, page 217
¾ cup TVP (Grape-Nuts–size granules)
1¼ cups apple cider (or apple juice)
4 cups baking apples like Macintosh or Rome
¾ cup raisins
1¾ teaspoons cinnamon
½ teaspoons nutmeg
¾ teaspoon ground cloves
½ teaspoon allspice (optional)

. . . .

MAKES 8 SERVINGS
PREPARATION TIME:
    "MINCE" FILLING: 10 minutes
    CRUST: 10 minutes
BAKING TIME: 30 minutes

. . . .

- Preheat oven to 400°F. Coat an 8-inch pie plate with nonstick cooking spray.
- Prepare Standard Vegan Double Pie Crust.
- Place TVP in a small bowl and cover with ¾ cup hot cider. Cover and set aside. Peel, core, and slice apples. Place apples in a heavy cooking pot with raisins and ½ cup apple cider. Cover pot and cook until apples are soft. Add spices and drained TVP to apples and stir to combine. Remove from heat. Pour filling into prepared crust.
- Remove top piece of wax paper from top crust that you rolled out earlier and then set aside. Invert onto pie and remove other sheet of wax paper. Press dough down around edges of pie plate. Cut edges of dough off both upper and lower crusts to fit pie plate. Crimp together with your fingers. With a sharp knife, make decorative slits in top of crust. If desired, brush crust with soy milk and sprinkle with sugar.
- Bake for 30 minutes, or until crust begins to brown. Serve warm with a scoop of non-dairy vanilla ice cream if desired.

PER SERVING: 315 calories, 12g fat (1g saturated), 47g carbohydrate, 4g dietary fiber, 7g protein, 0mg cholesterol, 17mg sodium, 394mg potassium. Calories from fat: 32 percent.

FALL HARVEST PIE

*T*HIS PIE IS a unique blend of foods that are bountiful in the fall—sweet potatoes, apples, and cranberries—whose flavors naturally compliment each other.

Standard Vegan Single Pie Crust, page 216
3 medium sweet potatoes
4 medium baking apples such as Macintosh or Rome
½ cup water
2 tablespoons arrowroot
½ cup maple syrup
1 tablespoon vanilla
1 cup dried cranberries
⅓ cup chopped walnuts

CRUMB TOPPING:

¼ cup canola oil
⅓ cup Sucanat (or brown sugar)
⅓ cup whole wheat flour

. . . .

MAKES 10 SERVINGS
PREPARATION TIME:
    FILLING: 15 minutes
    CRUST: 10 minutes
    CRUMBS: 5 minutes
BAKING TIME: 25 minutes

. . . .

- Preheat oven to 400°F. Coat an 8-inch pie plate with nonstick cooking spray.
- Prepare Standard Vegan Single Pie Crust. Weight pie crust with another empty pie plate filled with a little water or pie weights to keep the crust from bubbling or shrinking while it bakes. You can also line pie crust with aluminum foil and fill the foil with dry beans. Bake pie crust for 10 minutes or until edges begin to brown slightly.
- While crust is baking, make filling. Peel and dice sweet potatoes, place in small pot, and cover with water. Cook until soft when pricked with a fork. Drain potatoes and set aside. Peel, core, and slice apples and place in the same pot. Add ¼ cup water and 1 cup cranberries. Cook until apples begin to get soft. Return sweet potatoes to pot. Add maple syrup and vanilla.
- In a small cup, mix ¼ cup water with arrowroot. Add to hot filling mixture and stir until mixture thickens—do not boil. Remove from heat and stir in nuts.
- In another bowl, stir together topping ingredients. Put filling in prepared pie crust (having removed pie weights) and sprinkle crumbs on top.
- Bake for 15 minutes or until crumbs begin to brown.

PER SERVING: 534 calories, 17g fat (1g saturated), 92g carbohydrate, 7g dietary fiber, 10g sugar, 4g protein, 0mg cholesterol, 18mg sodium, 213mg potassium. Calories from fat: 26 percent.

STATE FAIR PEAR PIE

*T*HIS ISN'T JUST your average pear pie—you'll love this mouth-watering mixture of pears, apples, cranberries, nuts, and sweet vanilla syrup.

Standard Vegan Double Pie Crust, page 217
6 pears
4 medium baking apples such as Macintosh
¾ cup dried cranberries
¾ cup maple syrup
1 tablespoon vanilla
½ cup apple juice (or water)
2 tablespoons arrowroot
½ cup chopped walnuts

MAKES 10 SERVINGS
PREPARATION TIME:
    FRUIT FILLING: 20 minutes
    CRUST: 10 minutes
BAKING TIME: 30 minutes

- Preheat oven to 400°F. Coat an 8-inch pie plate with nonstick cooking spray.
- Prepare Standard Vegan Double Pie Crust.
- Peel, core and slice pears and apples. Place in a heavy cooking pot with cranberries and ¼ cup apple juice. Cover and cook until fruit is soft. Add maple syrup and vanilla and stir to combine.
- In a small cup, combine ¼ cup apple juice with arrowroot. Add to hot fruit and stir until thickened—do not boil. Remove from heat. Stir in walnuts and pour filling into prepared crust.
- Remove top piece of wax paper from top crust that you rolled out earlier and then set aside. Invert onto pie and remove other sheet of wax paper. Press dough down around edges of pie plate. Cut edges off dough of both upper and lower crusts to fit pie plate and crimp together with your fingers. With a sharp knife, make decorative slits in top of crust. If desired, brush crust with soy milk and sprinkle with sugar.
- Bake for 30 minutes, or until crust begins to brown. Serve warm with a scoop of non-dairy vanilla ice cream if desired.

PER SERVING: 572 calories, 16g fat (1g saturated), 104g carbohydrate, 8g dietary fiber, 15g sugar, 5g protein, 0mg cholesterol, 17mg sodium, 340mg potassium. Calories from fat: 23 percent.

CONFETTI FRUIT PIE

*T*HIS PIE DOESN'T just taste good, it's festive-looking with its contrast of golden peaches and bright colorful raspberries.

Standard Vegan Single Pie Crust, page 216
8 medium peaches (about 5 cups sliced)
1 cup raspberries
½ cup water
1 tablespoon arrowroot

CRUMB TOPPING:

½ cup unbleached white flour
½ cup granulated sweetener
2 tablespoons vegetable shortening (non-hydrogenated such as Spectrum)

. . . .

MAKES 10 SERVINGS
PREPARATION TIME:
   PEELING, PITTING, SLICING
   PEACHES: 15 minutes
   FRUIT FILLING: 10 minutes
   TOPPING: 5 minutes
   CRUST: 10 minutes
BAKING TIME: 25 minutes

. . . .

PER SERVING: 235 calories, 8g fat (3g saturated), 38g carbohydrate, 3g dietary fiber, 3g protein, 0mg cholesterol, 6mg sodium, 209mg potassium. Calories from fat: 31 percent.

Note: This analysis was made using hydrogenated shortening, not non-hydrogenated. Non-hydrogenated is more healthy.

- Preheat oven to 400°F. Coat an 8-inch pie plate with nonstick cooking spray.
- Prepare Standard Vegan Single Pie Crust. Weight pie crust with another empty pie plate filled with a little water or pie weights to keep the crust from bubbling or shrinking while it bakes. You can also line pie crust with aluminum foil and fill the foil with dry beans. Bake pie crust for 10 minutes or until edges begin to brown slightly.
- While crust is baking, make peach filling. Peel, pit, and slice peaches and place in a heavy cooking pot with raspberries. Add ¼ cup water to fruit. Cover and cook until fruit is soft, but not mushy. Remove from heat.
- Stir arrowroot into ¼ cup water. Stir arrowroot mixture into hot peaches. Mixture will thicken from the heat of the fruit—do not boil. Pour fruit into prepared crust when it is ready, making sure to remove pie pan weight or pie weights before filling.
- *To prepare topping:* Place all topping ingredients in bowl and cut shortening into flour with 2 knives until shortening pieces are pea-sized. Sprinkle peaches with topping.
- Bake for 15 minutes, or until crumbs begin to brown. Serve warm with a scoop of non-dairy vanilla ice cream if desired.

BEATS SINGIN' THE BLUES PIE

*T*HIS TASTY TREAT is made with fresh blueberries, and th[e]
the fruit makes for a lightly sweetened filling. A dusting of crumbs completes t[he]

Standard Vegan Single Pie Crust, page 216
6 cups fresh blueberries
½ cup water
1 tablespoon arrowroot

CRUMB TOPPING:
½ cup unbleached white flour
½ cup granulated sweetener
2 tablespoons vegetable shortening (non-hydrogenated such as Spectrum)

. . . .
MAKES 10 SERVINGS
PREPARATION TIME:
   PEELING, PITTING, SLICING
   PEACHES: 15 minutes
   FRUIT FILLING: 10 minutes
   TOPPING: 5 minutes
   CRUST: 10 minutes
BAKING TIME: 25 minutes
. . . .

PER SERVING: 240 calories, 9g fat (3g saturated), 40g carbohydrate, 3g dietary fiber, 3g protein, 0mg cholesterol, 11mg sodium, 101mg potassium. Calories from fat: 31 percent.

Note: This analysis was made using hydrogenated shortening, not non-hydrogenated. Non-hydrogenated is healthier.

- Preheat oven to 400°F. Coat an 8-inch pie plate with nonstick cooking spray.
- Prepare Standard Vegan Single Pie Crust. Weight pie crust with another empty pie plate filled with a little water or pie weights to keep the crust from bubbling or shrinking while it bakes. You can also line pie crust with aluminum foil and fill the foil with dry beans. Bake pie crust for 10 minutes or until edges begin to brown slightly.
- While crust is baking, make blueberry filling. Place blueberries in a heavy cooking pot. Add ¼ cup water to fruit. Cover and cook until fruit is soft, but not mushy, and remove from heat.
- Stir arrowroot into ¼ cup water. Stir arrowroot mixture into hot blueberries. Mixture will thicken from the heat of the fruit—do not boil. Pour fruit into prepared crust when it is ready, making sure to remove pie weights before putting filling in crust.
- *To prepare topping:* Place all topping ingredients in bowl and cut shortening into flour with two knives until shortening pieces are pea-sized. Sprinkle blueberries with topping.
- Bake for 15 minutes, or until crumbs begin to brown. Serve warm (with a scoop of non-dairy vanilla ice cream) if desired.

PUMPKIN PIE

HAT WOULD YOUR favorite holiday feast be without a traditional pumpkin pie? Here is a veganized version of the classic favorite. You won't even miss the eggs and milk.

Standard Vegan Single Pie
  Crust, page 216
1 15-ounce can pumpkin puree
  (or 2 cups fresh pumpkin)
1 cup soy milk
⅓ cup maple syrup
2 teaspoons pumpkin pie spice*
1 tablespoon arrowroot
2 teaspoons flax powder
½ cup water

. . . .

MAKES 10 SERVINGS
PREPARATION TIME:
  FILLING: 10 minutes
  CRUST: 10 minutes
BAKING TIME: 65 minutes

. . . .

- Preheat oven to 425°F. Coat an 8-inch pie plate with nonstick cooking spray.
- Prepare Standard Vegan Single Pie Crust. Weight pie crust with another empty pie plate filled with a little water or pie weights to keep the crust from bubbling or shrinking while it bakes. You can also line pie crust with aluminum foil and fill the foil with dry beans. Bake pie crust for 10 minutes or until edges begin to brown slightly. Set crust aside.
- *To make filling:* Place all ingredients except flax powder and ½ cup water in food processor or blender and process until smooth.
- Stir flax powder into ½ cup water. Add to pumpkin mixture and pulse to combine. Pour into prepared crust and sprinkle lightly with cinnamon.
- Bake for 15 minutes at 425°F. Reduce heat to 350°F and bake for 50 minutes. Pie will become firm as it cools. Cool at least 4 hours before serving.

Variation: For something different, try substituting either 2 cups cooked and pureed carrots or sweet potatoes for the pumpkin. The only difference I notice when I do this is in the texture. I actually like the texture of the sweet potato pie better—it's smoother. The carrots make a pie filling with a coarser consistency, more like the pumpkin.

*You can substitute 1 teaspoon cinnamon + ½ teaspoon ground ginger + ½ teaspoon ground cloves for the 2 teaspoons pumpkin pie spice.

PER SERVING: 188 calories, 6g fat (<1g saturated), 31g carbohydrate, 2g dietary fiber, 13g sugar, 3g protein, 0mg cholesterol, 121mg sodium, 191mg potassium. Calories from fat: 29 percent.

FUNNY CAKE

*T*HIS IS A veganized version of a Pennsylvania German treat that I grew up with. It's a moist yellow cake baked in a flaky pie crust with a layer of gooey chocolate on the bottom. It's a cake, but it looks like a pie—hence the name.

Standard Vegan Single Pie Crust, page 216
½ cup maple syrup
¼ cup + 1 tablespoon soy margarine
2¼ cups flour
¾ tablespoon baking powder
¼ teaspoon salt
1¼ cups soy milk, rice milk, or non-dairy milk of choice
1½ teaspoons vanilla

CHOCOLATE SAUCE:

1 cup powdered sugar
¼ cup canola oil
½ teaspoon vanilla
⅙ cup cocoa (use ⅓ cup measurer and only fill it half full)
3½ tablespoons arrowroot
½ cup water

. . . .

MAKES 10 SERVINGS
PREPARATION TIME:
  CAKE: 10 minutes
  CHOCOLATE SAUCE:
  10 minutes
  CRUST: 10 minutes
BAKING TIME: 35–40 minutes
. . . .

PER SERVING: 410 calories, 16g fat (1.6g saturated), 60g carbohydrate, 2g dietary fiber, 10g sugar, 6g protein, 0mg cholesterol, 900mg sodium, 148mg potassium. Calories from fat: 35 percent.

- Preheat oven to 375°F. Coat an 8-inch pie plate with nonstick cooking spray.
- Prepare Standard Vegan Single Pie Crust. Weight pie crust with another empty pie plate filled with a little water or pie weights to keep the crust from bubbling or shrinking while it bakes. You can also line pie crust with aluminum foil and fill the foil with dry beans. Bake pie crust for 10 minutes or until edges begin to brown slightly.
- *To make chocolate sauce:* Place powdered sugar, canola oil, vanilla, cocoa, and arrowroot in small saucepan and stir to combine, using a wire whisk for best results. Stir in water. Turn on heat and bring almost to boil stirring constantly. Keep stirring until mixture starts to thicken—do not boil. Remove from heat and set aside while you prepare cake.
- Allow margarine to soften to room temperature or soften in microwave. Do not melt. (If you cannot find soy margarine, any vegetable-based margarine will work.) Place margarine in bowl and cream. Slowly add maple syrup and beat until light and fluffy. Add vanilla and mix. In another bowl, combine flour, baking powder, and salt and mix to combine. Alternately add flour mixture and soy milk to maple/margarine mixture and stir well.
- Pour chocolate sauce in prepared crust. Spoon cake batter onto chocolate sauce. Evenly space 5 mounds around pie pan. Mixture will spread during baking. Bake for 35–40 minutes or until toothpick inserted into cake comes out clean. Allow to cool completely before serving.

ISLAND BREEZES CREAM PIE

*T*HIS SCRUMPTIOUS, FLUFFY coconut cream pie conjures up images of tropical paradise in my mind.

Standard Vegan Single Pie Crust, page 216
¾ cup water
2 tablespoons agar
32 ounces (3 boxes) firm silken tofu
2 cups powdered sugar
4 teaspoons coconut extract
2¼ cups shredded unsweetened coconut

. . . .

MAKES 10 SERVINGS
PREPARATION TIME:
  FILLING: 15 minutes
  CRUST: 10 minutes
BAKING TIME: 10 minutes

. . . .

PER SERVING: 486 calories, 18g fat (6g saturated), 67g carbohydrate, 3g dietary fiber, 3g sugar, 16g protein, 0mg cholesterol, 82mg sodium, 778mg potassium. Calories from fat: 32 percent.

- Preheat oven to 400°F. Coat an 8-inch pie plate with nonstick cooking spray.
- Prepare Standard Vegan Single Pie Crust. Weight pie crust with another empty pie plate filled with a little water or pie weights to keep the crust from bubbling or shrinking while it bakes. You can also line pie crust with aluminum foil and fill the foil with dry beans. Bake pie crust for 10 minutes or until edges begin to brown slightly.
- Remove from oven and set aside. Meanwhile, place water in small pan and bring to boil. Sprinkle agar over water and stir to combine. Simmer 10–15 minutes, or until agar has completely dissolved.
- While agar is simmering, place tofu in a food processor. Process until smooth, scraping down sides as necessary. Add sugar and coconut extract. Process until combined. Add agar mixture when it is ready. Process until mixture is smooth and creamy. Stir coconut in by hand, reserving ¼ cup for garnish.
- Pour into prepared crust. Sprinkle with reserved coconut. Refrigerate at least 8 hours before serving so that filling sets.

Variation: For an interesting coconut flavor, toast the coconut before adding it to the filling and using it for a garnish. To toast coconut, you can spread it out in a thin layer on foil that has been coated with nonstick cooking spray. Place it under broiler until it begins to brown. Stir and place under broiler again. Keep stirring until all coconut is a light brown color. Replace powdered sugar with brown sugar. Keep the rest of the recipe the same.

PEPPERMINT PATTY CREAM PIE

TOFU CREAM PIES are always light and fluffy because the tofu provides a creamy base from which to work. All tofu pies should be made the day before you plan to serve them so they have time to set. This winning combination of chocolate and mint reminds me of a York Peppermint Patty.

Standard Vegan Single Pie Crust, page 216
16 ounces (1½ boxes) firm silken tofu
1 cup powdered sugar
2 teaspoons vanilla
1½ cups vegan chocolate chips

TOPPING:

16 ounces (1½ boxes) firm silken tofu
1 cup powdered sugar
1½ teaspoon peppermint extract
¼ cup unbleached white flour

. . . .

MAKES 10 SERVINGS
PREPARATION TIME:
  FILLING: 15 minutes
  TOPPING: 10 minutes
  CRUST: 10 minutes
BAKING TIME: 10 minutes

. . . .

- Preheat oven to 400°F. Coat an 8-inch pie plate with nonstick cooking spray.
- Prepare Standard Vegan Single Pie Crust. Weight pie crust with another empty pie plate filled with a little water or pie weights to keep the crust from bubbling or shrinking while it bakes. You can also line pie crust with aluminum foil and fill the foil with dry beans. Bake pie crust for 10 minutes or until edges begin to brown slightly.
- Remove from oven and set aside. Meanwhile, place tofu in a food processor and process until smooth, scraping down sides as necessary. Add sugar and vanilla. Melt chocolate chips in microwave or double boiler. Pour into food processor and blend until combined. Pour into prepared crust.
- *To prepare topping:* Rinse and dry food processor. Place tofu in a food processor and process until smooth, scraping down sides as necessary. Add sugar, flour, and peppermint extract and mix. Carefully mound onto chocolate layer.
- Refrigerate at least 8 hours before serving so that filling sets. You may want to refrigerate the topping in a separate container to allow it to set before putting it on the pie. It will be easier to mound onto the filling.

PER SERVING: 423 calories, 20g fat (6g saturated), 50g carbohydrate, 2g dietary fiber, 3g sugar, 14g protein, 0mg cholesterol, 22mg sodium, 488mg potassium. Calories from fat: 41 percent.

A Hint of Mint Cream Pie

HIS PIE WAS inspired by one of my favorite ice cream flavors—mint chocolate chip. It has all the flavor of that delicious ice cream but none of the startling green color, which is achieved by adding artificial coloring.

Standard Vegan Single Pie
  Crust, page 216
¾ *cup water*
2 *tablespoon agar*
32 *ounces (3 boxes) firm*
  silken tofu
2 *cup powdered sugar*
3 *teaspoons peppermint extract*
1½ *cups vegan chocolate chips*

. . . .

MAKES 10 SERVINGS
PREPARATION TIME:
  FILLING: 15 minutes
  CRUST: 10 minutes
BAKING TIME: 10 minutes

. . . .

- Preheat oven to 400°F. Coat an 8-inch pie plate with nonstick cooking spray.
- Prepare Standard Vegan Single Pie Crust. Weight pie crust with another empty pie plate filled with a little water or pie weights to keep the crust from bubbling or shrinking while it bakes. You can also line pie crust with aluminum foil and fill the foil with dry beans. Bake pie crust for 10 minutes or until edges begin to brown slightly.
- Remove from oven and set aside. Meanwhile, place water in small pan and bring to boil. Sprinkle agar over water and stir to combine. Simmer for 15 minutes, or until agar has completely dissolved.
- While agar is simmering, place tofu in a food processor. Process until smooth, scraping down sides as necessary. Add sugar and peppermint extract. Add agar mixture when it is ready. Process until mixture is smooth and creamy. Stir in chocolate chips by hand. Pour into prepared crust.
- Refrigerate at least 8 hours before serving so that filling sets.

PER SERVING: 478 calories, 20g fat (6g saturated), 62g carbohydrate, 2g dietary fiber, 3g sugar, 16g protein, 0mg cholesterol, 22mg sodium, 504mg potassium. Calories from fat: 36 percent.

You Got Your Chocolate in My Peanut Butter Cream Pie

LUFFY PEANUT BUTTER cream mounded on a dark chocolate filling will make this a favorite for both chocolate and peanut butter lovers.

Standard Vegan Single Pie
  Crust, page 216
16 ounces (1½ boxes) firm
  silken tofu
1 cup powdered sugar
2 teaspoons vanilla
1½ cups vegan chocolate chips

TOPPING:
16 ounces (1½ boxes) firm
  silken tofu
1 cup powdered sugar
1½ teaspoon vanilla
¾ cup smooth natural peanut
  butter
¼ cup unbleached white flour or
  2 teaspoons xanthan gum*

. . . .

MAKES 10 SERVINGS
PREPARATION TIME:
  FILLING: 15 minutes
  TOPPING: 10 minutes
  CRUST: 10 minutes
BAKING TIME: 10 minutes

. . . .

PER SERVING: 482 calories, 20g fat
(6g saturated), 62g carbohydrate, 2g
dietary fiber, 3g sugar, 16g protein, 0mg
cholesterol, 22mg sodium, 506mg
potassium. Calories from fat: 36 percent.

- Preheat oven to 400°F. Coat an 8-inch pie plate with nonstick cooking spray.
- Prepare Standard Vegan Single Pie Crust. Weight pie crust with another empty pie plate filled with a little water or pie weights to keep the crust from bubbling or shrinking while it bakes. You can also line pie crust with aluminum foil and fill the foil with dry beans. Bake pie crust for 10 minutes or until edges begin to brown slightly.
- Remove from oven and set aside. Meanwhile, place tofu in a food processor and process until smooth, scraping down sides as necessary. Add sugar and vanilla. Melt chocolate chips in microwave or double boiler. Pour into food processor and blend until combined. Pour into prepared crust.
- *To make topping:* Rinse and dry food processor. Place tofu in a food processor and process until smooth, scraping down sides as necessary. Add sugar, flour, and vanilla. Add peanut butter and process until smooth and creamy. Carefully mound onto chocolate layer.
- Refrigerate at least 8 hours before serving so that filling sets. You may want to refrigerate the topping in a separate container to allow it to set before putting it on the pie. It will be easier to mound onto the filling.

*Xanthan gum will make a softer topping, but will not give the mild flour taste that you may get when using the ¼ cup flour.

BLACK AND WHITE CREAM PIE

I NAMED THIS cream pie Black and White because that's exactly what it is—
classic dark chocolate filling topped with fluffy vanilla cream. Simple and delicious.

Standard Vegan Single Pie
    Crust, page 216
16 ounces (1½ boxes) firm
    silken tofu
1 cup powdered sugar
2 teaspoons vanilla
1½ cups vegan chocolate chips

TOPPING:
16 ounces (1½ boxes) firm
    silken tofu
1 cup powdered sugar
1 tablespoon vanilla
¼ cup unbleached white flour or
    2 teaspoons xanthan gum*

. . . .

MAKES 10 SERVINGS
PREPARATION TIME:
    FILLING: 15 minutes
    TOPPING: 10 minutes
    CRUST: 10 minutes
BAKING TIME: 10 minutes

. . . .

- Preheat oven to 400°F. Coat an 8-inch pie plate with nonstick cooking spray.
- Prepare Standard Vegan Single Pie Crust. Weight pie crust with another empty pie plate filled with a little water or pie weights to keep the crust from bubbling or shrinking while it bakes. You can also line pie crust with aluminum foil and fill the foil with dry beans. Bake pie crust for 10 minutes or until edges begin to brown slightly.
- Remove from oven and set aside. Meanwhile, place tofu in a food processor and process until smooth, scraping down sides as necessary. Add sugar and vanilla. Melt chocolate chips in microwave or double boiler. Pour into food processor and blend until combined. Pour into prepared crust.
- *To make topping:* Rinse and dry food processor. Place tofu in a food processor and process until smooth, scraping down sides as necessary. Add sugar, flour, and vanilla. Carefully mound onto chocolate layer.
- Refrigerate at least 8 hours before serving so that filling sets. You may want to refrigerate the topping in a separate container to allow it to set before putting it on the pie. It will be easier to mound onto the filling.

PER SERVING: 484 calories, 20g fat (6g saturated), 62g carbohydrate, 2g dietary fiber, 3g sugar, 16g protein, 0mg cholesterol, 23mg sodium, 507mg potassium. Calories from fat: 36 percent.

*Xanthan gum will make a softer topping, but you will not get the mild flour flavor that you may get if you use the ¼ cup flour.

MONKEY'S CHOICE CREAM PIE

OR ALL YOU banana lovers out there, this combination of sliced bananas, creamy banana filling, and fluffy vanilla cream topping will be a dream come true!

Standard Vegan Single Pie Crust, page 216
½ cup water
1 tablespoon agar
16 ounces (1½ boxes) firm silken tofu
1 cup powdered sugar
2 teaspoons vanilla
½ teaspoon lemon juice
1½ cups ripe bananas, peeled and mashed (about 2 bananas)

TOPPING:

16 ounces (1½ boxes) firm silken tofu
1 cup powdered sugar
1 tablespoon vanilla
¼ cup unbleached white flour or 2 teaspoons xanthan gum*
2 medium yellow bananas, peeled and sliced

. . . .

MAKES 10 SERVINGS
PREPARATION TIME:
   FILLING: 15 minutes
   TOPPING: 10 minutes
   CRUST: 10 minutes
BAKING TIME: 10 minutes

. . . .

PER SERVING: 425 calories, 13g fat (1g saturated), 62g carbohydrate, 2g dietary fiber, 3g sugar, 16g protein, 0mg cholesterol, 31mg sodium, 754mg potassium. Calories from fat: 27 percent.

- Preheat oven to 400°F. Coat an 8-inch pie plate with nonstick cooking spray.
- Prepare Standard Vegan Single Pie Crust. Weight pie crust with another empty pie plate filled with a little water or pie weights to keep the crust from bubbling or shrinking while it bakes. You can also line pie crust with aluminum foil and fill the foil with dry beans. Bake pie crust for 10 minutes or until edges begin to brown slightly.
- Remove from oven and set aside. Meanwhile, place water in small pan and bring to boil. Sprinkle agar over water and stir to combine. Simmer 10–15 minutes, or until agar has completely dissolved.
- While agar is simmering, place tofu in a food processor and process until smooth, scraping down sides as necessary. Add sugar, lemon juice, and vanilla. Add mashed bananas and puree until smooth and creamy. Add agar mixture when it is ready. Process until mixture is combined. Slice peeled yellow bananas and place evenly around the bottom of the prepared pie crust. Pour filling over sliced bananas.
- *To make topping:* Rinse and dry food processor. Place tofu in food processor and process until smooth scraping down sides as necessary. Add sugar, flour, and vanilla and mix. Carefully mound onto banana layer.
- Refrigerate at least 8 hours before serving so that filling sets. You may want to refrigerate the topping in a separate container to allow it to set before putting it on the pie. It will be easier to mound onto the filling.

*Xanthan gum will give a softer topping, but you will not get the mild flour taste that you may have if you use the flour.

THAT'S ONE NUTTY BANANA!

*A*S A CHILD, I used to love slices of banana smeared with peanut butter, and this pie reminds me of that snack.

Standard Vegan Single Pie Crust, page 216
½ *cup water*
1 *tablespoon agar*
16 *ounces (1½ boxes) firm silken tofu*
1 *cup powdered sugar*
1 *teaspoon vanilla*
½ *teaspoon lemon juice*
1½ *cups ripe bananas, peeled and mashed (about 2 bananas)*

PEANUT BUTTER SAUCE:
16 *ounces (1½ boxes) firm silken tofu*
1 *cup powdered sugar*
1½ *teaspoons vanilla*
¾ *cup smooth natural peanut butter*
¼ *cup unbleached white flour or 2 teaspoons xanthan gum**

- Preheat oven to 400°F. Coat an 8-inch pie plate with nonstick cooking spray.
- Prepare Standard Vegan Single Pie Crust. Weight pie crust with another empty pie plate filled with a little water or pie weights to keep the crust from bubbling or shrinking while it bakes. You can also line pie crust with aluminum foil and fill the foil with dry beans. Bake pie crust for 10 minutes or until edges begin to brown slightly. Remove from oven and set aside.
- *To make filling:* Place water in small pan and bring to boil. Sprinkle agar over water and stir to combine. Simmer 10–15 minutes, or until agar has completely dissolved. While agar is simmering, place tofu in a food processor and process until smooth, scraping down sides as necessary. Add sugar, lemon juice, and vanilla. Add mashed bananas and puree until smooth and creamy. Add agar mixture when it is ready and process until mixture is combined. Transfer filling to another bowl so you can use the food processor to make peanut butter sauce.

*Xanthan gum will produce a slightly softer topping, but it will not have the mild flour flavor that you may get if you use the ¼ cup flour.

- Slice peeled yellow bananas and place evenly around the bottom of the prepared pie crust. Prepare peanut butter sauce by blending all sauce ingredients in food processor. Pour peanut butter sauce over bananas, reserving about ¼ cup for drizzling over top of pie if desired. Pour filling over sliced bananas and peanut butter sauce.
- *To make Peanut Butter Sauce:* Rinse and dry food processor. Place tofu in a food processor and process until smooth, scraping down sides as necessary. Add sugar, flour, and vanilla. Add peanut butter and blend until smooth. Carefully mound onto banana layer. Drizzle with reserved peanut butter sauce if desired.
- Refrigerate at least 8 hours before serving so that filling sets. You may want to refrigerate the topping in a separate container to allow it to set before putting it on the pie. It will be easier to mound onto the filling.

PEANUT BUTTER SAUCE:

¼ cup maple syrup

¼ cup smooth natural peanut butter

½ teaspoon vanilla

¼ cup water

2 medium yellow bananas, peeled and sliced

. . . .

MAKES 10 SERVINGS

PREPARATION TIME:

FILLING: 15 minutes

TOPPING: 10 minutes

CRUST: 10 minutes

BAKING TIME: 10 minutes

. . . .

PER SERVING: 655 calories, 30g fat (5g saturated), 79g carbohydrate, 4g dietary fiber, 13g sugar, 24g protein, 0mg cholesterol, 182mg sodium, 1000mg potassium. Calories from fat: 38 percent.

MIDNIGHT MONKEY CREAM PIE

*T*HIS PIE IS like a fluffy chocolate-covered banana. Don't be alarmed if the topping turns from a nice creamy white to a faded yellow color—it's because of the banana.

Standard Vegan Single Pie
  Crust, page 216
16 ounces (1½ boxes) firm
  silken tofu
1 cup powdered sugar
2 teaspoons vanilla
1½ cups vegan chocolate chips
2 medium yellow bananas, peeled

TOPPING:
16 ounces (1½ boxes) firm
  silken tofu
½ cup powdered sugar
1 teaspoon vanilla
½ teaspoon lemon juice
1½ cup mashed very ripe
  banana (about 2 bananas)
¼ cup unbleached white flour or
  2 teaspoons xanthan gum*

. . . .

MAKES 10 SERVINGS
PREPARATION TIME:
  FILLING: 15 minutes
  TOPPING: 10 minutes
  CRUST: 10 minutes
BAKING TIME: 10 minutes
. . . .

- Preheat oven to 400°F. Coat an 8-inch pie plate with nonstick cooking spray.
- Prepare Standard Vegan Single Pie Crust. Weight pie crust with another empty pie plate filled with a little water or pie weights to keep the crust from bubbling or shrinking while it bakes. You can also line pie crust with aluminum foil and fill the foil with dry beans. Bake pie crust for 10 minutes or until edges begin to brown slightly.
- Remove from oven and set aside. Meanwhile, place tofu in a food processor and process until smooth, scraping down sides as necessary. Add sugar and vanilla. Melt chocolate chips in microwave or double boiler. Pour into food processor and blend until combined.
- Slice peeled yellow bananas and arrange evenly around the bottom of the prepared pie crust. Pour filling into prepared crust on top of sliced bananas
- *To make topping:* Rinse and dry food processor. Place tofu in a food processor and process until smooth, scraping down sides as necessary. Add sugar, mashed banana, flour, lemon juice, and vanilla. Carefully mound onto chocolate layer.
- Refrigerate at least 8 hours before serving so that filling sets. You may want to refrigerate the topping in a separate container to allow it to set before putting it on the pie. It will be easier to mound onto the filling.

PER SERVING: 511 calories, 21g fat (6g saturated), 70 g carbohydrate, 4g dietary fiber, 3g sugar, 16g protein, 0mg cholesterol, 23mg sodium, 733mg potassium. Calories from fat: 34 percent.

*Xanthan gum will produce a slightly softer topping, but it will not have the mild flour flavor that you may have if you use the ¼ cup flour.

BERRY CHIP CREAM PIE

*C*REAMY RASPBERRY FILLING and dark chocolate chips make this a mouth-watering blend worthy of any dinner party.

Standard Vegan Single Pie Crust, page 216
¾ cup water
2 tablespoon agar
32 ounces (3 boxes) firm silken tofu
2 cups powdered sugar
1 teaspoon vanilla
½ cup raspberry jam or ¾ cup fresh raspberries
1½ cups vegan chocolate chips

. . . .

MAKES 10 SERVINGS
PREPARATION TIME:
   FILLING: 15 minutes
   CRUST: 10 minutes
BAKING TIME: 10 minutes

. . . .

- Preheat oven to 400°F. Coat an 8-inch pie plate with nonstick cooking spray.
- Prepare Standard Vegan Single Pie Crust. Weight pie crust with another empty pie plate filled with a little water or pie weights to keep the crust from bubbling or shrinking while it bakes. You can also line pie crust with aluminum foil and fill the foil with dry beans. Bake pie crust for 10 minutes or until edges begin to brown slightly.
- Remove from oven and set aside. Meanwhile, place water in small pan and bring to boil. Sprinkle agar over water and stir to combine. Simmer 10–15 minutes, or until agar has completely dissolved.
- While agar is simmering, place tofu in a food processor and process until smooth, scraping down sides as necessary. Add sugar, raspberry jam, and vanilla extract. Add agar mixture when it is ready. Process until mixture is smooth and creamy. Stir in chocolate chips by hand and pour into prepared crust.
- Refrigerate at least 8 hours before serving so that filling sets.

PER SERVING: 533 calories, 20g fat (6g saturated), 77g carbohydrate, 4g dietary fiber, 3g sugar, 17g protein, 0mg cholesterol, 43mg sodium, 740mg potassium. Calories from fat: 33 percent.

PUCKER-UP CREAM PIE

*T*HIS OLD-TIME CLASSIC—tangy lemon filling topped with fluffy vanilla cream—will definitely make your taste buds tingle.

Standard Vegan Single Pie
    Crust, page 216
½ cup lemon juice
1 tablespoon agar
16 ounces (1½ boxes) firm
    silken tofu
1 cup powdered sugar
1 tablespoon lemon extract
¼ teaspoon tumeric (for color
    only)

TOPPING:

16 ounces (1½ boxes) firm
    silken tofu
1 cup powdered sugar
1 tablespoon vanilla
¼ cup unbleached white flour or
    2 teaspoons xanthan gum*

. . . .

MAKES 10 SERVINGS
PREPARATION TIME:
    FILLING: 15 minutes
    TOPPING: 10 minutes
    CRUST: 10 minutes
BAKING TIME: 10 minutes

. . . .

- Preheat oven to 400°F. Coat an 8-inch pie plate with nonstick cooking spray.
- Prepare Standard Vegan Single Pie Crust. Weight pie crust with another empty pie plate filled with a little water or pie weights to keep the crust from bubbling or shrinking while it bakes. You can also line pie crust with aluminum foil and fill the foil with dry beans. Bake pie crust for 10 minutes or until edges begin to brown slightly.
- Remove from oven and set aside. Meanwhile, place lemon juice in small pan and bring to boil. Sprinkle agar over juice and stir to combine. Simmer 10–15 minutes, or until agar has completely dissolved. While agar is simmering, place tofu in a food processor. Process until smooth, scraping down sides as necessary. Add sugar and lemon extract. Add agar mixture when it is ready. Process until mixture is smooth and creamy. Pour into prepared crust.
- *To prepare topping:* Rinse and dry food processor. Place tofu in food processor and process until smooth, scraping down sides as necessary. Add sugar, flour, and vanilla. Carefully mound onto lemon layer. You may want to refrigerate the topping in a separate container to allow it to set before putting it on the pie. It will be easier to mound onto the filling.
- Refrigerate at least 8 hours before serving so that filling sets.

PER SERVING: 395 calories, 13g fat (1g saturated), 55g carbohydrate, 1g dietary fiber, 3g sugar, 15g protein 0mg cholesterol, 30mg sodium, 634mg potassium. Calories from fat: 29 percent.

*Xanthan will produce a slightly softer topping, but it will not have the mild flour flavor that you may have if you use the ¼ cup flour.

CLOUDS OF STRAWBERRY PIE

Y SON, A strawberry lover, asked if I could make strawberry cream pie—so how could I refuse? I created this pie for him as well as to make the most of fresh strawberries in June (although jam or frozen strawberries may be used as well). The light whipped topping adds just the right touch.

Standard Vegan Single Pie
  Crust, page 216
½ *cup water*
1 *tablespoon agar*
16 *ounces (1½ boxes) firm*
  silken tofu
1 *cup powdered sugar*
1 *teaspoon vanilla*
¼ *cup strawberry jam or* ¾ *cup*
  fresh or frozen strawberries
4–5 *fresh mint leaves*

TOPPING:
16 *ounces (1½ boxes) firm*
  silken tofu
1 *cup powdered sugar*
1 *tablespoon vanilla*
¼ *cup unbleached white flour or*
  2 *teaspoons xanthan gum**

. . . .

MAKES 10 SERVINGS
PREPARATION TIME:
  FILLING: 15 minutes
  TOPPING: 10 minutes
  CRUST: 10 minutes
BAKING TIME: 10 minutes

. . . .

PER SERVING: 396 calories, 13g fat (1g saturated), 55g carbohydrate, 2g dietary fiber, 3g sugar, 15g protein, 0mg cholesterol, 30mg sodium, 638mg potassium. Calories from fat: 29 percent.

- Coat an 8-inch pie plate with nonstick cooking spray. Preheat oven to 400°F.
- Prepare Standard Vegan Single Pie Crust. Weight pie crust with another empty pie plate filled with a little water or pie weights to keep the crust from bubbling or shrinking while it bakes. You can also line pie crust with aluminum foil and fill the foil with dry beans. Bake pie crust for 10 minutes or until edges begin to brown slightly.
- Remove from oven and set aside. Meanwhile, Place water in small pan and bring to boil. Sprinkle agar over water and stir to combine. Simmer 10–15 minutes, or until agar has completely dissolved. While agar is simmering, place tofu in a food processor.
- Process until smooth, scraping down sides as necessary. Add sugar and strawberry jam or fruit and vanilla. Add agar mixture when it is ready. Process until mixture is smooth and creamy. Pour into prepared crust.
- *To make topping:* Rinse and dry food processor. Place tofu in food processor and process until smooth, scraping down sides as necessary. Add sugar, flour, and vanilla. Carefully mound onto strawberry layer. You may want to refrigerate the topping in a separate container to allow it to set before putting it on the pie. It will be easier to mound onto the filling. Garnish with fresh strawberries and mint leaves if desired.
- Refrigerate at least 8 hours before serving so that filling may set.

*Xanthan gum will produce a slightly softer topping, but it will not have the mild flour flavor that you may have if you use the ¼ cup flour.

STRAWBERRY SURPRISE CREAM PIE

*T*HIS IS ONE of my favorite cream pies, even though it contains no chocolate. I always liked strawberry cake topped with coconut icing so I started to think that maybe I could add just a bit of coconut to the strawberry base that I use for the Clouds of Strawberry Pie. I tried it, made a few other adjustments, and the Strawberry Surprise Cream Pie was born!

Standard Vegan Single Pie Crust, page 216
¾ cup water
2 tablespoon agar
32 ounces (3 boxes) firm silken tofu
2 cups powdered sugar
1 teaspoon coconut extract
½ cup strawberry jam or 1½ cups fresh or frozen strawberries
1 cup shredded unsweetened coconut
4–5 fresh mint leaves for garnish (optional)

. . . .

MAKES 10 SERVINGS
PREPARATION TIME:
   FILLING: 15 minutes
   CRUST: 10 minutes
BAKING TIME: 10 minutes

. . . .

- Preheat oven to 400°F. Coat an 8-inch pie plate with nonstick cooking spray.
- Prepare Standard Vegan Single Pie Crust. Weight pie crust with another empty pie plate filled with a little water or pie weights to keep the crust from bubbling or shrinking while it bakes. You can also line pie crust with aluminum foil and fill the foil with dry beans. Bake pie crust for 10 minutes or until edges begin to brown slightly.
- Remove from oven and set aside. Meanwhile, place water in small pan and bring to boil. Sprinkle agar over water and stir to combine. Simmer 10–15 minutes, or until agar has completely dissolved.
- While agar is simmering, place tofu in a food processor. Process until smooth, scraping down sides as necessary. Add sugar and strawberry jam or fruit and coconut extract. Add agar mixture when it is ready. Process until mixture is smooth and creamy. Stir in ¾ cup coconut by hand, reserving ¼ cup to sprinkle on top of pie. Pour into prepared crust. Garnish with shredded coconut, fresh strawberries, and mint leaves if desired.
- Refrigerate at least 8 hours before serving so that filling sets.

Variation: Substitute fresh peaches for strawberries for a scrumptious coconut peach pie.

PER SERVING: 449 calories, 15g fat (3g saturated), 65g carbohydrate, 3g dietary fiber, 4g sugar, 16g protein., 0mg cholesterol, 59mg sodium, 787mg potassium. Calories from fat: 30 percent.

Piña Colada Cream Pie

F YOU ENJOY a frosty piña colada on a hot summer day, then you'll love this creamy tropical pineapple and coconut concoction.

Standard Vegan Single Pie
    Crust, page 216
¾ cup pineapple juice
2 tablespoon agar
32 ounces (3 boxes) firm
    silken tofu
2 cups powdered sugar
1 teaspoon coconut extract
¾ cup crushed pineapple
1 cup shredded unsweetened
    coconut
4–5 fresh mint leaves for
    garnish (optional)

. . . .
MAKES 10 SERVINGS
PREPARATION TIME:
    FILLING: 15 minutes
    CRUST: 10 minutes
BAKING TIME: 10 minutes
. . . .

- Preheat oven to 400°F. Coat an 8-inch pie plate with nonstick cooking spray.
- Prepare Standard Vegan Single Pie Crust. Weight pie crust with another empty pie plate filled with a little water or pie weights to keep the crust from bubbling or shrinking while it bakes. You can also line pie crust with aluminum foil and fill the foil with dry beans. Bake pie crust for 10 minutes or until edges begin to brown slightly.
- Remove from oven and set aside. Meanwhile, place juice in small pan and bring to boil. Sprinkle agar over juice and stir to combine. Simmer 10–15 minutes, or until agar has completely dissolved. While agar is simmering, place tofu in a food processor. Process until smooth, scraping down sides as necessary. Add sugar, ½ cup pineapple and coconut extract. Add agar mixture when it is ready. Process until mixture is smooth and creamy. Stir in ¾ cup coconut by hand (reserving ¼ cup to sprinkle on top of pie). Stir in ¼ cup crushed pineapple mix by hand.
- Pour into prepared crust. Garnish with shredded coconut and mint leaves if desired.
- Refrigerate at least 8 hours before serving so that filling sets.

PER SERVING: 464 calories, 15g fat (3g saturated), 69g carbohydrate, 3g dietary fiber, 4g sugar, 16g protein, 0mg cholesterol, 60mg sodium, 798mg potassium. Calories from fat: 29 percent.

PATRIOTIC CREAM PIE

I HAVE ALWAYS loved the taste of blueberry crumb pie so I got to wondering if blueberries would taste good in a cream pie. I tried it and loved it. This pie is similar to the Clouds of Strawberry Cream Pie, page 129, except it calls for blueberries instead of strawberries.

Standard Vegan Single Pie
    Crust, page 216
½ cup water juice
1 tablespoon agar
16 ounces (1½ boxes) firm
    silken tofu
1 cup powdered sugar
1 teaspoon vanilla
½ cup fresh or frozen blueberries
4–5 fresh mint leaves for
    garnish (optional)

TOPPING:
16 ounces (1½ boxes) firm
    silken tofu
1 cup powdered sugar
1 tablespoon vanilla
¼ cup unbleached white flour or
    2 teaspoons xanthan gum*

. . . .

MAKES 10 SERVINGS
PREPARATION TIME:
    FILLING: 15 minutes
    TOPPING: 10 minutes
    CRUST: 10 minutes
BAKING TIME: 10 minutes

. . . .

PER SERVING: 349 calories, 7g fat (1g saturated), 55g carbohydrate, 2g dietary fiber, 3g sugar, 15g protein, 0mg cholesterol, 31mg sodium, 626mg potassium. Calories from fat: 19 percent.

- Coat an 8-inch pie plate with nonstick cooking spray. Preheat oven to 400°F.
- Prepare Standard Vegan Single Pie Crust. Weight pie crust with another empty pie plate filled with a little water or pie weights to keep the crust from bubbling or shrinking while it bakes. You can also line pie crust with aluminum foil and fill the foil with dry beans. Bake pie crust for 10 minutes or until edges begin to brown slightly.
- Remove from oven and set aside. Meanwhile, place water in small pan and bring to boil. Sprinkle agar over water and stir to combine. Simmer 10–15 minutes, or until agar has completely dissolved. While agar is simmering, place tofu in food processor. Process until smooth, scraping down sides as necessary. Add sugar, ½ cup fruit, and vanilla. Add agar mixture when it is ready. Process until mixture is smooth and creamy. Pour into prepared crust.
- *To make topping:* Rinse and dry food processor. Place tofu in a food processor and process until smooth, scraping down sides as necessary. Add sugar, flour, and vanilla. Carefully mound onto blueberry layer. Garnish with ¼ cup fresh blueberries and mint leaves if desired.
- Refrigerate at least 8 hours before serving so that filling sets. You may want to refrigerate the topping in a separate container to allow it to set before putting it on the pie. It will be easier to mound onto the filling.

*Xanthan gum will produce a slightly softer topping, but it will not have the mild flour flavor that you may have if you use the ¼ cup flour.

A FRUIT TART is a light, refreshing dessert that looks spectacular. The following tarts are made with a crisp crust that is baked in an 11-inch tart pan with a removable bottom. Each has a small amount of tofu cream on the bottom not only to add a creamy flavor, but also to help hold the fruit in place to truly showcase it. Sliced fruit is arranged on top of the cream and brushed with a thin glaze of warm jam to give it a professional look. I have suggested several combinations, but feel free to vary the kinds of fruit depending on your personal taste and the availability of quality fresh fruit. Have fun and create beautiful, delicious masterpieces! You'll be surprised at how simple it is.

THE QUEEN OF TARTS

*T*HIS CRISPY TART is filled with strawberry cream and topped with a stunning array of glazed seasonal fruit. It looks spectacular, tastes delicious, and is simple to make.

Tart Crust, page 218
18 ounces (1½ boxes) firm
    silken tofu
1 cup powdered sugar
1 teaspoon vanilla
¼ cup strawberry jam or ¾ cup
    fresh or frozen strawberries
2 tablespoons unbleached
    white flour

FRUIT:

1 cup fresh strawberries
3 kiwi
1 cup fresh raspberries or
    blueberries

GLAZE:

½ cup plum or seedless rasp-
    berry preserve

. . . .
MAKES 12 SERVINGS
PREPARATION TIME:
    FILLING: 5 minutes
    FRUIT: 30 minutes
    CRUST: 10 minutes
ASSEMBLY: 15 minutes
BAKING TIME: 20 minutes
. . . .

PER SERVING: 229 calories, 8g fat
(<1g saturated), 33g carbohydrate, 4g
dietary fiber, 2g sugar, 8g protein, 0mg
cholesterol, 8mg sodium, 396mg
potassium. Calories from fat: 31 percent.

- Preheat oven to 375°F. Coat an 11-inch tart pan (with removable bottom) with nonstick cooking spray. Prepare Tart Crust.
- While pie shell is cooling, prepare filling. Place tofu in food processor and blend until smooth, scraping sides as necessary. Add other ingredients and blend until smooth. Set aside.
- *To prepare fruit:* Hull strawberries and cut in slices the long way, then set aside. Peel kiwi and slice, making several triangular cuts evenly spaced along the kiwi holding it the long way. When you slice the kiwi into rounds, it will have petal shaped edges. Set aside. Wash berries and set aside.
- When crust is cool, spread filling in it. Arrange prepared fruit so that all of filling is covered. Warm preserve and use a pastry brush to brush it over tops of fruit to glaze it.
- Refrigerate until serving.

TANGY TASTY TART

*T*HIS TANGY TREAT—tart lemon cream and artfully arrayed glazed fresh fruit—is a wonderful dessert to serve at a dinner party because it looks so beautiful.

Tart Crust, page 218
18 ounces (1½ boxes) firm silken tofu
1 cup powdered sugar
1 tablespoon lemon extract
¼ teaspoon tumeric (for color only)
2 tablespoons unbleached white flour

FRUIT:
1 cup fresh blueberries
4 kiwi
1 cup fresh raspberries

GLAZE:
½ cup plum or seedless raspberry preserve

. . . .

MAKES 12 SERVINGS
PREPARATION TIME:
   FILLING: 5 minutes
   FRUIT: 30 minutes
   CRUST: 10 minutes
ASSEMBLY: 15 minutes
BAKING TIME: 20 minutes

. . . .

PER SERVING: 265 calories, 8g fat (<1g saturated), 43g carbohydrate, 4g dietary fiber, 2g sugar, 8g protein, 0mg cholesterol, 14mg sodium, 404mg potassium. Calories from fat: 27 percent.

- Preheat oven to 375°F. Coat an 11-inch tart pan (with removable bottom) with nonstick cooking spray.
- Prepare Tart Crust.
- While pie shell is cooling, prepare filling. Place tofu in food processor and blend until smooth, scraping sides as necessary. Add other ingredients and blend until smooth. Set aside.
- *To prepare fruit:* Peel kiwi and slice, making several triangular cuts evenly spaced along the kiwi holding it the long way. When you slice the kiwi into rounds, it will have petal-shaped edges. Set aside. Wash berries and set aside.
- When crust is cool, spread filling in it. Arrange prepared fruit so that all of filling is covered. Warm preserve and use a pastry brush to brush it over tops of fruit to glaze it.
- Refrigerate until serving.

FRUITY ARTISTRY

OTHING BEATS THE simple yet elegant combination of seasonal glazed fresh fruit arranged in vanilla cream.

Tart Crust, page 218
18 ounces (1½ boxes) firm silken tofu
1 cup powdered sugar
1 tablespoon vanilla
2 tablespoons unbleached white flour

FRUIT:
1 cup fresh cherries
3 kiwi
1 cup fresh strawberries
½ cup fresh blueberries

GLAZE:
½ cup plum or seedless raspberry preserve

. . . .

MAKES 12 SERVINGS
PREPARATION TIME:
   FILLING: 5 minutes
   FRUIT: 30 minutes
   CRUST: 10 minutes
ASSEMBLY: 15 minutes
BAKING TIME: 20 minutes

. . . .

PER SERVING: 268 calories, 8g fat (<1g saturated), 43g carbohydrate, 4g dietary fiber, 2g sugar, 8g protein, 0mg cholesterol, 14mg sodium, 408mg potassium. Calories from fat: 27 percent.

- Preheat oven to 375°F. Coat an 11-inch tart pan (with removable bottom) with nonstick cooking spray.
- Prepare Tart Crust.
- While pie shell is cooling, prepare filling. Place tofu in food processor and blend until smooth, scraping sides as necessary. Add other ingredients and blend until smooth. Set aside.
- *To prepare fruit:* Peel kiwi and slice, making several triangular cuts evenly spaced along the kiwi holding it the long way. When you slice the kiwi into rounds, it will have petal shaped edges. Set aside. Hull strawberries and slice the long way, then set aside. Pit and half cherries, wash berries, and set aside.
- When crust is cool, spread filling in it. Arrange prepared fruit so that all of filling is covered. Warm preserve and use a pastry brush to brush it over tops of fruit to glaze it.
- Refrigerate until serving.

A TASTE OF THE TROPICS

*T*HIS FRUIT TART is my personal favorite because I adore the taste of coconut. I can't think of anything better than fresh tropical fruit arranged over a sweet coconut cream (except maybe for chocolate!).

Tart Crust, page 218
18 ounces (1½ boxes) firm
   silken tofu
1 cup powdered sugar
2 teaspoons coconut extract
1 cup shredded unsweetened
   coconut

FRUIT:
1 cup fresh pineapple cut in
   chunks
3 kiwi
1 cup fresh papaya cut in strips
   with diagonal edges

GLAZE:
½ cup plum or seedless raspberry preserve

. . . .

MAKES 12 SERVINGS
PREPARATION TIME:
  FILLING: 5 minutes
  FRUIT: 30 minutes
  CRUST: 10 minutes
ASSEMBLY: 15 minutes
BAKING TIME: 20 minutes

. . . .

PER SERVING: 230 calories, 5g fat (2g saturated), 41g carbohydrate, 4g dietary fiber, 2g sugar, 8g protein, 0mg cholesterol, 14mg sodium, 409mg potassium. Calories from fat: 19 percent.

- Preheat oven to 375°F. Coat an 11-inch tart pan (with removable bottom) with nonstick cooking spray.
- Prepare Tart Crust.
- While pie shell is cooling, prepare filling. Place tofu in food processor and blend until smooth, scraping sides as necessary. Add other ingredients except coconut and blend until smooth. Stir in coconut by hand, reserving 2 tablespoons for garnish if desired. Set aside.
- *To prepare fruit:* Peel kiwi and slice, making several triangular cuts evenly spaced along the kiwi holding it the long way. When you slice the kiwi into rounds, it will have petal shaped edges. Set aside. Peel and core pineapple (or better yet, buy a fresh pineapple that is already cored and peeled), cut into chunks and set aside. Peel and slice papaya, cut into strips with diagonal cut edges, and set aside.
- When crust is cool, spread filling in it. Arrange prepared fruit so that all of filling is covered. Warm preserve and use a pastry brush to brush it over tops of fruit to glaze it. Sprinkle with reserved shredded coconut if desired.
- Refrigerate until serving.

I'M NUTS FOR PEANUT BUTTER TART

HIS DOUBLY "PEANUTTY" dessert—with peanut butter filling placed in a peanut butter crust—is both spectacular looking and tasty. If you like the taste of peanut butter cookies, you'll love this tart.

CRUST:

1½ cups whole-wheat
    pastry flour
¼ cup granulated sweetener
¼ cup canola oil
¼ cup smooth natural peanut
    butter
1 tablespoon maple syrup
2 tablespoons water

FILLING:

½ cup water
1 tablespoon agar
18 ounces (1½ boxes) firm
    silken tofu
1 cup smooth natural peanut
    butter
¾ cup brown sugar

PEANUT BUTTER ORNA-MENTAL ICING:

6 ounces (½ box) firm
    silken tofu
½ cup powdered sugar
1 teaspoon vanilla
½ cup smooth natural peanut
    butter
2 tablespoons flour

- Preheat oven to 375°F. Coat an 11-inch tart pan (with removable bottom) with nonstick cooking spray.
- *To make crust:* In a small bowl, stir flour, granulated sweetener, and oil until it resembles coarse crumbs. Cut in peanut butter with two knives. Slowly stir in water and stir until mixture forms a ball in the bowl. Place flour on a piece of wax paper. Put the ball of dough onto the floured wax paper and roll in flour to coat. Put another piece of wax paper on top of ball of dough. Roll dough between two pieces of wax paper until very thin. Remove the top piece of wax paper. Flip the dough onto tart pan. Press the dough around the bottom and up the sides of the pan. Cut to fit at the top. Place pie weights (see Suggested Kitchen Equipment on page 16) in bottom of pan and bake for 15 minutes. Combine maple syrup and water in a small bowl. After 15 minutes, remove crust from oven and brush the maple/water mixture over it, then bake 5 more minutes to glaze.
- Set on cooling rack. Cool in pan for 10 minutes. Remove from pan and allow to cool completely before assembling.
- *To make filling:* While pie shell is cooling, put water in small pan and bring to boil. Sprinkle agar on top of water and stir to combine. Simmer until agar is completely dissolved, about 10–15 minutes. Place tofu in food processor and blend until smooth, scraping sides as necessary. Add other ingredients including agar mixture and blend until smooth. Set aside.

- *To make peanut butter ornamental icing:* Place tofu in food processor and blend until smooth, scraping sides as necessary. Add peanut butter and process until smooth. Add other ingredients and blend until smooth.
- When crust is cool, spread filling in it. Pipe frosting in shell design around outside perimeter of pie. Refrigerate until serving.

MAKES 16 SERVINGS
PREPARATION TIME:
FILLING: 5 minutes
ORNAMENTAL ICING:
5 minutes
CRUST: 10 minutes
ASSEMBLY: 10 minutes
BAKING TIME: 20 minutes

PER SERVING: 362 calories, 19g fat (3g saturated), 37g carbohydrate, 3g dietary fiber, 2g sugar, 14g protein, 0mg cholesterol, 130mg sodium, 544mg potassium. Calories from fat: 45 percent.

JUST PEEKIN' PIE

ONE OF MY favorite pre-veganism treats was pecan pie. I worked for a long time trying to duplicate that same texture and taste with vegan ingredients, and Just Peekin' Pie is the result. It's very similar to its high-fat non-veganized "cousin" in taste, but of course it's much healthier!

Standard Vegan Single Pie Crust, page 216
2 cups whole pecans
1 cup maple syrup
½ teaspoon salt
½ cup brown sugar
½ cup canola oil
½ cup arrowroot
¾ cup water
1 tablespoon vanilla

. . . .
MAKES 10 SERVINGS
PREPARATION TIME:
    FILLING: 15 minutes
    CRUST: 10 minutes
BAKING TIME: 10 minutes
. . . .

- Preheat oven to 400°F. Coat an 8-inch pie plate with nonstick cooking spray.
- Prepare Standard Vegan Single Pie Crust. Weight pie crust with another empty pie plate filled with a little water or pie weights to keep the crust from bubbling or shrinking while it bakes. You can also line pie crust with aluminum foil and fill the foil with dry beans. Bake pie crust for 10 minutes or until edges begin to brown slightly.
- Remove from oven and set aside. Meanwhile, bring maple syrup, salt, brown sugar, and canola oil to a boil in a small pan. Combine arrowroot and water in a small bowl. Pour into hot sugar mixture. Stir until thickened—**do not allow mixture to boil after arrowroot has been added**. Add vanilla.
- Put nuts in bottom of prepared pie crust. Pour sugar mixture over nuts. Place in refrigerator to thicken.
- Refrigerate at least 8 hours before serving so that filling sets.

PER SERVING: 471 calories, 29g fat (2g saturated), 52g carbohydrate, 2g dietary fiber, 21g sugar, 3g protein, 0mg cholesterol, 25mg sodium, 193mg potassium. Calories from fat: 53 percent.

APPLE DUMPLINGS

I GREW UP in a Pennsylvania German household, and one of my favorite dishes as a child was apple dumplings, which are pieces of apple covered with sugar and cinnamon and wrapped in flaky dough. My mother used to make them for dinner, so it was like eating pie for dinner! Try them in a bowl covered with soy milk. They're also delicious served warm with a glass of cold soy milk or a scoop of non-dairy vanilla ice cream.

CRUST:
1¼ cup unbleached flour
¼ cup canola oil or coconut oil
   if desired
¼ teaspoon sea salt
½ cup + 2 tablespoons water
   or apple juice (cold)

FILLING:
2 medium baking apples such
   as Macintosh
1 teaspoon cinnamon
1 teaspoon granulated sweetener
1 teaspoon vegan butter spread
   (optional)

. . . .

MAKES 4 SERVINGS
PREPARATION TIME:
   PEELING, CORING, SLICING
   APPLES: 10 minutes
   CRUST: 10 minutes
ASSEMBLY: 15 minutes
BAKING TIME: 20 minutes
. . . .

PER SERVING: 308 calories, 14g fat (1g saturated), 42g carbohydrate, 3g dietary fiber, <1g sugar, 4g protein, 0mg cholesterol, 15mg sodium, 124mg potassium. Calories from fat: 40 percent.

- Preheat oven to 400°F. Coat an 8-inch pie plate with nonstick cooking spray.
- *To make crust:* Put flour and salt for crust in small bowl. Add canola oil. Stir into flour until oil is distributed in pea-sized pieces. (If using the coconut oil, which is solid at room temperature like vegetable shortening, cut oil into flour with two knives until oil is pea-sized or smaller). Add *cold* water (or juice). Stir just until mixture forms a ball (add more water if necessary). Refrigerate for 10 minutes. Place ball of dough on a piece of floured wax paper. Place another piece of wax paper on top of ball of dough and push down to flatten. Using a rolling pin, roll dough as thin as possible between the two sheets of paper. Remove the top sheet of paper carefully and cut dough into quarters.
- *To prepare filling:* Coat a baking sheet with nonstick cooking spray or line it with parchment paper. Cut apples in half, peel, and core. Place 1 apple half on each quarter of dough, cut side down. Sprinkle each apple with ¼ teaspoon cinnamon and granulated sweetener. Place ¼ teaspoon vegan butter spread on each apple if desired.
- Draw up sides of dough and press closed around apple so that apple is completely sealed in dough. Place on greased or parchment lined baking sheet.
- Bake 15–20 minutes, or until golden brown.

TANTALIZING TRUFFLE PIE

*H*ERE'S ANOTHER WONDERFULLY creamy chocolate and peanut butter concoction. This was the first pie that I veganized and is still one of my favorites.

CRUST:

½ cup maple syrup
¼ cup canola oil
½ cup natural peanut butter
1 teaspoons vanilla
1 cup unbleached flour

FILLING:

2 boxes (24 ounces) firm silken tofu
¼ cup smooth natural peanut butter
1 teaspoon vanilla
¾ cup powdered sugar
1¼ cup vegan chocolate chips

PEANUT BUTTER TOPPING:

6 ounces firm silken tofu
½ cup powdered sugar
1 teaspoon vanilla
½ cup smooth natural peanut butter
2 tablespoons flour

MAKES 12 SERVINGS
PREPARATION TIME:
  CRUST: 10 minutes
  FILLING: 10 minutes
  TOPPING: 10 minutes
REFRIGERATE AT LEAST 8
HOURS BEFORE SERVING

- Preheat oven to 375°F. Coat a 9-inch springform pan with nonstick cooking spray.
- *To make crust:* In a food processor or small bowl, combine all crust ingredients and mix thoroughly. Press into the bottom of the prepared spring form pan. Prick with a fork and bake for 10 minutes. Remove from oven and set aside.
- *To make filling:* Place tofu in food processor and process until smooth, scraping down sides as necessary. Add peanut butter, sugar, and vanilla and blend. Melt chocolate chips in double boiler or microwave. Add to tofu mixture and blend. Pour onto prepared crust.
- *To make peanut butter topping:* Place tofu in food processor and process until smooth, scraping down sides of processor as necessary. Add sugar, vanilla, and peanut butter. If desired, pipe peanut butter topping in a lattice design using a plain round decorating tip and use a star tip to pipe a decorative border around outside edge of pie.
- Refrigerate at least 8 hours or overnight before serving.

Hint: Refrigerate peanut butter topping overnight before piping on pie.

PER SERVING: 527 calories, 29g fat (7g saturated), 53g carbohydrate, 3g dietary fiber, 11g sugar, 19g protein, 0mg cholesterol, 139mg sodium, 599mg potassium. Calories from fat: 47 percent.

CHEESECAKES

CARAMEL APPLE STREUSEL CHEESECAKE

*T*HIS IS ACTUALLY two luscious desserts in one—a yummy cinnamon swirl cheesecake and a delicious apple crumb pie drizzled with caramel sauce. It has several parts, but don't be put off—it is well worth the effort!

CRUST:

1¼ cups whole wheat flour
½ cup maple syrup
¼ cup canola oil
½ teaspoon baking soda
1 tablespoons molasses
½ cup vegan butter spread
   (such as Spectrum)
Pinch of sea salt

FILLING:

1 box (12 ounces) firm
   silken tofu
4 8-ounce containers soy cream
   cheese (such as Tofutti, which
   has no casein)
1 cup granulated sweetener
1 teaspoon vanilla
⅓ cup unbleached white flour

CINNAMON FILLING:

1 cup reserved filling
1 tablespoon Sucanat (or brown
   sugar)
2½ teaspoons cinnamon

APPLE TOPPING:

6 medium baking apples such
   as Macintosh or Rome
½ cup water
1 tablespoon arrowroot
1½ teaspoons cinnamon

- Preheat oven to 375°F. Coat a 9-inch springform pan with nonstick cooking spray.
- *To make crust:* Combine all crust ingredients in a food processor or small bowl and mix thoroughly. Press into the bottom of the prepared spring form pan. Prick with a fork and bake for 10 minutes. Remove from oven, reduce oven heat to 350°F, and set crust aside.
- *To make filling and cinnamon filling:* Combine all filling ingredients in food processor and process until smooth and creamy. Take out 1 cup of filling mixture and add 1 tablespoon Sucanat and 2½ teaspoons cinnamon to it. Mix to combine. Pour ½ of plain filling onto crust. Drop spoonfuls of cinnamon filling onto plain filling. Pour remaining plain filling mixture on top. Lightly swirl filling with knife—do not completely mix. Place cheesecake on middle rack in oven. Place a shallow pan filled with water on the lower rack of the oven. Bake cheesecake for 1 hour.
- *To make apple topping:* While cheesecake is baking, peel, core, and slice apples. Place in a pan with ¼ cup water. Bring to boil and simmer until apples are soft, but still hold their shape. Add cinnamon and stir. In a small bowl, mix arrowroot and remaining ¼ cup water and add to apple mixture. Heat and stir just until mixture thickens—do not boil. Set aside
- *To make streusel topping:* In another bowl, combine all streusel ingredients. Stir to combine. (Mixture should form crumbs.) Remove cheesecake from oven after it has baked 1 hour. Top with apples and sprinkle with streusel topping. (Be careful because cheesecake will

be soft.) Return to oven and bake another 20 minutes or until crumbs are lightly browned. Turn off the oven and allow the cheesecake to remain in the oven without opening the door for another hour. Remove from the oven and allow to cool completely.

- *To make caramel topping:* Just prior to serving, place corn syrup and brown sugar in small pan and bring to a boil. Simmer until mixture reaches soft ball stage or 240°F on a candy thermometer. Remove from heat and stir in soy milk, vanilla, and salt. Allow to cool to room temperature before drizzling over cake.
- *To serve:* Refrigerate cake at least 8 hours before serving. Remove collar from spring form pan before serving and drizzle room temperature caramel sauce over cheesecake or drizzle directly on each slice.

STREUSEL TOPPING:

1 cup unbleached flour
¼ cup granulated sweetener
⅓ cup Sucanat (or brown sugar)
¼ cup canola oil

CARAMEL TOPPING:

⅓ cup corn syrup
⅓ cup brown sugar
2 teaspoons vanilla
3 tablespoons soy milk
¼ teaspoon salt

. . . .

MAKES 16 SERVINGS
PREPARATION TIME:
    CRUST: 10 minutes
    FILLING: 5 minutes
    CINNAMON FILLING:
    5 minutes
    APPLE TOPPING: 15 minutes
    (including peeling, coring,
    slicing apples)
    STREUSEL TOPPING:
    5 minutes
    CARAMEL TOPPING:
    10 minutes
BAKING TIME: 1 hour, 30
minutes
COOLING TIME: 1 hour in oven
with heat off and door closed
REFRIGERATE AT LEAST 8
HOURS BEFORE SERVING
. . . .

PER SERVING: 541 calories, 26g fat (4g saturated), 72g carbohydrate, 4g dietary fiber, 8g sugar, 8g protein, 0mg cholesterol, 352mg sodium, 344mg potassium. Calories from fat: 18 percent.

NEW YORK–STYLE CHEESECAKE

CHEESECAKE IS SO delicious, there's no reason you can't enjoy it as a vegan. This recipe captures all the good taste of a New York-style cheesecake without using dairy products or eggs. Try it. I think you'll be pleasantly surprised.

CRUST:
½ cup maple syrup
¼ cup canola oil
1¾ cup whole wheat flour
½ teaspoon vanilla

FILLING:
4 8-ounce containers soy cream
  cheese (such as Tofutti, which
  has no casein)
1 box (12 ounces) firm
  silken tofu
1 cup granulated sweetener
1 teaspoon vanilla
⅓ cup unbleached white flour

TOPPING:
½ box (6 ounces) firm
  silken tofu
1 tablespoon canola oil
1½ teaspoons lemon juice
¼ teaspoon salt
¾ cup granulated sweetener
¾ teaspoon vanilla

- Preheat oven to 375°F. Coat a 9-inch springform pan with nonstick cooking spray.
- *To make crust:* In a food processor or small bowl, combine all crust ingredients and mix thoroughly. Press into the bottom of the prepared springform pan. Prick with a fork and bake for 10 minutes. Remove from oven, reduce oven heat to 350°F, and set crust aside.
- *To make filling:* Combine cream cheese and tofu in food processor and process until smooth, scraping down sides as necessary. Add granulated sweetener and blend until creamy. Add flour and vanilla, blend, and pour into prepared crust. Place on top rack of oven. Place a shallow pan filled with water on lower rack of oven and bake for 50 minutes.
- *To make topping:* While cheesecake is baking, place tofu in processor and process until smooth, scraping down sides as necessary. Add other ingredients and process to blend.

- After 50 minutes, pull cheesecake out of oven and carefully spread on topping. Return to oven and bake an additional 10 minutes. Turn the oven off and leave the cheesecake in the oven for an additional hour. Remove from oven and allow to cool completely.
- Refrigerate at least 8 hours or overnight before serving.

MAKES 16 SERVINGS
PREPARATION TIME:
   CRUST: 10 minutes
   FILLING: 10 minutes
   TOPPING: 5 minutes
BAKING TIME: 1 hour, 10 minutes
COOLING TIME: 1 hour in oven with heat off and door closed
REFRIGERATE AT LEAST 8 HOURS BEFORE SERVING

PER SERVING: 389 calories, 19g fat (4g saturated), 44g carbohydrate, <1g dietary fiber, 7g sugar, 9g protein, 0mg cholesterol, 327mg sodium, 101mg potassium. Calories from fat: 11 percent.

THREE CHEERS FOR CHERRY CHEESECAKE

CHEESECAKE WITH CHERRIES on top is a classic dessert that I just had to veganize. I developed a basic cheesecake, topped it with fresh cherries, and it turned out beautifully. Fresh cherries really do make all the difference.

CRUST:
½ cup maple syrup
¼ cup canola oil
1¾ cups whole wheat flour
½ teaspoon vanilla

FILLING:
4 8-ounce containers soy cream cheese (such as Tofutti, which has no casein)
1 box (12 ounces) firm silken tofu
1 cup granulated sweetener
1 teaspoon vanilla
⅓ cup unbleached white flour

TOPPING:
2 cups fresh cherries
½ cup apple juice
1 tablespoon arrowroot

. . . .

MAKES 16 SERVINGS
PREPARATION TIME:
   CRUST: 10 minutes
   FILLING: 10 minutes
   TOPPING: 10 minutes
BAKING TIME: 60 minutes
COOLING TIME: 1 hour in oven with heat off and door closed
REFRIGERATE at least 8 hours before serving

. . . .

- Preheat oven to 375°F. Coat a 9-inch springform pan with nonstick cooking spray.
- *To make crust:* In a food processor or small bowl, combine all crust ingredients and mix thoroughly. Press into the bottom of the prepared springform pan. Prick with a fork and bake for 10 minutes. Remove from oven, reduce oven heat to 350°F, and set crust aside.
- *To make filling:* Combine cream cheese and tofu in food processor and process until smooth, scraping down sides as necessary. Add granulated sweetener and blend until creamy. Add flour and vanilla, blend, and pour into prepared crust. Place on top rack of oven. Place a shallow pan filled with water on lower rack of oven and bake for 60 minutes. Then turn off oven and leave the cheesecake in oven for an additional hour.
- *To make topping:* While cheesecake is cooling, pit cherries and cut in half. Place in a small pan with ½ cup juice. Bring to boil and simmer until cherries are soft. In a small bowl, combine arrowroot and ½ cup juice or water. Add to hot cherries and stir until thickened—do not boil. (Mixture will thicken more as it cools.) Set aside.
- Remove cheesecake from oven and carefully spread on cherry topping. Allow to cool completely. Refrigerate at least 8 hours or overnight before serving.

PER SERVING: 321 calories, 18g fat (4g saturated), 37g carbohydrate, 2g dietary fiber, 6g sugar, 4g protein, 0mg cholesterol, 243mg sodium, 127mg potassium. Calories from fat: 10 percent.

SWIRLED RASPBERRY CHEESECAKE

*T*HIS UNIQUE CREATION consists of raspberry sauce swirled through creamy cheesecake and topped with tangy sweet raspberries—I think you'll really enjoy this deliciously different taste.

CRUST:

½ cup maple syrup
¼ cup canola oil
1¾ cups whole wheat flour
½ teaspoon vanilla

RASPBERRY TOPPING:

1 12-ounce package frozen
    raspberries (or 2 cups fresh
    raspberries)
¼ cup water
⅓ cup granulated sweetener
1 tablespoon arrowroot
2 tablespoons water

FILLING:

4 8-ounce containers soy cream
    cheese (such as Tofutti, which
    has no casein)
1 box (12 ounces) firm silken
    tofu
1 cup granulated sweetener
1 teaspoon vanilla
⅓ cup unbleached white flour

. . . .

MAKES 16 SERVINGS
PREPARATION TIME:
    CRUST: 10 minutes
    FILLING: 10 minutes
    TOPPING: 10 minutes
BAKING TIME: 60 minutes
COOLING TIME: 1 hour in oven
with heat off and door closed
REFRIGERATE AT LEAST 8
HOURS BEFORE SERVING
. . . .

- Preheat oven to 375°F. Coat a 9-inch springform pan with nonstick cooking spray.
- *To make crust:* In a food processor or small bowl, combine all crust ingredients and mix thoroughly. Press into the bottom of the prepared springform pan. Prick with a fork and bake for 10 minutes. Remove from oven, reduce oven heat to 350°F, and set crust aside.
- *To make topping:* Bring first three ingredients to boil in medium saucepan. (If using fresh raspberries, simmer until berries are soft.) Dissolve arrowroot in 2 tablespoons of water and add to hot raspberry mixture. Heat just until thickened—do not boil (mixture will thicken more as it cools). Set aside.
- *To make filling:* Combine cream cheese and tofu in food processor and process until smooth, scraping down sides as necessary. Add granulated sweetener and blend until creamy. Add flour and vanilla and blend. Pour half of filling into prepared crust. Spoon ½ cup of raspberry sauce over filling. Pour the rest of the filling in the pan and swirl with knife—be careful not to mix completely. Place on top rack of oven. Place a shallow pan filled with water on lower rack of oven and bake for 60 minutes.
- After 50 minutes, turn oven off, pull out cheesecake, and carefully spread on raspberry topping. Return the cheesecake to the oven and allow it to remain there for an additional hour.
- Remove from oven and allow to cool completely. Refrigerate at least 8 hours or overnight before serving.

PER SERVING: 354 calories, 19g fat (4g saturated), 42g carbohydrate, 1g dietary fiber, 6g sugar, 5g protein, 0mg cholesterol, 244mg sodium, 87mg potassium. Calories from fat: 11 percent.

I Dream of Lemon Cream Cheesecake

TANGY LEMON CHEESECAKE is a refreshing treat anytime. This dessert looks impressive if garnished with a mound of fresh blueberries and twists of lemon.

CRUST:
½ cup maple syrup
¼ cup canola oil
1¾ cups whole wheat flour
½ teaspoon vanilla

FILLING:
4 8-ounce containers soy cream cheese (such as Tofutti, which has no casein)
1 box (12 ounces) firm silken tofu
1 cup granulated sweetener
½ cup lemon juice
1 tablespoon lemon extract
½ teaspoon tumeric (for color only)
⅓ cup unbleached white flour

TOPPING:
½ box (6 ounces) firm silken tofu
1 tablespoon canola oil
1½ teaspoon lemon juice
¼ teaspoon salt
¾ cup granulated sweetener
¾ teaspoon lemon extract

GARNISH: (OPTIONAL)
2 lemons
1 cup fresh blueberries

- Preheat oven to 375°F. Coat a 9-inch springform pan with nonstick cooking spray.
- *To make crust:* In a food processor or small bowl, combine all crust ingredients and mix thoroughly. Press into the bottom of the prepared springform pan. Prick with a fork and bake for 10 minutes. Remove from oven, reduce oven heat to 350°F, and set crust aside.
- *To make filling:* Combine cream cheese and tofu in food processor and process until smooth, scraping down sides as necessary. Add granulated sweetener and blend until creamy. Add remaining ingredients, blend, and pour into prepared crust.
- Place on top rack of oven. Place a shallow pan filled with water on lower rack of oven and bake for 50 minutes. While cheesecake is baking, make topping by placing all topping ingredients in food processor and processing to combine. Set aside.
- After 50 minutes, pull cheesecake out of the oven and spread topping on evenly. Return it to oven and bake for 10 more minutes. Then turn oven off and leave the cheesecake in there for an additional hour. Remove from oven and allow to cool completely.

- Slice lemon(s) into very thin slices. (Number of slices will depend on the size of the lemon.) Cut these slices in half so they are semi-circle shapes. Remove the collar of the pan. (Slide a sharp knife around the inside of the pan so the cheesecake does not stick to it as you remove the collar.) Firmly press semi-circle lemon slices onto side of cheesecake with flat, cut edge lining up along the bottom of the cheesecake and rounded edge near the top of the cheesecake. Clean off the collar of the pan and put it back on the cheesecake. Refrigerate at least 8 hours or overnight before serving.
- *To garnish:* Just before serving, mound washed and dried blueberries on top of cheesecake. Make a slit along the radius of several lemon slices. Twist lemon slices and place randomly on top of blueberries. Sprinkle with a little sugar if desired.

. . . .

MAKES 16 SERVINGS
PREPARATION TIME:
　　CRUST: 10 minutes
　　FILLING: 10 minutes
　　BAKING TIME: 60 minutes
COOLING TIME: 1 hour in oven with heat off and door closed
REFRIGERATE AT LEAST 8 HOURS BEFORE SERVING

. . . .

PER SERVING: 303 calories, 21g fat (4g saturated), 22g carbohydrate, 2g dietary fiber, 7g sugar, 9g protein, 0mg cholesterol, 249mg sodium, 176mg potassium. Calories from fat: 18 percent.

MINTY CHOCOLATE CHIP CHEESECAKE

Y OLDEST DAUGHTER can't get enough of mint chocolate chip ice cream, and I was inspired by that flavor to create this cheesecake. I guarantee you're going to love this mint-flavored cheesecake full of vegan chocolate chips in a chocolate cookie crust.

CRUST:
½ cup maple syrup
¼ cup canola oil
½ cup cocoa
1¼ cups whole wheat flour
½ teaspoon vanilla

FILLING:
4 8-ounce containers soy cream cheese (such as Tofutti, which has no casein)
1 box (12 ounces) firm silken tofu
1 cup granulated sweetener
4½ tablespoons peppermint extract
⅓ cup unbleached white flour
1 cup vegan chocolate chips

MINT TOPPING:
6 ounces (½ box) tofu
1 tablespoon canola oil
1½ teaspoon lemon juice
¼ teaspoon salt
¾ cup sugar
¾ teaspoon peppermint extract

- Preheat oven to 375°F. Coat a 9-inch springform pan with nonstick cooking spray.
- *To make crust:* In a food processor or small bowl, combine all crust ingredients and mix thoroughly. Press into the bottom of the prepared springform pan. Prick with a fork and bake for 10 minutes. Remove from oven, reduce oven heat to 350°F, and set crust aside
- *To make filling:* Combine cream cheese and tofu in food processor and process until smooth, scraping down sides as necessary. Add granulated sweetener and blend until creamy. Add flour and peppermint extract and blend. Stir in 1 cup chocolate chips by hand. Place on top rack of oven. Place a shallow pan filled with water on lower rack of oven and bake for 50 minutes.
- *To make mint topping:* While cheesecake is baking, combine all topping ingredients in food processor and mix to combine. Set aside. After cheesecake has baked 50 minutes, pull it out and spread on topping evenly. Return to oven and bake for 10 more minutes.

- Turn the oven off, leaving the cheesecake there for an additional hour. Remove from oven and allow to cool completely. Refrigerate at least 8 hours or overnight before serving.

MAKES 16 SERVINGS
PREPARATION TIME:
  CRUST: 10 minutes
  FILLING: 10 minutes
  TOPPING: 5 minutes
BAKING TIME: 1 hour
COOLING TIME: 1 hour in oven with heat off and door closed
REFRIGERATE AT LEAST 8 HOURS BEFORE SERVING

PER SERVING: 358 calories, 22g fat (6g saturated), 38g carbohydrate, 3g dietary fiber, 6g sugar, 6g protein, 0mg cholesterol, 246mg sodium, 128mg potassium. Calories from fat: 18 percent.

PUMPKIN PIE CHEESECAKE

MAKE THIS cheesecake every year for dessert on Thanksgiving Day. The delightful combination of pumpkin and spices tastes just like the holidays to me.

CRUST:
¼ cup vegetable shortening (non-hydrogenated such as Spectrum)
¼ cup brown sugar
¼ cup molasses
1½ teaspoons vinegar
1 tablespoon applesauce
½ cup + 2 tablespoons unbleached white flour
½ cup + 2 tablespoons whole wheat flour
½ teaspoon baking soda
¼ teaspoon salt
2 teaspoons fresh ginger or ¾ teaspoon ground ginger (optional)
¼ teaspoon ground cinnamon
¼ teaspoon ground cloves

FILLING:
4 8-ounce containers soy cream cheese (such as Tofutti, which has no casein)
1 box (12 ounces) firm silken tofu
1 cup granulated sweetener
1 teaspoon vanilla
1 cup fresh pureed pumpkin or ¾ cup canned pumpkin puree
⅓ cup unbleached white flour

(continued on next page)

- Preheat oven to 375°F. Coat a 9-inch springform pan with nonstick cooking spray.
- *To make crust:* Cream shortening and sugar together in a large bowl. Add applesauce, molasses, fresh ginger, and vinegar to shortening and sugar mixture and beat until combined. Sift together dry ingredients, including spices, add to shortening/sugar mixture, and stir to combine. Press into the bottom of the prepared springform pan. Prick with a fork and bake for 10 minutes. Remove from oven, reduce oven heat to 350°F, and set crust aside.
- *To make filling:* Combine cream cheese and tofu in food processor and process until smooth, scraping down sides as necessary. Add granulated sweetener and blend until creamy. Add remaining ingredients, blend, and pour into prepared crust. Place on top rack of oven. Place a shallow pan filled with water on lower rack of oven and bake for 50 minutes.

- *To prepare topping:* While cheesecake is baking, place tofu in processor and process until smooth, scraping down sides as necessary. Add other ingredients and process to blend. After 50 minutes, pull cheesecake out of oven and carefully spread on topping.
- Return to oven and bake an additional 10 minutes. Turn the oven off and leave the cheesecake there for an additional hour. Remove from oven and allow to cool completely. Refrigerate at least 8 hours or overnight before serving.

1 teaspoon cinnamon

1 teaspoon pumpkin pie spice

TOPPING:

½ box (6 ounces) firm
　silken tofu

1 tablespoon canola oil

1½ teaspoons lemon juice

¼ teaspoon salt

¾ cup granulated sweetener

¾ teaspoon vanilla

¼ cup fresh pureed or canned
　pumpkin

½ teaspoon cinnamon

. . . .

MAKES 16 SERVINGS

PREPARATION TIME:
　CRUST: 10 minutes
　FILLING: 10 minutes
　TOPPING: 5 minutes

BAKING TIME: 1 hour

COOLING TIME: 1 hour in oven with heat off and door closed

REFRIGERATE AT LEAST 8 HOURS BEFORE SERVING

. . . .

PER SERVING: 394 calories, 21g fat (5g saturated), 44g carbohydrate, 2g dietary fiber, 1g sugar, 8g protein, 0mg cholesterol, 318mg sodium, 323mg potassium. Calories from fat: 15 percent.

INSIDE-OUT
PEANUT BUTTER CUP CHEESECAKE

ERE'S ANOTHER CHEESECAKE that combines the flavors of chocolate and peanut butter. Unlike the Peanut Butter Cup Cheesecake, page 158, which has peanut butter–flavored filling and a chocolate topping that mimics a peanut butter cup, this cheesecake takes the peanut butter cup idea and turns it inside out, using chocolate filling and a peanut butter topping. You're going to love this switch!

CRUST:

½ cup maple syrup
¼ cup canola oil
½ cup natural peanut butter
1 teaspoons vanilla
1 cup unbleached flour

FILLING:

4 8-ounce containers soy cream cheese (such as Tofutti, which has no casein)
1 box (12 ounces) firm silken tofu
1 cup granulated sweetener
1 teaspoon vanilla
2 cups vegan chocolate chips
½ cup smooth natural peanut butter
⅓ cup unbleached white flour

- Preheat oven to 375°F. Coat a 9-inch springform pan with nonstick cooking spray.
- *To make crust:* In a food processor or small bowl, combine all crust ingredients and mix thoroughly. Press into the bottom of the prepared springform pan. Prick with a fork and bake for 10 minutes. Remove from oven, reduce oven heat to 350°F, and set crust aside.
- *To make filling:* Combine cream cheese and tofu in food processor and mix until smooth, scraping down sides as necessary. Add peanut butter and granulated sweetener and blend until creamy. Add flour and vanilla and blend. Melt chocolate chips in double boiler or microwave. Add to cream cheese mixture, blend, and pour into prepared pan. Place on top rack of oven. Place a shallow pan filled with water on lower rack of oven and bake for 50 minutes.

- *To make peanut butter topping:* While cheesecake is baking, combine all topping ingredients in food processor and mix to combine. Set aside. After cheesecake has baked 50 minutes, pull it out and spread on topping evenly.
- Return to oven and bake for 10 more minutes. Turn the oven off and leave the cheesecake in there for an additional hour. Remove from oven and cool completely. Refrigerate at least 8 hours or overnight before serving.

PEANUT BUTTER TOPPING:

6 ounces (½ box) tofu
1 tablespoon canola oil
1½ teaspoons lemon juice
¼ teaspoon salt
¾ cup sugar
¼ cup smooth natural peanut butter

. . . .

MAKES 16 SERVINGS
PREPARATION TIME:
   CRUST: 10 minutes
   FILLING: 10 minutes
   TOPPING: 10 minutes
BAKING TIME: 1 hour
COOLING TIME: 1 hour in oven with heat off and door closed
REFRIGERATE AT LEAST 8 HOURS BEFORE SERVING

. . . .

PER SERVING: 534 calories, 38g fat (10g saturated), 40g carbohydrate, 3g dietary fiber, 7g sugar, 13g protein, 0mg cholesterol, 347mg sodium, 347mg potassium. Calories from fat: 37 percent.

PEANUT BUTTER CUP CHEESECAKE

HIS CHEESECAKE TASTES just like a gooey Reese's Peanut Butter Cup.

CRUST:
½ cup maple syrup
¼ cup canola oil
½ cup natural peanut butter
1 teaspoons vanilla
1 cup unbleached flour

FILLING:
4 8-ounce containers soy cream
  cheese (such as Tofutti, which
  has no casein)
1 box (12 ounces) firm
  silken tofu
1 cup granulated sweetener
1 teaspoon vanilla
1 cup smooth natural peanut
  butter
⅓ cup unbleached white flour

CHOCOLATE TOPPING:
½ cup cocoa
½ cup maple syrup
1 teaspoon vanilla

. . . .

MAKES 16 SERVINGS
PREPARATION TIME:
   CRUST: 10 minutes
   FILLING: 10 minutes
   TOPPING: 10 minutes
BAKING TIME: 60 minutes
COOLING TIME: 1 hour in oven
with heat off and door closed
REFRIGERATE AT LEAST 8
HOURS BEFORE SERVING
. . . .

- Preheat oven to 375°F. Coat a 9-inch springform pan with nonstick cooking spray.
- *To make crust:* In a food processor or small bowl, combine all crust ingredients and mix thoroughly. Press into the bottom of the prepared springform pan. Prick with a fork and bake for 10 minutes. Remove from oven, reduce oven heat to 350°F, and set crust aside
- *To make filling:* Combine cream cheese and tofu in food processor and process until smooth, scraping down sides as necessary. Add peanut butter and process until combined. Add granulated sweetener and blend until creamy. Add flour and vanilla, blend, and pour into prepared pan. Place on top rack of oven. Place a shallow pan filled with water on lower rack of oven and bake for 50 minutes.
- After 60 minutes, turn the oven off and leave the cheesecake in there for an additional hour. Remove from oven and allow to cool completely.
- *To make chocolate topping:* While cheesecake is cooling, combine all topping ingredients in a small bowl and stir until combined and smooth. Spread evenly on top of cheesecake before refrigerating. (If topping is too thick, heat for about 10 seconds in the microwave.) Refrigerate at least 8 hours or overnight before serving.

PER SERVING: 416 calories, 31g fat (7g saturated), 30g carbohydrate, 3g dietary fiber, 12g sugar, 10g protein, 0mg cholesterol, 357mg sodium, 255mg potassium. Calories from fat: 33 percent.

COCONUT DREAM CHEESECAKE

I LOVE THE taste of coconut, and I wanted to see if it would work when combined with a creamy cheesecake filling. Did it ever!

CRUST:
¾ cup shredded unsweetened
   coconut
½ cup flour
½ cup maple syrup
⅛ cup canola oil

FILLING:
4 8-ounce containers soy cream
   cheese (such as Tofutti, which
   has no casein)
1 box (12 ounces) firm
   silken tofu
1 cup granulated sweetener
1 tablespoon coconut extract
1 cup shredded unsweetened
   coconut
⅓ cup unbleached white flour

TOPPING:
½ box (6 ounces) firm silken tofu
1 tablespoon canola oil
1½ teaspoons lemon juice
¼ teaspoon salt
¾ cup granulated sweetener
¾ teaspoon vanilla extract

. . . .

MAKES 16 SERVINGS
PREPARATION TIME:
   CRUST: 10 minutes
   FILLING: 10 minutes
   TOPPING: 5 minutes
BAKING TIME: 1 hour
COOLING TIME: 1 hour in oven
with heat off and door closed
REFRIGERATE AT LEAST 8
HOURS BEFORE SERVING

. . . .

- Preheat oven to 375°F. Coat a 9-inch springform pan with nonstick cooking spray.
- *To make crust:* In a small bowl, combine all crust ingredients and mix thoroughly. Press into the bottom of the prepared springform pan and bake for 15 minutes. Remove from oven, reduce oven heat to 350°F, and set crust aside.
- *To make filling:* Combine cream cheese and tofu in food processor and mix until smooth, scraping down sides as necessary. Add granulated sweetener and blend until creamy. Add flour and coconut extract and blend. Stir in coconut by hand, and then pour filling into prepared crust. Place on top rack of oven. Place a shallow pan filled with water on lower rack of oven and bake for 50 minutes.
- *To make topping:* While cheesecake is baking, place tofu in food processor and process until smooth, scraping down sides as necessary. Add other ingredients and process to blend. After 50 minutes, pull cheesecake out of oven and carefully spread on topping. Return to oven and bake an additional 10 minutes.
- Turn the oven off and leave the cheesecake in there for an additional hour. Remove from oven and allow to cool completely. Refrigerate at least 8 hours or overnight before serving.

PER SERVING: 376 calories, 21g fat (6g saturated), 39g carbohydrate, <1g dietary fiber, 7g sugar, 7g protein, 0mg cholesterol, 252mg sodium, 216mg potassium Calories from fat: 16 percent.

Tropical Chocolate Chip Cheesecake

*O*NE DAY I was eating a chocolate-covered coconut cream egg (vegan, of course) and it occurred to me that this would make a wonderful cheesecake flavor! I have to say that this is my all-time favorite cheesecake.

CRUST:
¾ cup shredded unsweetened
   coconut
½ cup unbleached white flour
½ cup maple syrup
⅛ cup canola oil

FILLING:
4 8-ounce containers soy cream
   cheese (such as Tofutti, which
   has no casein)
1 box (12 ounces) firm
   silken tofu
1 cup granulated sweetener
1 tablespoon coconut extract
1 cup shredded unsweetened
   coconut
1 cup vegan chocolate chips
⅓ cup unbleached white flour

CHOCOLATE TOPPING:
½ cup cocoa
½ cup maple syrup
1 teaspoon vanilla

MAKES 16 SERVINGS
PREPARATION TIME:
   CRUST: 10 minutes
   FILLING: 10 minutes
   TOPPING: 5 minutes
BAKING TIME: 60 minutes
COOLING TIME: 1 hour in oven
with heat off and door closed
REFRIGERATE AT LEAST 8
HOURS BEFORE SERVING

- Preheat oven to 375°F. Coat a 9-inch springform pan with nonstick cooking spray.
- *To make crust:* In a small bowl combine, all crust ingredients and mix thoroughly. Press into the bottom of the prepared springform pan and bake for 15 minutes. Remove from oven, reduce oven heat to 350°F, and set crust aside.
- *To make filling:* Combine cream cheese and tofu in food processor and mix until smooth, scraping down sides as necessary. Add granulated sweetener and blend until creamy. Add flour and coconut extract and blend. Stir in coconut and chocolate chips by hand and pour filling into prepared crust. Place on top rack of oven. Place a shallow pan filled with water on lower rack of oven and bake for 60 minutes. Turn the oven off and leave the cheesecake there for an additional hour. Remove from oven.
- *To make chocolate topping:* Combine all topping ingredients in a bowl. Using a wire whisk, mix until combined and creamy. Gently pour chocolate topping over cheesecake. Spread out evenly. (If chocolate is too thick to spread, heat in the microwave for about 10 seconds.) Refrigerate at least 8 hours or overnight before serving.

PER SERVING: 395 calories, 23g fat (8g saturated), 43g carbohydrate, 2g dietary fiber, 13g sugar, 7g protein, 0mg cholesterol, 249mg sodium, 219mg potassium. Calories from fat: 19 percent.

Peanut Butter Chocolate Chip Cheesecake

ERE'S ANOTHER TWIST on the chocolate and peanut butter combination. This one is lighter on the chocolate with just a spattering of chocolate chips dotting the rich peanut butter filling. If you like, you could use the chocolate topping from the Peanut Butter Cup Cheesecake, page 158, or the peanut butter topping from the Inside-Out Peanut Butter Cup Cheesecake, page 156, to add a little extra something.

CRUST:
1/4 cup maple syrup
1/8 cup canola oil
1/4 cup natural peanut butter
1/2 teaspoons vanilla
1/2 cup + 2 tablespoons
  unbleached flour

FILLING:
4 8-ounce containers soy cream
  cheese (such as Tofutti, which
  has no casein)
1 box (12 ounces) firm
  silken tofu
1 cup granulated sweetener
1 teaspoon vanilla
1 cup smooth natural peanut
  butter
1/3 cup unbleached white flour
3/4 cup vegan chocolate chips

....

MAKES 16 SERVINGS
PREPARATION TIME:
CRUST: 10 minutes
FILLING: 10 minutes
BAKING TIME: 50 minutes
COOLING TIME: 1 hour in oven
with heat off and door closed
REFRIGERATE AT LEAST 8
HOURS BEFORE SERVING
....

- Preheat oven to 375°F. Coat an 9-inch springform pan with nonstick cooking spray.
- *To make crust:* In a food processor or small bowl, combine all crust ingredients and mix thoroughly. Press into the bottom of the prepared springform pan, prick with a fork, and bake for 10 minutes. Remove from oven, reduce oven heat to 350°F, and set crust aside.
- *To make filling:* Combine cream cheese and tofu in food processor and mix until smooth, scraping down sides as necessary. Add peanut butter and process until combined. Add granulated sweetener and blend until creamy. Add flour and vanilla and blend. Stir in chocolate chips by hand and pour filling into prepared pan. Place on top rack of oven. Place a shallow pan filled with water on lower rack of oven and bake for 50 minutes.
- Turn the oven off and leave the cheesecake there for an additional hour. Remove from oven and allow to cool completely. Refrigerate at least 8 hours or overnight before serving.

PER SERVING: 437 calories, 30g fat (7g saturated), 34g carbohydrate, 2g dietary fiber, 4g sugar, 11g protein, 0mg cholesterol, 340mg sodium, 281mg potassium. Calories from fat: 31 percent.

BLACK FOREST CHEESECAKE

F YOU LIKE chocolate cheesecake, you've got to try this luscious combination of rich chocolate filling and creamy cherry topping. It can also be made with a raspberry topping if you prefer. Both fruits blend wonderfully with chocolate! You might also want to try the Chocolate-Covered Cherry Cheesecake, page 164, which also combines the tastes of chocolate and cherry, but more closely resembles a chocolate-covered cherry.

CRUST:
½ cup maple syrup
¼ cup canola oil
½ cup cocoa
1¼ cups whole wheat flour
½ teaspoon vanilla

FILLING:
3 8-ounce containers soy cream cheese (such as Tofutti, which has no casein)
1½ boxes (18 ounces) firm silken tofu
1 cup granulated sweetener
1 teaspoon vanilla
2 cups vegan chocolate chips
⅓ cup unbleached white flour

TOPPING:
2 cups fresh cherries
½ cup apple juice
1 tablespoon arrowroot

- Preheat oven to 375°F. Coat a 9-inch springform pan with nonstick cooking spray.
- *To make crust:* In a food processor or small bowl, combine all crust ingredients and mix thoroughly. Press into the bottom of the prepared springform pan. Prick with a fork and bake for 10 minutes. Remove from oven, reduce oven heat to 350°F, and set crust aside.
- *To make filling:* Combine cream cheese and tofu in food processor and mix until smooth, scraping down sides as necessary. Add granulated sweetener and blend until creamy. Add flour and vanilla and blend. Melt chocolate chips in microwave or double boiler. Pour into food processor with cream cheese mixture and blend. Pour into prepared crust. Place on top rack of oven. Place a shallow pan filled with water on lower rack of oven and bake for 50 minutes.
- *To make topping:* While cheesecake is baking, pit cherries and cut in half. Place in a small pan with ½ cup juice. Bring to boil and simmer until cherries are soft. In a small bowl, combine arrowroot and ½ cup juice or water. Add to hot cherries and stir until thickened—do not boil. (Mixture will thicken more as it cools.) Set aside.
- After 60 minutes, turn the oven off and leave the cheesecake in the oven for an additional hour. Remove from oven and carefully spread on cherry topping. Allow to cool completely. Refrigerate at least 8 hours or overnight before serving.

Variation: Use a raspberry topping instead of cherry.

RASPBERRY TOPPING:

1 12-ounce package frozen raspberries (or 2 cups fresh raspberries)
¼ cup water
⅓ cup granulated sweetener
1 tablespoon arrowroot
2 tablespoons water

- Bring first 3 ingredients to boil in medium saucepan. (If using fresh raspberries, simmer until berries are soft.) Dissolve arrowroot in 2 tablespoons of water and add to hot raspberry mixture. Heat just until thickened—do not boil. (Mixture will thicken more as it cools.)

MAKES **16** SERVINGS
PREPARATION TIME:
  CRUST: 10 minutes
  FILLING: 10 minutes
  TOPPING: 10 minutes
BAKING TIME: 60 minutes
COOLING TIME: 1 hour in oven with heat off and door closed
REFRIGERATE AT LEAST **8** HOURS BEFORE SERVING

CHEESECAKE WITH CHERRY TOPPING
PER SERVING: 431 calories, 24g fat (7g saturated), 51g carbohydrate, 4g dietary fiber, 7g sugar, 9g protein, 0mg cholesterol, 190mg sodium, 323mg potassium. Calories from fat: 25 percent.

CHEESECAKE WITH RASPBERRY TOPPING
PER SERVING: 446 calories, 24g fat (7g saturated), 55g carbohydrate, 4g dietary fiber, 7g sugar, 9g protein, 0mg cholesterol, 190mg sodium, 297mg potassium. Calories from fat: 24 percent.

CHOCOLATE-COVERED CHERRY CHEESECAKE

T HIS CHEESECAKE WAS inspired by my love for a good dark chocolate-covered cherry. I think this cheesecake comes pretty close.

CRUST:
½ cup maple syrup
¼ cup canola oil
½ cup cocoa
1¼ cup whole wheat flour
½ teaspoon vanilla

FILLING:
4 8-ounce containers soy cream cheese (such as Tofutti, which has no casein)
1 box (12 ounces) firm silken tofu
1 cup granulated sweetener
1½ tablespoons cherry extract
1½ cups fresh cherries (pitted and chopped)
⅓ cup unbleached white flour

- Preheat oven to 375°F. Coat a 9-inch springform pan with nonstick cooking spray.
- *To make crust:* In a food processor or small bowl, combine all crust ingredients and mix thoroughly. Press into the bottom of the prepared springform pan, prick with a fork, and bake for 10 minutes. Remove from oven, reduce oven heat to 350°F, and set crust aside.
- *To make filling:* Combine cream cheese and tofu in food processor and mix until smooth, scraping down sides as necessary. Add granulated sweetener and blend until creamy. Add flour and cherry extract and blend. Pit and chop cherries (reserving 16 for garnish if desired). Add ¼ cup of pitted, chopped cherries to food processor and process. Stir remaining cherries into filling mixture by hand. Pour into prepared pan and place on top rack of oven. Place a shallow pan filled with water on lower rack of oven and bake for 60 minutes. Turn the oven off and leave the cheesecake there an additional hour. Remove from oven and allow to cool completely.

- *To make chocolate topping:* While cheesecake is cooling, combine all topping ingredients in a small bowl and stir until combined and smooth. Spread evenly on top of cheesecake before refrigerating. If topping is too thick, place in the microwave for about 10 seconds. Refrigerate at least 8 hours or overnight before serving.
- *To garnish:* Pit cherries, leaving stems attached. Trim stems to length of about ½ inch. Melt ½ cup vegan chocolate chips in microwave or in double boiler. Dip each cherry halfway into chocolate and place on wax or parchment paper lined pan. Put pan of cherries in freezer to harden for 10 minutes. Arrange evenly around perimeter of cheesecake.

CHOCOLATE TOPPING:

½ cup cocoa
½ cup maple syrup
1 teaspoon vanilla

GARNISH (OPTIONAL):

16 whole fresh cherries
*   with stems*
½ cup vegan chocolate chips

. . . .

MAKES 16 SERVINGS
PREPARATION TIME:
   CRUST: 10 minutes
   FILLING: 10 minutes
   TOPPING: 10 minutes
   CHERRIES: 10 minutes
BAKING TIME: 60 minutes
COOLING TIME: 1 hour in oven with heat off and door closed
REFRIGERATE AT LEAST 8 HOURS BEFORE SERVING

. . . .

PER SERVING: 375 calories, 20g fat (4g saturated), 43g carbohydrate, 3g dietary fiber, 13g sugar, 7g protein, 0mg cholesterol, 248mg sodium, 309mg potassium. Calories from fat: 14 percent.

CHOCOLATE TUXEDO CHEESECAKE

*T*HIS CHEESECAKE CONSISTS of a chocolate cookie crust with creamy chocolate filling and a light vanilla topping—almost like an Oreo cookie!

CRUST:
½ cup maple syrup
¼ cup canola oil
½ cup cocoa
1¼ cups whole wheat flour
½ teaspoon vanilla

FILLING:
3 8-ounce containers soy cream cheese (such as Tofutti which has no casein)
1½ boxes (18 ounces) firm silken tofu
1 cup granulated sweetener
1 teaspoon vanilla
2 cups vegan chocolate chips
⅓ cup unbleached white flour

TOPPING:
½ box (6 ounces) firm silken tofu
1 tablespoon canola oil
1½ teaspoons lemon juice
¼ teaspoon salt
¾ cup granulated sweetener
¾ teaspoon vanilla

. . . .

MAKES 16 SERVINGS
PREPARATION TIME:
   CRUST: 10 minutes
   FILLING: 10 minutes
   TOPPING: 10 minutes
BAKING TIME: 60 minutes
COOLING TIME: 1 hour in oven with heat off and door closed
REFRIGERATE AT LEAST 8 HOURS BEFORE SERVING

. . . .

- Preheat oven to 375°F. Coat a 9-inch springform pan with nonstick cooking spray.
- *To make crust:* In a food processor or small bowl, combine all crust ingredients and mix thoroughly. Press into the bottom of the prepared springform pan. Prick with a fork and bake for 10 minutes. Remove from oven, reduce oven heat to 350°F, and set crust aside
- *To make filling:* Combine cream cheese and tofu in food processor and mix until smooth, scraping down sides as necessary. Add granulated sweetener and blend until creamy. Add flour and vanilla and blend. Melt chocolate chips in microwave or double boiler. Pour into food processor with cream cheese mixture and blend. Pour into prepared crust. Place on top rack of oven. Place a shallow pan filled with water on lower rack of oven and bake for 50 minutes.
- *To make topping:* While cheesecake is baking, place tofu in food processor and process until smooth, scraping down sides as necessary. Add other ingredients and process to blend. Set aside.
- After 50 minutes, pull cheesecake out of oven and carefully spread on topping. Return to oven and bake an additional 10 minutes. Turn the oven off and leave the cheesecake there for an additional hour. Remove from oven and allow to cool completely. Refrigerate at least 8 hours or overnight before serving.

PER SERVING: 474 calories, 25g fat (7g saturated), 57g carbohydrate, 3g dietary fiber, 8g sugar, 10g protein, 0mg cholesterol, 195mg sodium, 330mg potassium. Calories from fat: 26 percent.

PUDDINGS

*T*OFU PUDDINGS ARE easy and delicious. Unlike traditional puddings, no cooking or thickening is involved. The tofu gives the pudding a nice creamy texture. If you want to get creative, you can layer several of the following pudding recipes to make a parfait. For example, you can layer chocolate and peanut butter or chocolate and coconut. Lemon, orange, and coconut make a nice tropical parfait and look pretty garnished with fresh citrus fruit, sprinkled coconut, and mint leaves. Use your imagination! I usually serve pudding in inexpensive small wine goblets for a festive look.

CHOCOLATE LOVER'S PUDDING

*T*HIS IS A treat that I like to make when I'm craving chocolate. It's very versatile and may be used as a dessert on its own, a pie filling, or a topping for a cake.

1 pound (16 ounces) firm
   silken tofu
1 cup powdered sugar
2 teaspoons vanilla
2 cups vegan chocolate chips,
   melted (use double boiler or
   microwave)
¼ cup vegan chocolate chips
   finely ground for garnish
   (optional)

. . . .

MAKES 8 SERVINGS
PREPARATION TIME: 5 minutes

. . . .

- Place tofu in food processor and mix until smooth, scraping down sides of processor as necessary. Add sugar and vanilla.
- Melt chocolate chips in microwave or double boiler. Pour melted chocolate into food processor and process until combined.
- Pour into serving dishes. Sprinkle with finely ground chocolate chips if desired. Refrigerate until ready to serve.

Variation: Add ¾ cup vegan chocolate chips or ½ cup coarsely chopped peanuts to pudding for an interesting dessert.

PER SERVING: 297 calories, 14g fat (8g saturated), 43g carbohydrate, 3g dietary fiber, <1g sugar, 5g protein, 0mg cholesterol, 9mg sodium, 70mg potassium. Calories from fat: 39 percent.

Guiltless Pudding

*T*HIS PUDDING IS a healthier version of Chocolate Lover's Pudding, page 169, because I use stevia to sweeten it. (See Stocking Your Vegan Pantry on page 11 for more information on stevia). The raisins are optional, but keep in mind that they will add some extra sweetness to the pudding. This dessert is also a good source of potassium and iron.

*24 ounces (2 boxes) firm or
extra firm silken tofu*
¼ cup carob
1 teaspoon stevia
¼ cup organic raisins

. . . .

MAKES 8 SERVINGS
PREPARATION TIME: 5 minutes

. . . .

- Place tofu in food processor and process until smooth, scraping down sides of processor as necessary. Add sugar and vanilla.
- Add carob and stevia to food processor and process until combined. Stir in raisins by hand.
- Pour into serving dishes and refrigerate until ready to serve.

PER SERVING: 37 calories, <1g fat (<1g saturated), 7g carbohydrate, 1g dietary fiber, <1g sugar, 2g protein, 0mg cholesterol, 3mg sodium, 114mg potassium. Calories from fat: 20 percent.

Peanut Butter and No Jelly Pudding

*S*MOOTH, CREAMY PEANUT butter pudding makes for a quick, easy, and delicious treat any time.

1 pound (16 ounces) firm
   silken tofu
1 cup powdered sugar
2 teaspoons vanilla
¾ cup smooth natural peanut
   butter
¼ cup peanut finely ground for
   garnish (optional)

. . . .

MAKES 8 SERVINGS
PREPARATION TIME: 5 minutes

. . . .

- Place tofu in food processor and process until smooth, scraping down sides of processor as necessary. Add sugar, vanilla, and peanut butter.
- Pour into serving dishes and sprinkle with finely ground peanuts, if desired.
- Refrigerate until ready to serve.

Variation: Add ¾ cup vegan chocolate chips to pudding for an interesting twist.

PER SERVING: 239 calories, 14g fat (3g saturated), 21g carbohydrate, 2g dietary fiber, <1g sugar, 10g protein, 0mg cholesterol, 117mg sodium, 231mg potassium. Calories from fat: 50 percent.

BAHAMA MAMA PUDDING

COCONUT PUDDING IS creamy and tropical-tasting and is wonderful served alone or with chocolate chips added. Being a chocoholic myself, I always add the chocolate chips!

1 pound (16 ounces) firm
   silken tofu
1 cup powdered sugar
2 teaspoons coconut extract
¾ cup shredded unsweetened
   coconut
Fresh mint leaves for garnish
   (optional)

. . . .
MAKES 8 SERVINGS
PREPARATION TIME: 5 minutes
. . . .

- Place tofu in food processor and process until smooth, scraping down sides of processor as necessary. Add sugar and coconut extract. Stir coconut in by hand.
- Pour into serving dishes. Refrigerate until ready to serve.
- Garnish with fresh mint leaves.

Variation: Add ½ cup vegan chocolate chips to the pudding after it has been processed in the food processor. Stir it into the pudding along with the coconut.

PER SERVING: 113 calories, 4g fat (2g saturated), 17g carbohydrate, <1g dietary fiber, <1g sugar, 4g protein, 0mg cholesterol, 6mg sodium, 84mg potassium. Calories from fat: 28 percent.

THE BERRY BEST PUDDING

RASPBERRY PUDDING IS light and fruity and, in my opinion, provides a simple and elegant end to a delicious meal.

1 pound (16 ounces) firm
  silken tofu
1 cup powdered sugar
¼ cup raspberry jam
fresh raspberries and mint leaves
  for garnish (optional)

. . . .

MAKES 8 SERVINGS
PREPARATION TIME: 5 minutes

. . . .

- Place tofu in food processor and process until smooth, scraping down sides of processor as necessary. Add sugar and jam.
- Pour into serving dishes and refrigerate until ready to serve.
- Garnish with fresh raspberries and mint leaves.

PER SERVING: 117 calories, 2g fat (<1g saturated), 22g carbohydrate, <1g dietary fiber, <1g sugar, 4g protein, 0mg cholesterol, 9mg sodium, 76mg potassium. Calories from fat: 15 percent.

CREAMY RICE PUDDING

SMOOTH RICE PUDDING is always a crowd pleaser, and this recipe is a great way to use up any leftover rice you may have from last night's stir-fry!

1 pound (16 ounces) firm
silken tofu
¾ cup maple syrup
2 teaspoons vanilla extract
1½ teaspoons cinnamon
2 cups cooked brown rice (I like
short-grain brown rice or
brown basmati.)
½ cup raisins
¾ cup apple juice (or water)

. . . .

MAKES 8 SERVINGS
PREPARATION TIME:
    PUDDING: 5 minutes
    RICE: 45 minutes

. . . .

- *To cook rice:* Put 1 cup rice with 2 cups water in a saucepan and bring to boil. Lower heat, cover, and simmer for 45 minutes.
- While rice is cooking, place apple juice in small pan and bring to boil. Add raisins, cover, and simmer for 5 minutes. Remove from heat and allow to soak until you are ready to add them to the pudding.
- Place tofu in food processor and process until smooth, scraping down sides of processor as necessary. Add sugar, vanilla, and cinnamon and process until smooth. Pour into bowl. Add rice and raisins. (Discard apple juice that raisins were soaking in.) Stir to combine. Sprinkle with more cinnamon.
- Refrigerate until cold.

Variation: Substitute brandy for apple juice when soaking raisins for a festive alternative.

PER SERVING: 197 calories, 3g fat (<1g saturated), 40g carbohydrate, 2g dietary fiber, 19g sugar, 5g protein, 0mg cholesterol, 11mg sodium, 221mg potassium. Calories from fat: 11 percent.

ORANGE CHOCOLATE CHIP PUDDING

I LIKE TO combine flavors that are unusual, such as tangy orange and bittersweet chocolate. If you like the taste of this pudding, you should definitely try the Orange You Glad It Has Chocolate Chips Cake, page 79.

1 pound (16 ounces) firm silken tofu
1 cup powdered sugar
2 teaspoons orange extract
1½ cups vegan chocolate chips
4 thin orange slices and mint leaves for garnish (optional)

. . . .
MAKES 8 SERVINGS
PREPARATION TIME: 5 minutes
. . . .

- Place tofu in food processor and process until smooth scraping down sides of processor as necessary. Add sugar and orange extract and blend. Stir chocolate chips in by hand.
- Pour into serving dishes and refrigerate until ready to serve.
- Garnish with fresh orange slices and mint leaves.

PER SERVING: 246 calories, 12g fat (6g saturated), 36g carbohydrate, 2g dietary fiber, <1g sugar, 5g protein, 0mg cholesterol, 8mg sodium, 70mg potassium. Calories from fat: 37 percent.

TANGY LEMON PUDDING

THIS PUDDING WORKS well as a light dessert, or it may be used as a pie filling or topping for a cake.

1 pound (16 ounces) firm
  silken tofu
1 cup powdered sugar
2 teaspoons lemon extract
¼ teaspoon tumeric (for
  color only)
4 thin lemon slices and mint
  leaves for garnish (optional)

MAKES 8 SERVINGS
PREPARATION TIME: 5 minutes

- Place tofu in food processor and process until smooth, scraping down sides of processor as necessary. Add sugar, lemon extract, tumeric and blend.
- Pour into serving dishes and refrigerate until ready to serve.
- Garnish with fresh lemon slices and mint leaves.

PER SERVING: 96 calories, 2g fat (<1g saturated), 16 carbohydrate, <1g dietary fiber, <1g sugar, 4g protein, 0mg cholesterol, 5mg sodium, 70mg potassium. Calories from fat: 18 percent.

STRAWBERRY FIELDS PUDDING

*T*HIS SIMPLE BUT tasty strawberry pudding can be used on its own as a dessert, layered with other flavors to make a parfait, put in a pie shell, or mounded onto a cake.

1 pound (16 ounces) firm
    silken tofu
1 cup powdered sugar
¼ cup strawberry jam or ¾ cup
    fresh or frozen strawberries
Fresh strawberries and mint
    leaves for garnish (optional)

. . . .
MAKES 8 SERVINGS
PREPARATION TIME: 5 minutes
. . . .

- Place tofu in food processor and process until smooth, scraping down sides of processor as necessary. Add sugar and jam or fruit.
- Pour into serving dishes and refrigerate until ready to serve.
- Garnish with fresh strawberries and mint leaves.

PER SERVING: 97 calories, 2g fat (<1g saturated), 17g carbohydrate, <1g dietary fiber, <1g sugar, 4g protein, 0mg cholesterol, 5mg sodium, 92mg potassium. Calories from fat: 18 percent.

Donuts and Candy

FASNACHTS

THE FOLLOWING THREE recipes are variations on a donut recipe called fasnachts. Fasnachts are traditionally made in Pennsylvania German households on Fat Tuesday, the day before Ash Wednesday, which is the start of the season of Lent leading up to Easter. The idea is to eat as much delicious (albeit fattening) food as you can before Lent begins, when foods become more restricted for a few weeks. Fasnachts are pieces of potato dough deep-fried to a golden brown. They are traditionally eaten plain or with molasses. I like to dust them with powdered sugar so they are more like glazed and powdered donuts.

3 packages dry yeast
1 cup lukewarm water
4 cups scalded soy milk
2 cups plain mashed potatoes
    (no soy milk added)*
1 cup canola oil
1 cup granulated sweetener
17–18 cups unbleached white
    flour
2 teaspoons flax powder
½ cup water
1 teaspoon salt
1-pound bag powdered sugar
    (optional)

. . . .

MAKES ABOUT 8 DOZEN
FASNACHTS
PREPARATION TIME:
    MIXING DOUGH: 30 minutes
    RAISING TIME: 20 minutes
    1 hour
    45 minutes
FRYING TIME: 1–2 hours
depending on the size of the
pan that you use

. . . .

- Dissolve yeast in 1 cup lukewarm water. Allow to sit for about 5 minutes. Meanwhile, heat soy milk until almost boiling, but don't boil. Pour into a very large bowl and mix with 2 cups mashed potatoes, canola oil, and granulated sweetener. Allow to cool to lukewarm (or you will kill the yeast when you add it).
- Add yeast mixture and 6 cups of flour. Stir to combine. Allow mixture to stand for 20 minutes— mixture will look foamy on top.
- In a small bowl, mix flax powder in ½ cup water. Add to flour mixture and stir to combine. Add salt and 10 cups of flour. Add the last cup or 2 of flour slowly. Dough should be firm enough to stir, yet soft—it will stiffen as you knead. You want tender flaky donuts, not tough ones! When you can no longer stir dough, turn out onto floured counter and knead until satiny. If dough is too sticky to work with, add more flour. Coat a large mixing bowl with nonstick cooking spray and place dough in this bowl. Cover and allow to rise in a warm place until doubled in bulk (at least 1 hour).

*You may cook potatoes and mash them. The number of potatoes it will take to make 2 cups mashed will vary depending on the size of the potato—5 medium potatoes will probably be enough. I usually use potato flakes because I find that they make a lighter donut and they're easier to make. If you choose to use potato flakes, you will need four ½-cup servings of the potatoes. I use 1⅓ cups of water mixed with ½ cup soy milk. I heat the liquid and add 1½ cups potato flakes. Check the back of the box of the potato flakes that you use for further direction.

- *To make fasnachts:* Roll out dough (in small batches) to about ½-inch thickness. Cut dough with a sharp knife or pizza cutter into about 2 inches by 1 inch rectangles. Place rectangles of dough on trays lined with wax or parchment paper (less sticking with parchment paper). With a sharp knife, cut an X in the center of each piece of dough. This will prevent the center from being too thick and not cooking through entirely.

- Cover and allow to rise until not quite doubled in size, about 45 minutes. (I find that by the time I am finished cutting all the donuts, the first ones are ready to fry.) Heat vegetable oil to 375°F. You can either use a pan with a cooking thermometer clipped on the side or a wok. I find that my electric wok works well for this. It has its own thermostat and a wide area in which to cook the donuts. When oil is proper temperature, carefully drop in rectangles of dough. (Don't overcrowd cooking area.) Donuts will float. When bottom sides are golden brown, turn over.

- Remove from oil with a slotted spoon when both sides are golden brown. Drain on paper towels or cut up brown paper bags, with the inside of the bag facing up. (To make cleanup easier, I always place aluminum foil beneath the brown paper bags.)

- Allow to cool until donuts can be handled before coating with powdered sugar (if desired). Put powdered sugar in plastic or paper bag. Drop 3–4 donuts in bag. Shake carefully to cover with sugar. Remove and cool completely. The consistency of the powdered sugar covering is directly related to the temperature of the donuts at the time of the coating. If you want more of a glaze, coat them when they are warmer. If you want more of a powdered sugar covering, allow them to cool almost completely before coating.

Variation: You may place some of the dough in a greased 8-inch baking dish. Punch holes in the dough (not all the way through). Sprinkle with sugar, maple syrup, and/or vegan butter if desired. Bake at 400°F until top is golden brown, about 15–20 minutes. This will make one breakfast cake.

PER SERVING: 133 calories, 3g fat (<1g saturated), 24g carbohydrate, <1g dietary fiber, 3g protein, 0mg cholesterol, 4mg sodium, 47mg potassium. Calories from fat: 19 percent.

JELLY-FILLED DONUTS

OTHING COMPARES TO a freshly baked donut. If you love jelly donuts and have never made them—here's your chance. You will be glad you did, and you'll never want to buy another donut again! These treats take a lot of work, but they are worth it.

1 package dry yeast
⅓ cup lukewarm water
1⅓ cups scalded soy milk
½ cup plain mashed potatoes
   (no soy milk added)*
⅓ cup canola oil
⅓ cup granulated sweetener
5 cups unbleached white flour
1 teaspoon flax powder
¼ cup water
⅓ teaspoon salt
1 16-ounce jar of jelly or seedless jam such as raspberry
3 cups powdered sugar (optional)

. . . .

MAKES ABOUT 3 DOZEN DONUTS
PREPARATION TIME:
   MIXING DOUGH: 30 minutes
RAISING TIME: 20 minutes
   1 hour
   45 minutes
FRYING TIME: 1 hour depending on the size of the pan
that you use
. . . .

- Dissolve yeast in 1 cup lukewarm water. Allow to sit for about 5 minutes. Meanwhile, heat soy milk until almost boiling, but don't boil. Pour into a very large bowl and mix with mashed potatoes, canola oil, and granulated sweetener. Allow to cool to lukewarm (or you will kill the yeast when you add it).

- Add yeast mixture and 1 cup of flour. Stir to combine. Allow mixture to stand for 20 minutes.

- In a small bowl, mix flax powder in ¼ cup water. Add to flour mixture and stir to combine. Add salt and 3 cups of flour. Add the last cup of flour slowly. Dough should be firm enough to stir, yet soft—it will stiffen as you knead. You want tender flaky donuts, not tough ones! When you can no longer stir dough, turn out onto floured counter and knead until satiny. Coat a large mixing bowl with nonstick cooking spray and place dough in this bowl. Cover and allow to rise in a warm place until doubled in bulk (at least 1 hour).

*You may cook potatoes and mash them. The number of potatoes it will take to make ½ cup mashed will vary depending on the size of the potato—2 medium potatoes will probably be enough. I usually use potato flakes because I find that they make a lighter donut and they're easier to make. If you choose to use potato flakes, you'll need one ½-cup serving of the potatoes. I use ⅓ cup of water mixed with 2 tablespoons soy milk. I heat the liquid and add ¼ cup + 2 tablespoons potato flakes. Check the back of the box of the potato flakes that you use for further directions.

- *To make donuts:* Roll out dough (in small batches) to about ½-inch thickness. Cut with a 2-inch round cutter (or a glass with about a 2-inch diameter). Place circles of dough on trays lined with wax or parchment paper (less sticking with parchment paper). Cover and allow to rise until not quite doubled in size, about 45 minutes. (I find that by the time I am finished cutting all the donuts, the first ones are ready to fry.)
- Heat vegetable oil to 375°F. You can either use a pan with a cooking thermometer clipped on the side or a wok. I find that my electric wok works well for this. It has its own thermostat and a wide area in which to cook the donuts. When oil is proper temperature, carefully drop in circles of dough. (Don't overcrowd cooking area.) Donuts will float. When bottom sides are golden brown, turn over. Remove from oil with a slotted spoon when both sides are golden brown. Drain on paper towels or cut up brown paper bags, with the inside of the bag facing up. (To make cleanup easier, I always place aluminum foil under the brown bags.) Allow to cool enough so that you can handle them.
- Push handle of wooden spoon about 2½ to 3 inches into the side of each donut to make a hole. Be careful not to push it all the way through the donut. Put jelly into pastry bag fitted with large round tip (or use a resealable plastic bag, snip 1 corner). Squeeze about 2 teaspoons of jelly into the hole in each donut. Dust the donuts with powdered sugar.

PER SERVING: 168 calories, 2g fat (<1g saturated), 34g carbohydrate, <1g dietary fiber, 2g protein, 0mg cholesterol, 9mg sodium, 49mg potassium. Calories from fat: 13 percent.

BOSTON CREAM–FILLED DONUTS

THESE DELICIOUS TENDER donuts are filled with creamy vanilla filling and topped with dark chocolate. Yum!

DONUTS:

1 package dry yeast
⅓ cup lukewarm water
1⅓ cups scalded soy milk
*½ cup plain mashed potatoes
   (no soy milk added)**
⅓ cup canola oil
⅓ cup granulated sweetener
5 cups unbleached white flour
1 teaspoons flax powder
¼ cup water
⅓ teaspoon salt

VANILLA FILLING:

*1 pound (16 ounces) firm
   silken tofu*
1 cup powdered sugar
2 teaspoons vanilla
¼ cup unbleached white flour

CHOCOLATE GLAZE TOPPING:

1 cup powdered sugar
¼ cup canola oil
½ teaspoon vanilla
*⅙ cup cocoa (use ⅓ cup meas-
   urer and only fill it half full)*
3½ tablespoons arrowroot
½ cup water

- Dissolve yeast in 1 cup lukewarm water. Allow to sit for about 5 minutes. Meanwhile, heat soy milk until almost boiling, but don't boil. Pour into a very large bowl and mix with mashed potatoes, canola oil, and granulated sweetener. Allow to cool to lukewarm (or you will kill the yeast when you add it). Add yeast mixture and 1 cup of flour. Stir to combine. Allow mixture to stand for 20 minutes.
- In a small bowl, mix flax powder in ¼ cup water. Add to flour mixture and stir to combine. Add salt and 3 cups of flour. Add the last cup of flour slowly. Dough should be firm enough to stir, yet soft—it will stiffen as you knead. You want tender flaky donuts, not tough ones! When you can no longer stir dough, turn out onto floured counter and knead until satiny. Coat a large mixing bowl with nonstick cooking spray and place dough in this bowl. Cover and allow to rise in a warm place until doubled in bulk (at least 1 hour).
- *To make filling:* While dough is rising, place tofu in food processor. Whip until smooth, scraping down sides several times. Add sugar, flour, and vanilla and process. Refrigerate until ready to use.

*You may cook potatoes and mash them. The number of potatoes it will take to make ½ cup mashed will vary depending on the size of the potato—2 medium potatoes will probably be enough. I usually use potato flakes because I find that they make a lighter donut and they're easier to make. If you choose to use potato flakes, you'll need one ½-cup serving of the potatoes. I use ⅓ cup of water mixed with 2 tablespoons soy milk. I heat the liquid and add ¼ cup + 2 tablespoons potato flakes. Check the back of the box of the potato flakes that you use for further directions.

- *To make donuts:* Roll out dough (in small batches) to about ½-inch thickness. Cut with a 2-inch round cutter (or a glass with about a 2-inch diameter). Place circles of dough on trays lined with wax or parchment paper (less sticking with parchment paper). Cover and allow to rise until not quite doubled in size, about 45 minutes. (I find that by the time I am finished cutting all the donuts, the first ones are ready to fry.)

- Heat vegetable oil to 375°F. You can either use a pan with a cooking thermometer clipped on the side or a wok. I find that my electric wok works well for this. It has its own thermostat and a wide area in which to cook the donuts. When oil is proper temperature, carefully drop in circles of dough. (Don't overcrowd cooking area.) Donuts will float. When bottom sides are golden brown, turn over. Remove from oil with a slotted spoon when both sides are golden brown. Drain on paper towels or cut up brown paper bags with the inside of the bag facing up. (To make cleanup easier, I always place aluminum foil beneath the brown bags.) Allow to cool. Push handle of wooden spoon about 2½ to 3 inches into the side of each donut to make a hole. Be careful not to push it all the way through the donut. Put cream into pastry bag fitted with large round tip (or use a resealable plastic bag, snip one corner). Squeeze about 2 teaspoons of cream into the hole in each donut and then refrigerate.

- *To make chocolate topping:* Place powdered sugar, canola oil, vanilla, cocoa, and arrowroot in small saucepan and stir to combine, using a wire whisk for best results. Stir in water. Turn on heat and bring almost to boil, stirring constantly. Do not boil. Keep stirring until mixture starts to thicken. Allow to cool until mixture is of a good spreading consistency. Pour 1–2 tablespoons of chocolate topping over each donut and refrigerate. (Topping will thicken as it cools.)

. . . .

MAKES ABOUT 3 DOZEN
DONUTS
PREPARATION TIME:
  MIXING DOUGH: 30 minutes
RAISING TIME: 20 minutes
  1 hour
  45 minutes
FRYING TIME: 1 hour depending on the size of the pan that you use

. . . .

PER SERVING: 152 calories, 5g fat (<1g saturated), 23g carbohydrate, <1g dietary fiber, <1g sugar, 4g protein, 0mg cholesterol, 6mg sodium, 110mg potassium. Calories from fat: 29 percent.

PEANUT BUTTER BALLS

HO CAN RESIST creamy peanut butter covered in dark chocolate? These are truly delicious candies—my kids can vouch for that!

1 cup smooth natural peanut
   butter
½ cup pureed pumpkin
½ cup powdered sugar
1 10-ounce bag vegan chocolate chips
½ cup chopped peanuts
   (optional)

. . . .

MAKES 3 DOZEN
PREPARATION TIME:
   FILLING: 5 minutes
   ROLLING INTO BALLS:
   15 minutes
   COATING: 15 minutes
. . . .

- Mix peanut butter and pumpkin together. Add pow-dered sugar. (You may want to use a food processor to mix filling.) Roll filling into ¾-inch balls. Place on wax- or parchment-lined tray. Place in freezer for 15 minutes so that filling is hard and easier to coat with the warm chocolate.

- Melt chocolate chips in microwave or double boiler until smooth and creamy. (If using double boiler, keep water in double boiler on low so that chocolate remains hot and thin.) Pierce each ball of filling with a toothpick to use as a handle. Dip filling ball in chocolate and place on wax or parchment paper lined tray.

- If desired, sprinkle with chopped peanuts. Refrigerate to harden chocolate.

- Store candy in the refrigerator in airtight container.

PER SERVING: 100 calories, 7g fat (2g saturated), 9g carbohydrate, 1g dietary fiber, 3g protein, 0mg cholesterol, 43mg sodium, 68mg potassium. Calories from fat: 58 percent.

Coconut Cream Eggs

HERE'S MY VEGAN version of the traditional candy coconut cream eggs.

12 ounces (1 box) firm
   silken tofu
4 ounces soy cream cheese
1⅓ cups prepared mashed
   potatoes*
2 cups powdered sugar
3 cups shredded unsweetened
   coconut
1 teaspoon coconut extract
4 cups vegan chocolate chips

. . . .

MAKES 4 DOZEN
PREPARATION TIME:
   FILLING: 5 minutes
   ROLLING INTO LOGS:
   15 minutes
   COATING: 15 minutes
. . . .

- Place tofu in food processor and process until smooth, scraping down sides of bowl as necessary. Add cream cheese and process until smooth. Add mashed potatoes, sugar, and coconut extract and process until smooth. Stir in coconut by hand, mixing well. Chill filling for 10 minutes so that it is easier to handle.
- Roll or spoon filling into small log or egg-shaped pieces—about ¾-inch by ½-inch (filling may still be soft). Place logs of filling onto wax- or parchment-covered tray. Freeze for 15 minutes or until filling is easy to handle.
- Melt chocolate chips in microwave or double boiler until smooth and creamy. (If using double boiler, keep water in double boiler on low so that chocolate remains hot and thin.) Pierce each log of filling with a toothpick to use as a handle. Dip filling log in chocolate. Place on wax- or parchment-lined tray. Refrigerate to harden chocolate.
- Store candy in the refrigerator in airtight container.

*You may peel, boil, and mash potatoes. The number of potatoes needed will vary depending on size—3 or 4 medium potatoes will probably be enough. I use instant potato flakes because I think they are much easier and make a lighter filling. I use ¾ cup water mixed with ⅓ cup soy milk. I heat the liquid and add ¾ cup potato flakes. This makes 2 servings, which is equal to 1⅓ cups of potatoes. Check on the back of the box of the potato flakes that you use for further directions.

PER SERVING: 123 calories, 6g fat (4g saturated), 17g carbohydrate, 1g dietary fiber, <1g sugar, 2g protein, 0mg cholesterol, 13mg sodium, 83mg potassium. Calories from fat: 37 percent.

MELT IN YOUR MOUTH FUDGE

PON BECOMING A vegan, were you afraid that your days of enjoying a luscious, creamy piece of sinfully rich fudge were over? Well, have I got good news for you! This vegan fudge recipe is sure to satisfy even the most savage sweet tooth.

8 ounces soy cream cheese
4 cups powdered sugar
1 cup vegan chocolate chips
1 teaspoon vanilla

. . . .
MAKES 6–7 DOZEN PIECES OF FUDGE
PREPARATION TIME: 5 minutes
. . . .

- Place the cream cheese in a food processor and blend until smooth. Add powdered sugar and vanilla. Melt chocolate chips in microwave or double boiler. Pour into food processor and process until blended.
- Pour into 8-inch square pan that has been lined with wax paper. Refrigerate until firm.
- Pull wax paper out of pan. Cut fudge into bite-size pieces.
- Store fudge in refrigerator in airtight container.

PER SERVING: 45 calories, 1g fat (<1g saturated), 8g carbohydrate, <1g dietary fiber, <1g protein, 0mg cholesterol, 14mg sodium, <1mg potassium. Calories from fat: 12 percent.

Raisin and Peanut Clusters

THIS CANDY—PEANUTS and raisins nestled in rich, dark chocolate—can be made in a snap and tastes fantastic.

2½ cups vegan chocolate chips
1 cup whole roasted peanuts,
   salted
1 cup organic raisins

. . . .

MAKES 2 DOZEN
PREPARATION TIME:
   MIXING: 5 minutes
   FORMING INTO MOUNDS:
   10 minutes

. . . .

- Melt chocolate in microwave or double boiler. Mix in peanuts and raisins. Drop by teaspoonfuls onto wax- or parchment-lined trays.
- Refrigerate until hard. Store in the refrigerator in airtight container.

PER SERVING: 137 calories, 8g fat (3g saturated), 17g carbohydrate, 2g dietary fiber, 2g protein, 0mg cholesterol, 3mg sodium, 85mg potassium. Calories from fat: 49 percent.

CHOCOLATE COCONUT NESTS

*T*HIS DELICIOUS CANDY can be used as a basket or nest to hold other small candy or it can be eaten alone—take your pick.

2 cups vegan chocolate chips
1½ cups shredded coconut
½ teaspoon coconut extract

. . . .

MAKES 1 DOZEN
PREPARATION TIME:
   MIXING: 5 minutes
   FORMING INTO MOUNDS:
10 minutes

. . . .

- Melt chocolate in microwave or double boiler. Mix in coconut and coconut extract. Drop by tablespoonfuls onto wax- or parchment-lined trays.
- Press knuckle into center of candy to make and indentation. Refrigerate until hard. Store in the refrigerator in airtight container.

Variation: You can fill these nests with vegan jelly beans or vegan candy coated chocolates, if desired.

PER SERVING: 158 calories, 11g fat (7g saturated), 19g carbohydrate, 2g dietary fiber, 1g protein, 0mg cholesterol, 4mg sodium, 19mg potassium. Calories from fat: 54 percent.

BEVERAGES AND SMOOTHIES

AIN'T NO CHOCOLATE HERE SMOOTHIE

*T*HIS HEALTHY CREATION tastes so rich that it can just as easily be served as a sinful-tasting snack or dessert as it can be for breakfast. The carob is not as chocolatey as real chocolate, but it has more calcium and no caffeine. You may choose to substitute cocoa for the carob (use the same amount of cocoa as you would carob) for a real chocolate shake taste. The banana in this smoothie does not add much banana flavor, but it does add sweetness and a smooth texture.

1 cup crushed ice

1 cup soy milk, or non-dairy milk of your choice

1 yellow banana, peeled and broken into several small pieces (not too green and not overripe)

2 tablespoons carob powder (or cocoa powder)

. . . .

SERVES 1
PREPARATION TIME: 5 minutes

. . . .

- Place all ingredients in blender.
- Process at high speed until smooth.
- Pour into a tall glass and serve immediately.

PER SERVING: 279 calories, 5g fat (<1g saturated), 54g carbohydrate, 8g dietary fiber, 8g protein, 0mg cholesterol, 55mg sodium, 838mg potassium. Calories from fat: 15 percent.

ORANGE CREAMSICLE SMOOTHIE

I LIKE TO make this refreshing drink on a summer evening when I'm craving something sweet and cool. It tastes just like an orange sherbet shake.

1 cup crushed ice
3 tablespoons orange juice concentrate
1 cup vanilla soy milk, or non-dairy milk of your choice
1 teaspoon vanilla

SERVES 1
PREPARATION TIME: 5 minutes

- Place all ingredients in blender.
- Process at high speed until smooth.
- Pour into a tall glass and serve immediately.

PER SERVING: 203 calories, 5g fat (<1g saturated), 31g carbohydrate, 4g dietary fiber, 8g protein, 0mg cholesterol, 32mg sodium, 817mg potassium. Calories from fat: 19 percent.

BANANAS IN PAJAMAS SMOOTHIE

*T*HIS IS ONE of my morning favorites—I like to whip up one of these smoothies before work. It keeps me feeling satisfied until lunch—no mid-morning snack attacks. I think bananas truly are the perfect food, and a wonderful source of potassium to boot. Depending on the ripeness of the banana that you use, this smoothie can taste either like a banana milkshake or a vanilla milkshake.

1 yellow banana, peeled and broken into several small pieces (not too green and not overripe)
1 cup crushed ice
1 cup soy milk
1 teaspoon vanilla

SERVES 1
PREPARATION TIME: 5 minutes

- Place all ingredients in blender.
- Process at high speed until smooth.
- Pour into a tall glass and serve immediately.

PER SERVING: 202 calories, 5g fat (<1g saturated), 33g carbohydrate, 6g dietary fiber, 8g protein, 0mg cholesterol, 31mg sodium, 819mg potassium. Calories from fat: 21 percent.

GREEN (I SWEAR TO GOD IT'S GOOD!) SMOOTHIE

*T*HIS VERY-HEALTHY, great-tasting smoothie is perfect for when you need an energy boost. It's amazing, but I swear I can feel the energy from the enzymes, vitamins, and minerals as they go to work when I have one.

1 cup crushed ice

1¼ cups water or apple juice

¼ cup (1 scoop) soy based protein powder

2 yellow bananas, peeled and broken into several smaller pieces

1 tablespoon flax oil

2 tablespoons wheat germ

2 tablespoons powdered green supplement such as Green Magma, which is powdered barley grass juice

SERVES 2
PREPARATION TIME: 5 minutes

- Place all ingredients in blender.
- Process at high speed until smooth.
- Pour into a tall glass and serve immediately.

PER SERVING: 247 calories, 8g fat (<1g saturated), 41g carbohydrate, 4g dietary fiber, <1g sugar, 5g protein, 0mg cholesterol, 86mg sodium, 931mg potassium. Calories from fat: 30 percent.

BERRY DELICIOUS SMOOTHIE

*J*UST THE THING for a quick, nutritious morning breakfast or a healthy ending to any meal. Here's a helpful hint: If you use the berries when they are still frozen, you will make a thicker smoothie.

1 cup crushed ice
1 cup apple juice
¼ cup water
1 cup frozen berries (blueberries, blackberries, or raspberries)
1 yellow banana, peeled and broken into several small pieces

SERVES 1
PREPARATION TIME: 5 minutes

- Place all ingredients in blender.
- Process at high speed until smooth.
- Pour into a tall glass and serve immediately.

PER SERVING: 285 calories, 1g fat (<1g saturated), 71g carbohydrate, 11g dietary fiber, 2g protein, 0mg cholesterol, 8mg sodium, 949mg potassium. Calories from fat: 4 percent.

PINK PASSION SMOOTHIE

*T*HIS SMOOTHIE IS another healthy way to start the day or to use as a sweet, delicious ending to any meal.

1 cup frozen strawberries
1 cup crushed ice
1 cup apple juice
¼ cup water
1 yellow banana, peeled and broken in several small pieces

SERVES 1
PREPARATION TIME: 5 minutes

- Place all ingredients in blender.
- Process at high speed until smooth.
- Pour into a tall glass and serve immediately.

PER SERVING: 270 calories, 1g fat (<1g saturated), 67g carbohydrate, 6g dietary fiber, 2g protein, 0mg cholesterol, 10mg sodium, 1014mg potassium. Calories from fat: 4 percent.

CARIBBEAN CRUISE SMOOTHIE

THIS SMOOTHIE WILL tickle your taste buds with its smooth, rich-tasting combination of coconut and pineapple. If you kick back in your backyard or patio with this drink, you'll feel like you're on vacation.

1 cup crushed pineapple,
    drained
1 cup crushed ice
1 cup soy milk
2 tablespoons shredded
    unsweetened coconut
¼ teaspoon coconut extract

SERVES 1
PREPARATION TIME: 5 minutes

- Place all ingredients in blender.
- Process at high speed until smooth.
- Pour into a tall glass and serve immediately.

PER SERVING: 327 calories, 14g fat (9g saturated), 47g carbohydrate, 7g dietary fiber, 9g protein, 0mg cholesterol, 37mg sodium, 727mg potassium. Calories from fat: 35 percent.

RED BARON SMOOTHIE

I CREATED THIS smoothie when I was having a snack attack and it definitely did the trick. If you add more ice, you can make it extra thick and eat it with a spoon like ice cream.

1¼ cups vanilla soy milk
1 cup crushed ice
1 cup frozen, pitted cherries
2 tablespoons carob powder

SERVES 1
PREPARATION TIME: 5 minutes

- Place all ingredients in blender.
- Process at high speed until smooth.
- Pour into a tall glass and serve immediately.

PER SERVING: 241 calories, 7g fat (<1g saturated), 44g carbohydrate, 13g dietary fiber, 10g protein, 0mg cholesterol, 42mg sodium, 889mg potassium. Calories from fat: 25 percent.

RICH HOT COCOA (SINGLE SERVING)

Wheat Free

REMEMBER THE WARM feeling you get from a cup of hot cocoa on a cold winter day? You can recapture that same good taste and warm feeling with this vegan version. The recipe below is for one serving and is so easy because it's made in the microwave.

1 cup vanilla soy milk, or non-dairy milk of your choice
1 teaspoon vanilla
2 teaspoons sugar
1 tablespoon cocoa

MAKES 1 SERVING
PREPARATION TIME: 5 minutes

- Heat soy milk in microwave safe mug in microwave until it is steaming but not boiling (about 1 or 1½ minutes depending on the strength of your microwave). Add vanilla and sugar and stir. Put cocoa in another small cup. Add a small amount of the warm milk mixture to the cocoa. Stir to mix. Add more of the warm milk and stir.
- Pour cocoa mixture back into the rest of the soy milk in the mug and stir well.
- Serve immediately.

PER SERVING: 137 calories, 5g fat (1g saturated), 16g carbohydrate, 5g dietary fiber, 8g protein, 0mg cholesterol, 31mg sodium, 434mg potassium. Calories from fat: 33 percent.

RICH HOT COCOA (FOUR SERVINGS)

Wheat Free

IF YOU'RE HAVING friends over and want to make hot cocoa, this recipe is easier to use than making it one cup at a time. Same good taste as the single serving recipe!

4 cups vanilla soy milk, or other non-dairy milk of your choice
1½ tablespoons vanilla
2 tablespoons sugar +
*   2 teaspoons*
¼ cup cocoa

MAKES 4 SERVINGS
PREPARATION TIME: 5 minutes

- Heat soy milk in small pan until hot (steaming), but not boiling. Add vanilla and sugar and stir. Put cocoa in another small cup. Add a small amount of the warm milk mixture to the cocoa and stir to mix. Add more of the warm milk and stir.
- Pour cocoa mixture back into the rest of the soy milk in the pan. Stir well.
- Serve immediately.

PER SERVING: 122 calories, 5g fat (1g saturated), 12g carbohydrate, 5g dietary fiber, 8g protein, 0mg cholesterol, 31mg sodium, 435mg potassium. Calories from fat: 36 percent.

FROSTINGS, TOPPINGS, AND CRUSTS

*T*HIS SECTION CONTAINS frosting, topping, and pie and tart crust recipes for many of the dessert recipes in this book. I have paired each cake with a frosting or topping as indicated in each recipe. Please feel free to mix and match cakes with toppings or frostings and create your own masterpieces.

NOTE: It is a good idea, whenever possible, to prepare any tofu-based frosting the day before to allow the frosting to set. It will be firmer and easier to use.

CHERRY FILLING

2 cups fresh cherries (pitted and
    halved)
½ cup apple juice
3 teaspoons arrowroot
½ cup water

- Remove pits from cherries.
- Place in saucepan with ½ cup apple juice. Bring to boil and allow to simmer until cherries are soft, about 10 minutes.
- Dissolve arrowroot in water. Add to hot cherries and heat just until it thickens—do not boil.

Recommended for:
    Cherry, Cherry Not Contrary Cake, p. 38
    Triple Cherry Treat, p. 77
    Cherry + Chocolate = Delicious Cake, p. 85

PER SERVING: 25 calories, <1g fat
(<.1g saturated), 6g carbohydrate, <1g
dietary fiber, <1g protein, 0mg
cholesterol, <1mg sodium, 66mg
potassium. Calories from fat: 8 percent.

CHERRY TOPPING

1 cup fresh cherries (pitted and
    chopped)
¼ cup apple juice
1½ teaspoons arrowroot
¼ cup water

- Place cherries in saucepan with ¼ cup apple juice. Bring to boil and allow to simmer until cherries are soft, about 10 minutes.
- Dissolve arrowroot in water. Add to hot cherries and heat just until it thickens—do not boil.
- Refrigerate until ready to use.

Recommended for:
    Banana Split Cake, p. 63
    Cherry Vanilla Dream, p. 76

PER SERVING: 13 calories, <1g fat
(<.1g saturated), 3g carbohydrate, <1g
dietary fiber, <1g protein, 0mg
cholesterol, <1mg sodium, 33mg
potassium. Calories from fat: 8 percent.

WHIPPED CHERRY TOPPING

1 pound (16 ounces) firm
    silken tofu
1 cup powdered sugar
2 teaspoons cherry extract
½ cup fresh cherries (pitted and
    chopped)
¼ cup unbleached white flour or
    2 teaspoons xanthan gum*
    (optional for thickening)

- Place tofu in food processor and process until smooth, scraping down sides of processor as necessary. Add powdered sugar, cherry extract and flour and process until blended. Stir in cherries.
- Refrigerate until ready to use.

Recommended for:
Triple Cherry Treat, p. 77
Cherry Vanilla Dream, p. 76
Cherry, Cherry Not Contrary Cake, p. 38

PER SERVING: 60 calories, <1g fat (<.1g saturated), 13g carbohydrate, <1g dietary fiber, <1g sugar, <1g protein, 0mg cholesterol, <1mg sodium, 40mg potassium. Calories from fat: 6 percent.

*Xanthan gum will produce a slightly softer frosting, but will not give the mild flour taste that you may get if you use the flour.

WHIPPED CHOCOLATE FROSTING

1 pound (16 ounces) firm
    silken tofu
1 cup powdered sugar
2 teaspoons vanilla
2 cups vegan chocolate chips,
    melted (use double boiler or
    microwave)

- Place tofu in food processor and whip until smooth, scraping down sides several times.
- Add sugar and vanilla and process.
- Pour melted chocolate chips into tofu mixture and blend completely.
- If refrigerating cake overnight before serving, you may use frosting right away. If planning to frost cake and serve immediately, refrigerate frosting overnight to allow it to set.

Recommended for:
Cherry, Cherry Not Contrary Cake, p. 38
Nuts about Chocolate Cake, p. 43
Chocolate-Covered Gold, p. 46
Chocolate-Covered Mint, p. 60

PER SERVING: 182 calories, 9g fat (5g saturated), 28g carbohydrate, 2g dietary fiber, <1g sugar, 2g protein, 0mg cholesterol, 4 mg sodium, 25mg potassium. Calories from fat: 38 percent.

CHOCOLATE CREAM CHEESE FR[...]

12 ounces (1 box) firm
   silken tofu
8 ounces soy cream cheese
   (such as Tofutti, which has
   no casein)
3 cups powdered sugar
¼ cup unbleached flour
1½ cups vegan chocolate chips,
   melted

- Place tofu in food processor and proce[...]
  smooth, scraping down sides of process[...]
  sary. Add cream cheese and continue t[...]
  smooth. Add sugar and flour and proce[...]
- Melt chocolate chips in microwave or [...] double
  boiler. Add to other ingredients and combine.
- Refrigerate overnight for best results, so that icing
  has time to set.

Recommended for:
   Double Chocolate Delight, p. 74
   Chocolate-Covered Gold, p. 46
   Mellow Yellow Cake, p. 47
   Mint Madness, p. 75

PER SERVING: 237 calories, 7g fat (4g
saturated), 46g carbohydrate, 1g dietary
fiber, <1g sugar, 2g protein, 0mg
cholesterol, 6mg sodium, 22mg
potassium. Calories from fat: 22 percent.

VEGAN CHOCOLATE SYRUP

¼ cup maple syrup
2 tablespoons cocoa

- Combine maple syrup and cocoa in a small bowl.
  Stir with a wire whisk to combine until mixture is
  the consistency of commercial chocolate syrup. If it is
  too thick, you may add a little water. If it is too thin,
  add a little more cocoa.

Recommended for:
   Cherry, Cherry Not Contrary Cake, p. 38
   Nuts about Chocolate Cake, p. 43
   Just Loafing Around (pound cake), p. 44
   Banana Split Cake, p. 63
   Triple Cherry Treat, p. 77
   Cherry + Chocolate = Delicious Cake, p. 85

PER SERVING: 19 calories, <1g fat
(<.1g saturated), 5g carbohydrate, <1g
dietary fiber, 4g sugar, <1g protein,
0mg cholesterol, <1mg sodium.
Calories from fat: 5 percent.

Vanilla Tofu Whipped Topping

½ pound (8 ounces) firm silken tofu
½ cup powdered sugar
1 teaspoon vanilla extract
2 tablespoons unbleached white flour or 1 teaspoon xanthan gum* (optional for thickening)

- Place tofu in food processor and blend until smooth and creamy. Add powdered sugar and vanilla and blend.
- Refrigerate.

Recommended for:
Banana Split Cake, p. 63
Long on Flavor Shortcake, p. 64
Chocolate Lover's Pudding, p. 169
Peanut Butter and No Jelly Pudding, p. 171
Bahama Mama Pudding, p. 172
The Berry Best Pudding, p. 173
Creamy Rice Pudding, p. 174
Orange Chocolate Chip Pudding, p. 174
Tangy Lemon Pudding, p. 176
Strawberry Fields Pudding, p. 177

PER SERVING: 25 calories, <1g fat (<.1g saturated), 6g carbohydrate, <.1g dietary fiber, <.1g sugar, <1g protein, 0mg cholesterol, <1mg sodium, 3mg potassium. Calories from fat: 1 percent.

*Xanthan gum will produce a slightly softer frosting, but will not give the mild flour taste that you may get if you use the flour. If you are making the Banana Split Cake as a wheat-free cake, you should use the xanthan gum instead of the flour.

Vanilla Glaze

Wheat Free

¾ cup powdered sugar
2 tablespoons soy milk
½ teaspoon vanilla

- Mix together. Pour over cake before slicing.

Recommended for:
Just Loafing Around (pound cake), p. 44
You Can't Catch Me I'm the Gingerbread . . . Cake, p. 53
Cinn-sational Apple Cake, p. 66
"P" is for Pumpkin Cake, p. 67
Rootin' Tootin' Raisin Spice Cake, p. 84

PER SERVING: 31 calories, <1g fat (<.01g saturated), 8g carbohydrate, <.1g dietary fiber, <1g protein, 0mg cholesterol, <1mg sodium, 8mg potassium. Calories from fat: 2 percent.

PUMPKIN WHIPPED TOPPING

1 pound (16 ounces) firm
   silken tofu
1 cup powdered sugar
1 teaspoon vanilla
⅓ cup pureed pumpkin
1 teaspoon cinnamon

- Place tofu in food processor and process until
  smooth, scraping down sides as necessary. Add the
  rest of the ingredients and blend.
- Refrigerate until ready to use.

Recommended for:
   "P" is for Pumpkin Cake, p. 67
   Pumpkin Pie, p. 116

PER SERVING: 52 calories, <1g fat
(<.1g saturated), 12g carbohydrate, <1g
dietary fiber, <1g sugar, <1g protein,
0mg cholesterol, 34mg sodium, 54mg
potassium. Calories from fat: 7 percent.

STANDARD CHOCOLATE FROSTING

½ pound (8 ounces) firm
   silken tofu
½ cup powdered sugar
1 teaspoons vanilla
1½ cups vegan chocolate chips,
   melted (use double boiler or
   microwave)

- Place tofu in food processor and whip until smooth,
  scraping down sides several times.
- Add sugar and vanilla and process.
- Pour melted chocolate chips into tofu mixture and
  blend completely.
- If refrigerating cake overnight before serving, you
  may use frosting right away. If planning to frost cake
  and serve immediately, refrigerate frosting overnight
  to allow it to set.

Recommended for:
   Chocolate Raspberry Celebration Loaf, p. 40
   Mellow Yellow Cake, p. 47
   Double Chocolate Delight, p. 74
   Peanut Butter Kandy Kake, p. 82
   Chocolate-Covered Gold, p. 46

PER SERVING: 121 calories, 6g fat (4g
saturated), 18g carbohydrate, 1g dietary
fiber, <.1g sugar, 1g protein, 0mg
cholesterol, 2mg sodium, 2mg
potassium. Calories from fat: 41 percent.

COFFEE FROSTING

1 pound (16 ounces) firm
    silken tofu
1 cup powdered sugar
3 teaspoons instant coffee gran-
    ules or 3 teaspoons grain
    "coffee" like Roma
1 teaspoon coffee extract
    (optional, to give a more
    intense coffee flavor)
¼ cup unbleached white flour or
    2 teaspoons xanthan gum*

- Place tofu in food processor and whip until smooth,
  scraping down sides several times.
- Add sugar, coffee granules, and coffee extract and
  process. Add flour or xanthan gum. If possible, refrigerate over night before using.

Recommended for:
  Mocha Madness Cake, p. 42
  Nuts about Chocolate Cake, p. 43

PER SERVING: 57 calories, <1g fat
(<.1g saturated), 12g carbohydrate, <.1g
dietary fiber, <1g sugar, 1g protein, 0mg
cholesterol, mg sodium, 35mg
potassium. Calories from fat: 6 percent.

*Xanthan gum will produce a slightly softer frosting, but will not give the
mild flour taste that you may get if you use the ¼ cup flour.

CREAMY PEANUT BUTTER FROSTING

1 pound (16 ounces) firm
    silken tofu
1 cup powdered sugar
¾ cup creamy natural peanut
    butter
¼ cup unbleached white flour or
    2 teaspoons xanthan gum*

- Place tofu in food processor and whip until smooth,
  scraping down sides several times. Add sugar and
  peanut butter and process.
- Add flour or xanthan gum and mix.
- If possible, make ahead and refrigerate overnight so
  frosting can set.

Recommended for:
  Nuts about Chocolate Cake, p. 43
  Mocha Goober Cake, p. 45

PER SERVING: 151 calories, 9g fat (2g
saturated), 15g carbohydrate, 1g dietary
fiber, <1g sugar, 5g protein, 0mg
cholesterol, 76mg sodium, 135mg
potassium. Calories from fat: 47 percent.

*Xanthan gum will produce a slightly softer frosting, but will not give the
mild flour taste that you may get if you use the ¼ cup flour.

FLUFFY ORANGE FROSTING

*1 pound (16 ounces) firm
    silken tofu
1 cup powdered sugar
2 teaspoons orange extract
¼ cup unbleached white flour or
    2 teaspoons xanthan gum**

- Place tofu in food processor and whip until smooth, scraping down sides several times. Add sugar and orange extract and process. Add flour or xanthan gum and mix.
- If possible, make ahead and refrigerate overnight so frosting can set.

Recommended for:
    Citrus Orange Cake, p. 48
    Cherry Vanilla Dream, p. 76

PER SERVING: 58 calories, <1g fat (<.1g saturated), 12g carbohydrate, <.1g dietary fiber, <1g sugar, 1g protein, 0mg cholesterol, <1mg sodium, 28mg potassium. Calories from fat: 6 percent.

*Xanthan gum will produce a slightly softer frosting, but will not give the mild flour taste that you get if you use the ¼ cup flour.

LIGHT RASPBERRY FROSTING

*1 pound (16 ounces) firm
    silken tofu
1 cup powdered sugar
¼ cup raspberry jam
¼ cup unbleached white flour or
    2 teaspoons xanthan gum**

- Place tofu in food processor and whip until smooth, scraping down sides several times. Add sugar and raspberry jam and process. Add flour or xanthan gum and mix.
- If possible, make ahead and refrigerate overnight so frosting can set.

Recommended for:
    Mellow Yellow Cake, p. 47
    Double Chocolate Delight, p. 74

PER SERVING: 72 calories, <1g fat (<.1g saturated), 17g carbohydrate, <1g dietary fiber, <1g sugar, 1g protein, 0mg cholesterol, 3mg sodium, 32mg potassium. Calories from fat: 5 percent.

*Xanthan gum will produce a slightly softer frosting, but will not give the mild flour taste that you may get if you use the ¼ cup flour.

WHIPPED LEMON FROSTING

1 pound (16 ounces) firm
   silken tofu
1 cup powdered sugar
2 teaspoons lemon extract
¼ teaspoon tumeric
   (for color only)

- Place tofu in food processor and whip until smooth, scraping down sides several times. Add sugar. lemon extract, and tumeric and process.
- If possible, make ahead and refrigerate overnight so frosting can set.

Recommended for:
   Mellow Yellow Cake, p. 47
   Lemon Times Two Cake, p. 65

PER SERVING: 48 calories, <1g fat (<.1g saturated), 10g carbohydrate, <1g dietary fiber, <1g sugar, <1g protein, 0mg cholesterol, <1mg sodium, 26mg potassium. Calories from fat: 6 percent.

TOASTED COCONUT PECAN FROSTING

12 ounces soy cream cheese
1½ teaspoons tahini
1½ cups powdered sugar
1½ teaspoons vanilla
¼ cup unbleached flour
¾ cup toasted coconut (broil
   unsweetened coconut until
   golden brown)
1 cup chopped pecans

- *To toast coconut:* Line cookie sheet with aluminum foil and coat with nonstick cooking spray. Spread coconut in a thin layer on baking sheet and place under broiler. Stir as coconut begins to brown. Remove from oven immediately when golden brown.
- In a food processor, combine the soy cream cheese and tahini and puree until smooth. Add powdered sugar and process.
- Stir toasted coconut and pecans into the frosting by hand.

Recommended for:
   Mellow Yellow Cake, p. 47
   Toasted Coconut Pecan Cake, p. 50
   Double Chocolate Delight, p. 74

PER SERVING: 182 calories, 11g fat (2g saturated), 19g carbohydrate, 1g dietary fiber, <1g sugar, 2g protein, 0mg cholesterol, 49mg sodium, 57mg potassium. Calories from fat: 39 percent.

WHIPPED COCONUT CREAM FROSTING

1 pound (16 ounces) firm
    silken tofu
1 cup powdered sugar
2 teaspoons coconut extract
¾ cup shredded unsweetened
    coconut

- Place tofu in food processor and whip until smooth, scraping down sides several times. Add sugar and coconut extract and process. Stir in coconut by hand, reserving about 2 tablespoons for a garnish.
- If possible, make ahead and refrigerate overnight so frosting can set.

Recommended for:
Mellow Yellow Cake, p. 47
Tropical Mango Cake, p. 52

PER SERVING: 89 calories, 4g fat (4g saturated), 12g carbohydrate, 1g dietary fiber, <1g sugar, 1g protein, 0mg cholesterol, 3mg sodium, 59mg potassium. Calories from fat: 41 percent.

COCONUT CREAM CHEESE FROSTING

6 ounces firm silken tofu
12 ounces soy cream cheese
1 cup powdered sugar
1 teaspoon coconut extract
½ cup unsweetened coconut
¼ cup unbleached flour or 2
    teaspoons xanthan gum*
    (optional for thickening)

- Place all frosting ingredients except coconut in food processor and process until smooth. Stir in coconut by hand.
- If possible, make ahead and refrigerate overnight so frosting can set.

Recommended for:
Tropical Fruit Cake, p. 58
White on White Tropical Cake, p. 70

PER SERVING: 86 calories, 4g fat (1g saturated), 13g carbohydrate, <1g dietary fiber, <1g sugar, <1g protein, 0mg cholesterol, 49mg sodium, 11mg potassium. Calories from fat: 7 percent.

*Xanthan gum will produce a slightly softer frosting, but will not give the mild flour taste that you may get if you use the ¼ cup flour.

MEGA-COCONUT CREAM CHEESE FROSTING

9 ounces (¾ box) firm
   silken tofu
16 ounces (2 containers) soy
   cream cheese
1½ cups powdered sugar
1½ teaspoons coconut extract
1 cup unsweetened coconut
¼ cup unbleached flour or 2
   teaspoons xanthan gum*
   (optional for thickening)

- Place tofu in food processor and whip until smooth, scraping down sides several times.
- Add cream cheese and sugar and process. Add coconut extract and flour or xanthan gum and process until combined. Stir in coconut by hand.
- If possible, make ahead and refrigerate overnight so frosting can set.

Recommended for:
   Mellow Yellow Cake, p. 47
   Coconut-Covered Delight, p. 81

PER SERVING: 127 calories, 6g fat (2g saturated), 18g carbohydrate, <1g dietary fiber, <1g sugar, 1g protein, 0mg cholesterol, 66mg sodium, 30mg potassium. Calories from fat: 11 percent.

*Xanthan gum will produce a slightly softer frosting, but will not give the mild flour taste that you may get if you use the flour.

CREAM CHEESE FROSTING

12 ounces firm silken tofu
8 ounces soy cream cheese
1 cup powdered sugar
1 teaspoon vanilla

- Place all ingredients in food processor and process until smooth.
- If possible, make ahead and refrigerate overnight so frosting can set.

Recommended for:
   You Can't Catch Me I'm the Gingerbread . . . Cake,
      p. 53
   Hold the Wheat Carrot Cake, p. 54

PER SERVING: 47 calories, <1g fat (.1g saturated), 10g carbohydrate, <.1g dietary fiber, <1g sugar, <1g protein, 0mg cholesterol, 4mg sodium, 19mg potassium. Calories from fat: 5 percent.

SOY CREAM CHEESE GLAZE

4 ounces soy cream cheese (such
    as Tofutti, which has no
    casein)
½ cup maple syrup
½ teaspoon vanilla

- Blend all ingredients together in a food processor until smooth.

Recommended for:
    Hold the Wheat Carrot Cake, p. 54
    Applesauce Applause Cake, p. 56
    Cinn-sational Apple Cake, p. 66
    "P" is for Pumpkin Cake, p. 67
    Rootin' Tootin' Raisin Spice Cake, p. 84

PER SERVING: 36 calories, <1g fat
(<.1g saturated), 9g carbohydrate, 0g
dietary fiber, 8g sugar, <.1g protein,
0mg cholesterol, 3mg sodium, 27mg
potassium. Calories from fat: 0 percent.

MAPLE COCOA FROSTING

½ cup maple syrup
1 cup cocoa
⅓ cup whipped tofu

- Place tofu in food processor and blend until smooth.
- Add maple syrup and cocoa and continue blending until mixture is smooth and creamy.

Recommended for:
    Death by Chocolate Brownies, p. 30
    Nuts about Chocolate Cake, p. 43
    Bold Banana Cake, p. 55
    Double Chocolate Delight, p. 74

PER SERVING: 51 calories, 1g fat (<1g
saturated), 13g carbohydrate, 2g dietary
fiber, 8g sugar, 1g protein, 0mg
cholesterol, 3mg sodium, 137mg
potassium. Calories from fat: 16 percent.

WHIPPED CREAM CHEESE FROSTING

6 ounces firm silken tofu
12 ounces soy cream cheese
1 cup powdered sugar
1 teaspoon vanilla
¼ cup unbleached white flour or
  2 teaspoons xanthan gum*
  (optional for thickening)

- Place all frosting ingredients in food processor and process until smooth.
- If possible, make ahead and refrigerate overnight so frosting can set.

Recommended for:
  Applesauce Applause Cake, p. 56
  Orange Creamsicle Cake, p. 57
  Granny's Cranberry Cake, p. 59
  Cherry Vanilla Dream, p. 76
  Ten-Carat Gold Cake, p. 78

PER SERVING: 78 calories, 3g fat (<1g saturated), 12g carbohydrate, <.1g dietary fiber, <.1g sugar, <1g protein, 0mg cholesterol, 48mg sodium, 4mg potassium. Calories from fat: 0 percent.

*Xanthan gum will produce a slightly softer frosting, but will not give the mild flour taste that you might get if you use the ¼ cup flour.

CHOCOLATE DECORATIVE TOPPING

6 ounce (½ box) firm
  silken tofu
4 ounces vegan cream cheese
  (such as Tofutti, which has
  no casein)
1 cup powdered sugar
2 tablespoons unbleached
  white flour
½ cup vegan chocolate chips,
  melted (using microwave or
  double boiler)

- Place tofu and cream cheese in food processor and process until smooth and creamy. Add sugar and flour and process until combined. Add melted chocolate chips and process until smooth and creamy.
- Refrigerate overnight.

Recommended as a garnish for:
  Nuts about Chocolate Cake, p. 43
  Chocolate-Covered Mint, p. 60
  Richer than Fort Knox Cake, p. 68
  German Chocolate Cake, p. 71

PER SERVING: 78 calories, 2g fat (1g saturated), 15g carbohydrate, <1g dietary fiber, <.1g sugar, <1g protein, 0mg cholesterol, 2mg sodium, 2mg potassium. Calories from fat: 21 percent.

German Chocolate Coconut-Pecan Frosting

1 cup coconut milk
1 cup brown sugar
2 teaspoons flax powder
½ cup water
⅓ cup canola oil
1½ tablespoons arrowroot
¼ cup water
1 cup chopped pecans
1⅓ cups unsweetened shredded
   coconut
1 teaspoon vanilla
½ teaspoon salt

PER SERVING: 202 calories, 13g fat (6g saturated), 22g carbohydrate, 2g dietary fiber, <1g sugar, 2g protein, 0mg cholesterol, 23mg sodium, 167mg potassium. Calories from fat: 55 percent.

- Heat coconut milk, sugar, and oil over medium heat until it is steaming. In a small cup, mix flax powder and ½ cup water. Add to coconut milk mixture.
- In another small cup, mix arrowroot and ¼ cup water. Add to coconut milk mixture and heat until thickened (do not boil—mixture will thicken more as it cools).
- Stir in pecans, coconut, vanilla, and salt. Allow to cool completely.

Recommended for:
 Nuts about Chocolate Cake (use ½ recipe), p. 43
 Mellow Yellow Cake, p. 47
 German Chocolate Cake, p. 71

Fluffy Mint Frosting

1 pound (16 ounces) firm
   silken tofu
1 cup powdered sugar
2 teaspoons peppermint extract
¼ cup unbleached white flour or
   2 teaspoons xanthan gum*
   (optional for thickening)

PER SERVING: 58 calories, <1g fat (<.1g saturated), 12g carbohydrate, <1g dietary fiber, <1g sugar, <1g protein, 0mg cholesterol, <1mg sodium, 28mg potassium. Calories from fat: 6 percent.

- Place tofu in food processor and blend until smooth and creamy.
- Add powdered sugar, flour or xanthan gum, and peppermint extract and continue to blend.
- If possible, make ahead and refrigerate overnight so frosting can set.

Recommended for:
 Chocolate-Covered Mint, p. 60
 Mint Madness, p. 75

*Xanthan gum will produce a slightly softer frosting, but will not give the mild flour taste that you might get if you use the flour.

FUDGE ICE CREAM TOPPING

*T*HIS RICH FUDGE topping tastes great smothering a scoop of vanilla dairy-free dessert. If you want a real treat, try making I Can't Believe They're Not Sinful Brownies, page 29, and top a piece while it is still warm with a scoop of vanilla dairy-free dessert nestled under this delicious fudge topping. Being a vegan never tasted so good!

½ *cup cocoa*
¾ *cup maple syrup*
1 *teaspoon vanilla*

. . . .
MAKES ABOUT 1 CUP OF TOPPING
PREPARATION TIME: 5 minutes
. . . .

- Place all ingredients in a bowl and mix until smooth and creamy.
- Heat topping on low heat in microwave if you want a hot fudge topping.

PER SERVING: 182 calories, 2g fat (<1g saturated), 46g carbohydrate, 4g dietary fiber, 38g sugar, 2g protein, 0mg cholesterol, 8mg sodium, 286mg potassium. Calories from fat: 7 percent.

CARAMEL ICE CREAM TOPPING

*T*HIS GOOEY SWEET caramel-like topping tastes great on many of the non-dairy frozen desserts that are now available at most supermarkets and health food stores.

⅓ cup corn syrup
⅓ cup brown sugar
2 teaspoons vanilla
3 tablespoons soy milk
¼ teaspoon salt

. . . .

MAKES 10 SERVINGS
PREPARATION TIME:
    CARAMEL TOPPING:
    10 minutes
. . . .

- Place corn syrup and brown sugar in small pan and heat to boiling.
- Simmer until mixture reaches soft ball stage or 240°F on a candy thermometer.
- Remove from heat and stir in soy milk, vanilla, and salt. Allow to cool to room temperature before serving.

PER SERVING: 95 calories, <1g fat (<1g saturated), 23g carbohydrate, <1g dietary fiber, <1g protein, 0mg cholesterol, 24mg sodium, 47mg potassium. Calories from fat: 1 percent.

STANDARD VEGAN SINGLE PIE CRUST

1¼ cups unbleached flour
¼ cup canola oil or coconut oil
    if desired
¼ teaspoon sea salt
½ cup + 2 tablespoons water
    or apple juice (cold)

- Put flour and salt for crust in small bowl. Add canola oil and stir into flour until oil is distributed in pea-sized pieces. (If using the coconut oil, which is solid at room temperature like vegetable shortening, cut into flour with 2 knives until oil is pea-sized or smaller). Add *cold* water (or juice) and mix just until mixture forms a ball (add more water if necessary). Refrigerate for 10 minutes.
- Place ball of dough on a piece of floured wax paper. Sprinkle ball of dough with a little more flour. Place another piece of wax paper on top of ball of dough and push down to flatten. Using a rolling pin, roll dough as thin as possible between the two sheets of paper.
- Remove the top sheet of paper carefully. Flip the pie crust onto the pie plate. Carefully remove the last piece of wax paper. Fit crust into pie plate, allowing edges to hang over the edge. Cut edges of dough with sharp knife. Crimp edges of crust with fingers and prick bottom of crust with a fork.

PER SERVING: 110 calories, 6g fat (<1g saturated), 13g carbohydrate, <1g dietary fiber, 2g protein, 0mg cholesterol, 8mg sodium, 31mg potassium. Calories from fat: 44 percent.

STANDARD VEGAN DOUBLE PIE CRUST

2½ cups unbleached flour
½ cup canola oil or coconut oil
   if desired
½ teaspoon sea salt
1¼ cups water or apple
   juice (cold)

- Put flour and salt for crust in small bowl. Add canola oil and stir into flour until oil is distributed in pea-sized pieces. (If using the coconut oil, which is solid at room temperature like vegetable shortening, cut oil into flour with 2 knives until oil is pea-sized or smaller). Add *cold* water (or juice). Mix just until mixture forms a ball (add more water if necessary). Refrigerate for 10 minutes.
- Place ball of dough on a piece of floured wax paper. Sprinkle ball of dough with a little more flour. Place another piece of wax paper on top of ball of dough and push down to flatten. Using a rolling pin, roll dough as thin as possible between the two sheets of paper.
- Remove the top sheet of paper carefully. Flip the pie crust onto the pie plate. Carefully remove the last piece of wax paper. Fit crust into pie plate allowing edges to hang over the edge. Set pie plate with rolled dough in it in refrigerator until ready to fill.
- Roll out other half of crust between floured wax paper and set aside. If possible, place on cookie sheet and put in refrigerator until ready to use.

PER SERVING: 220 calories, 12g fat (<1g saturated), 26g carbohydrate, <1g dietary fiber, 4g protein, 0mg cholesterol, 16mg sodium, 62mg potassium. Calories from fat: 44 percent.

TART CRUST

1½ cups whole-wheat
    pastry flour
¼ cup granulated sweetener
¼ cup canola oil
1 tablespoon maple syrup
¼ cup + 2 tablespoons water

- In a small bowl, stir together flour, granulated sweetener, and oil until it resembles coarse crumbs. Slowly stir in water and stir until mixture forms a ball in the bowl.
- Place flour on a piece of wax paper. Put the ball of dough onto the floured wax paper and roll in flour to coat. Put another piece of wax paper on top of ball of dough. Roll dough between two pieces of wax paper until very thin. Remove the top piece of wax paper.
- Flip the dough onto tart pan. Press the dough around the bottom and up the sides of the pan. Cut to fit at the top of pan. Place pie weights in bottom of pan and bake for 15 minutes. (If pie crust is not weighted with commercial pie weights or dried beans placed on foil, the crust will bubble and shrink during baking.)
- Combine maple syrup and water in a small bowl. After 15 minutes, brush the maple/water mixture over the crust and bake 5 more minutes to glaze. Set on cooling rack. Cool in pan for 10 minutes. Remove from pan and allow to cool completely before assembling.

PER SERVING: 111 calories, 5g fat (<1g saturated), 15g carbohydrate, <1g dietary fiber, 1g sugar, 2g protein, 0mg cholesterol, <1mg sodium, 20mg potassium. Calories from fat: 37 percent.

CONVERSION TABLES FOR U.S. TO METRIC COOKING

THE RECIPES IN this book use U.S. measurements and oven temperatures. The following tables will help you to convert if you use another standard of measure.

OVEN TEMPERATURES

Fahrenheit degrees	Celsius degrees	Gas Mark
250	120	½
275	140	1
300	150	2
325	160	3
350	180	4
375	190	5
400	200	6
425	220	7
450	230	8

LIQUID AND DRY MEASURES

U.S.	Metric
¼ teaspoon	1.25 milliliters
½ teaspoon	2.5 milliliters
1 teaspoon	5 milliliters
1 tablespoon (3 teaspoons)	15 milliliters
1 fluid ounce (2 tablespoons)	30 milliliters
¼ cup	59 milliliters
⅓ cup	79 milliliters
1 cup	237 milliliters
1 pint (2 cups)	473 milliliters
1 quart (4 cups)	950 milliliters
1 gallon (4 quarts)	3.8 liters

WEIGHT MEASURES

U.S.	Metric
1 ounce	28 grams
1 pound	454 grams

$\mathcal{A}$cknowledgments

I'D LIKE TO thank my family, friends, co-workers, and neighbors who were faithful and honest taste testers. Without all of you, this book could never have been completed.

INDEX

A

agar, 11
Ain't No Chocolate Here Smoothie, 192
All-American Apple Crumb Pie, 106
apples
    All-American Apple Crumb Pie, 106
    Apple Dumplings, 141
    Applesauce Applause Cake, 56
    Caramel Apple Streusel Cheesecake, 144–45
    Cinn-sational Apple Cake, 66
    Fall Harvest Pie, 112
    Festive Apple Cranberry Pie, 109
    Fruit 'n' Nut Bread, 87
    Mom's Apple Crisp, 105
    Newfangled Mince Pie, 111
    State Fair Pear Pie, 113
arrowroot flour, 11
Award-Winning Peach Crumb Pie, 107

B

Bahama Mama Pudding, 172
bananas, 5
    Ain't No Chocolate Here Smoothie, 192
    Banana Split Cake, 63
    Bananas in Pajamas Smoothie, 194
    Berry Delicious Smoothie, 196
    Bold Banana Cake, 55
    Going Nuts for Banana Bread, 86
    Green (I Swear to God It's Good!) Smoothie, 195
    Midnight Monkey Cream Pie, 126
    Monkey's Choice Cream Pie, 123
    Pink Passion Smoothie, 196

    That's One Nutty Banana!, 124–25
barley flour, 11
Beats Singin' the Blues Pie, 115
Berry Best Pudding, The, 173
Berry Chip Cream Pie, 127
Berry Delicious Smoothie, 196
beverages
    See also smoothies
    Rich Hot Cocoa, 198
Black and White Cream Pie, 122
Black Forest Cheesecake, 162–63
blackberries
    Berry Delicious Smoothie, 196
blender, 16
blueberries
    Beats Singin' the Blues Pie, 115
    Berry Delicious Smoothie, 196
    Fruity Artistry, 136
    Patriotic Cream Pie, 132
    Queen of Tarts, The, 134
    Tangy Tasty Tart, 135
Bold Banana Cake, 55
Boston Cream-Filled Donuts, 184–85
breads
    Fruit 'n' Nut Bread, 87
    Going Nuts for Banana Bread, 86
brownies
    Death by Chocolate Brownies, 30
    Heavenly Brownie Torte, 32–33
    I Can't Believe They're Not Sinful Brownies, 29
    Peanut Butter Twist Brownies, 34
    Swirly Berry Brownies, 31
butter, 4, 9

C

cakes
  apple
    Applesauce Applause Cake, 56
    Cinn-sational Apple Cake, 66
  banana
    Banana Split Cake, 63
    Bold Banana Cake, 55
  carrot
    Hold the Wheat Carrot Cake, 54
    Ten-Carat Gold Cake, 78
  cherry
    Cherry, Cherry Not Contrary Cake, 38–39
    Cherry + Chocolate = Delicious Cake, 85
    Cherry Vanilla Dream, 76
    Triple Cherry Treat, 77
  chocolate
    Cherry, Cherry Not Contrary Cake, 38
    Cherry + Chocolate = Delicious Cake, 85
    Chocolate-Covered Gold, 46
    Chocolate-Covered Mint, 60
    Chocolate Raspberry Celebration Loaf, 40–41
    Coconut-Covered Delight, 81
    Double Chocolate Delight, 74
    German Chocolate Cake, 71
    Mint Madness, 75
    Mocha Goober Cake, 45
    Mocha Madness Cake, 42
    Nuts about Chocolate Cake, 43
    Richer than Fort Knox Cake, 68–69
  coconut
    Coconut-Covered Delight, 81
    Toasted Coconut Pecan Cake, 50–51
    White on White Tropical Cake, 70
  Cranberry Cake, Granny's, 59
  Crumb Cake, My Grandmother's, 61
  fruit
    Tropical Fruit Cake, 58
    Tropical Mango Cake, 52
  gingerbread
    You Can't Catch Me I'm the Gingerbread . . . Cake,
      53
  lemon
    Lemon Loaf, 36
    Lemon Times Two Cake, 65
  orange
    Citrus Orange Cake, 48–49
    Orange Creamsicle Cake, 57
    Orange You Glad It Has Chocolate Chips Cake, 79
  peanut butter
    Peanut Butter Kandy Kake, 82–83
    Peanut Butter Surprise, 72–73
  pineapple
    Oops, I Dropped My Cake, 62
  pound
    Just Loafing Around, 44
    Lemon Loaf, 36
  Pumpkin Cake, "P" Is for, 67
  Shortcake, Long on Flavor, 64
  Spice Cake, Rootin' Tootin', 84
  Sugar Cake, Raised, 80
  yellow
    Funny Cake, 117
    Mellow Yellow Cake, 47
candies
  Chocolate Coconut Nests, 190
  Coconut Cream Eggs, 187
  Melt in Your Mouth Fudge, 188
  Peanut Butter Balls, 186
  Raisin and Peanut Clusters, 189

caramel
  Caramel Apple Streusel Cheesecake, 144–45
  Caramel Ice Cream Topping, 215
  Caramel Sauce, 32
  Chocolate Caramel Boston Cream Pie, 98–99
Caribbean Cruise Smoothie, 197
carob, 11
  Ain't No Chocolate Here Smoothie, 192
  Red Baron Smoothie, 197
carrots, 5
  Hold the Wheat Carrot Cake, 54
  Ten-Carat Gold Cake, 78
cheesecakes
  Black Forest Cheesecake, 162–63
  Caramel Apple Streusel Cheesecake, 144–45
  Chocolate-Covered Cherry Cheesecake, 164–65
  Chocolate Tuxedo Cheesecake, 166
  Coconut Dream Cheesecake, 159
  I Dream of Lemon Cream Cheesecake, 150–51
  Inside-Out Peanut Butter Cup Cheesecake, 156–57
  Minty Chocolate Chip Cheesecake, 152–53
  New York-Style Cheesecake, 146–47
  Peanut Butter Chocolate Chip Cheesecake, 161
  Peanut Butter Cup Cheesecake, 158
  Pumpkin Pie Cheesecake, 154–55
  Swirled Raspberry Cheesecake, 149
  Three Cheers for Cherry Cheesecake, 148
  Tropical Chocolate Chip Cheesecake, 160
cherries
  Black Forest Cheesecake, 162–63
  Cherry, Cherry Not Contrary Cake, 38–39
  Cherry + Chocolate = Delicious Cake, 85
  Cherry Filling, 201
  Cherry Topping, 201
  Cherry Vanilla Dream, 76
  Chocolate-Covered Cherry Cheesecake, 164–65
  Fruity Artistry, 136
  Red Baron Smoothie, 197
  Three Cheers for Cherry Cheesecake, 148
  Triple Cherry Treat, 77
  Washington's Cherry Crumb Pie, 110
  Whipped Cherry Topping, 202
chickpea flour, 12, 15
chocolate
  brownies
    Death by Chocolate Brownies, 30
    Heavenly Brownie Torte, 32–33
    I Can't Believe They're Not Sinful Brownies, 29
    Peanut Butter Twist Brownies, 34
    Swirly Berry Brownies, 31
  cakes
    Cherry, Cherry Not Contrary Cake, 38–39
    Cherry + Chocolate = Delicious Cake, 85
    Chocolate-Covered Gold, 46
    Chocolate-Covered Mint, 60
    Chocolate Raspberry Celebration Loaf, 40–41
    Coconut-Covered Delight, 81
    Double Chocolate Delight, 74
    German Chocolate Cake, 71
    Granny's Cranberry Cake, 59
    Mint Madness, 75
    Mocha Goober Cake, 45
    Mocha Madness Cake, 42
    Nuts about Chocolate Cake, 43
    Orange You Glad It Has Chocolate Chips Cake, 79
    Peanut Butter Kandy Kake, 82–83
    Peanut Butter Surprise, 72–73
    Richer than Fort Knox Cake, 68–69
    Triple Cherry Treat, 77
  candies

Chocolate Coconut Nests, 190
Coconut Cream Eggs, 187
Melt in Your Mouth Fudge, 188
Peanut Butter Balls, 186
Raisin and Peanut Clusters, 189
cheesecakes
    Black Forest Cheesecake, 162–63
    Chocolate-Covered Cherry Cheesecake, 164–65
    Chocolate Tuxedo Cheesecake, 166
    Inside-Out Peanut Butter Cup Cheesecake, 156–57
    Minty Chocolate Chip Cheesecake, 152–53
    Peanut Butter Chocolate Chip Cheesecake, 161
    Peanut Butter Cup Cheesecake, 158
    Tropical Chocolate Chip Cheesecake, 160
Cocoa, Rich Hot, 198
cookies
    Chocolate-Coconut Crisps, 28
    Home-Style Chocolate Chip Cookies, 24
Donuts, Boston Cream-Filled, 184–85
frostings/toppings
    Chocolate Cream Cheese Frosting, 203
    Chocolate Decorative Topping, 212
    Chocolate Glaze Topping, 90
    Fudge Ice Cream Topping, 214
    German Chocolate Coconut-Pecan Frosting, 213
    Maple Cocoa Frosting, 211
    Standard Chocolate Frosting, 205
    Whipped Chocolate Frosting, 202
pies
    Berry Chip Cream Pie, 127
    Black and White Cream Pie, 122
    Chocolate Caramel Boston Cream Pie, 98–99
    Chocolate Peanut Butter Boston Cream Pie, 100
    Chocolate Raspberry Boston Cream Pie, 91
    Funny Cake, 117
    Hint of Mint Cream Pie, A, 120
    I Love Chocolate Cream Pie, 104
    Midnight Monkey Cream Pie, 126
    Peanut Butter Boston Cream Pie, 94–95
    Tantalizing Truffle Pie, 142
    Traditional Boston Cream Pie, 92–93
    Triple-Chocolate Boston Cream Pie, 96–97
    Wetzel's Pretzel Pie, 102–3
    You Got Your Chocolate in My Peanut Butter
        Cream Pie, 121
puddings
    Chocolate Lover's Pudding, 169
    Orange Chocolate Chip Pudding, 175
Syrup, Vegan Chocolate, 203
cholesterol, 3–7
Cinn-sational Apple Cake, 66
Citrus Orange Cake, 48–49
Clouds of Strawberry Pie, 129
Cocoa, Rich Hot, 198
coconut
    cakes
        Coconut-Covered Delight, 81
        Ten-Carat Gold Cake, 78
        Toasted Coconut Pecan Cake, 50–51
        Tropical Fruit Cake, 58
        White on White Tropical Cake, 70
    candies
        Chocolate Coconut Nests, 190
        Coconut Cream Eggs, 187
    cheesecakes
        Coconut Dream Cheesecake, 159
        Tropical Chocolate Chip Cheesecake, 160
    cookies
        Chocolate-Coconut Crisps, 28
    frostings

    Coconut Cream Cheese Frosting, 209
    German Chocolate Coconut-Pecan Frosting, 213
    Mega-Coconut Cream Cheese Frosting, 210
    Toasted Coconut Pecan Frosting, 208
    Whipped Coconut Cream Frosting, 209
    pies
        I Love Chocolate Cream Pie, 104
        Island Breezes Cream Pie, 118
        Piña Colada Cream Pie, 131
        Strawberry Surprise Cream Pie, 130
    Pudding, Bahama Mama, 172
    Smoothie, Caribbean Cruise, 197
    tarts
        Taste of the Tropics, A, 137
coconut oil, 7, 11–12, 14
coffee
    Coffee Frosting, 206
    Mocha Goober Cake, 45
    Mocha Madness Cake, 42
Confetti Fruit Pie, 114
conversion tables, 219–20
cookies
    Chocolate-Coconut Crisps, 28
    Home-Style Chocolate Chip Cookies, 24
    Little Oaties, 25
    Mom's Warm Peanut Butter Cookies, 26
    Snappy Ginger Cookies, 23
    Snickerdoodles, 27
    Vanilla Spritz Cookies, 22
cranberries
    Festive Apple Cranberry Pie, 109
    Fruit 'n' Nut Bread, 87
    Granny's Cranberry Cake, 59
    State Fair Pear Pie, 113
Cream Cheese Frosting, 210
Creamy Peanut Butter Frosting, 206
Creamy Rice Pudding, 174

D
Death by Chocolate Brownies, 30
donuts
    Boston Cream-Filled Donuts, 184–85
    Fasnachts, 180–81
    Jelly-Filled Donuts, 182–83
Double Chocolate Delight, 74
Dumplings, Apple, 141

E
eggs, 4, 10
electric mixer, 16
Ener-G Egg Replacer, 12, 15
equipment, kitchen, 16

F
Fall Harvest Pie, 112
famous vegans, 18–20
Fasnachts, 180–81
fats, 4
    amount needed of, 7–8
    types of, 6–7
Festive Apple Cranberry Pie, 109
Filling, Cherry, 201
flax oil, 4
flax powder, 5, 10, 12, 14
Fluffy Mint Frosting, 213
Fluffy Orange Frosting, 207
food processors, 16
frostings
    See also toppings
    chocolate

Chocolate Cream Cheese Frosting, 203
German Chocolate Coconut-Pecan Frosting, 213
Maple Cocoa Frosting, 211
Standard Chocolate Frosting, 205
Whipped Chocolate Frosting, 202
coconut
    Coconut Cream Cheese Frosting, 209
    German Chocolate Coconut-Pecan Frosting, 213
    Mega-Coconut Cream Cheese Frosting, 210
    Toasted Coconut Pecan Frosting, 208
    Whipped Coconut Cream Frosting, 209
    Coffee Frosting, 206
cream cheese
    Chocolate Cream Cheese Frosting, 203
    Cream Cheese Frosting, 210
    Mega-Coconut Cream Cheese Frosting, 210
    Whipped Cream Cheese Frosting, 212
Lemon Frosting, Whipped, 208
Mint Frosting, Fluffy, 213
Orange Frosting, Fluffy, 207
Peanut Butter Frosting, Creamy, 206
Raspberry Frosting, Light, 207
Fruit 'n' Nut Bread, 87
fruit tarts. *See* tarts
fruits
    See also specific fruits
    Confetti Fruit Pie, 114
    Fruit 'n' Nut Bread, 87
    Fruity Artistry, 136
    Tropical Fruit Cake, 58
fudge
    Fudge Ice Cream Topping, 214
    Melt in Your Mouth Fudge, 188
Funny Cake, 117

G
garbanzo bean flour, 12, 15
German Chocolate Cake, 71
German Chocolate Coconut-Pecan Frosting, 213
ginger
    Snappy Ginger Cookies, 23
    You Can't Catch Me I'm the Gingerbread . . .. Cake, 53
glazes. *See* toppings
Glueck, Charles, 4
Going Nuts for Banana Bread, 86
Granny's Cranberry Cake, 59
Green (I Swear to God It's Good!) Smoothie, 195
Guiltless Pudding, 170

H
handheld blender, 16
health benefits, of vegan desserts, 2–4
heart disease, 4
Heavenly Brownie Torte, 32–33
Hint of Mint Cream Pie, A, 120
Hold the Wheat Carrot Cake, 54
Home-Style Chocolate Chip Cookies, 24
hydrogenated fats, 4, 7

I
I Can't Believe They're Not Sinful Brownies, 29
I Dream of Lemon Cream Cheesecake, 150–51
I Love Chocolate Cream Pie, 104
ice cream
    toppings
        Caramel Ice Cream Topping, 215
        Fudge Ice Cream Topping, 214
    Wetzel's Pretzel Pie, 102–3
icings. *See* frostings

I'm Nuts for Peanut Butter Tart, 138–39
ingredients
    buying vegan, 10–11
    organic, 10–11
    replacing, with vegan, 9–10
    sources for vegan, 14–16
    staple, 11–14
Inside-Out Peanut Butter Cup Cheesecake, 156–57
Island Breezes Cream Pie, 118

J
Jelly-Filled Donuts, 182–83
Just Loafing Around, 44
Just Peekin' Pie, 140

K
kitchen equipment, 16
kiwis
    Fruity Artistry, 136
    Queen of Tarts, The, 134
    Tangy Tasty Tart, 135
    Taste of the Tropics, A, 137

L
lemon
    I Dream of Lemon Cream Cheesecake, 150–51
    Lemon Glaze, 37
    Lemon Loaf, 36
    Lemon Times Two Cake, 65
    Pucker-Up Cream Pie, 128
    Tangy Lemon Pudding, 176
    Tangy Tasty Tart, 135
    Whipped Lemon Frosting, 208
Light Raspberry Frosting, 207
lignans, 12
Little Oaties, 25
Long on Flavor Shortcake, 64

M
Mango Cake, Tropical, 52
Maple Cocoa Frosting, 211
measurement conversion tables, 220
Mega-Coconut Cream Cheese Frosting, 210
Mellow Yellow Cake, 47
Melt in Your Mouth Fudge, 188
metric conversion tables, 219–20
Midnight Monkey Cream Pie, 126
milk, 3, 5, 9
    soy, 9, 10, 13
mint
    Chocolate-Covered Mint, 60
    Fluffy Mint Frosting, 213
    Hint of Mint Cream Pie, A, 120
    Mint Madness, 75
    Minty Chocolate Chip Cheesecake, 152–53
    Peppermint Patty Cream Pie, 119
Mocha Goober Cake, 45
Mocha Madness Cake, 42
Mom's Apple Crisp, 105
Mom's Warm Peanut Butter Cookies, 26
Monkey's Choice Cream Pie, 123
monounsaturated fats, 4, 6
My Grandmother's Crumb Cake, 61

N
New York-Style Cheesecake, 146–47
Newfangled Mince Pie, 111
nutritional comparisons, 8–9
nuts
    German Chocolate Coconut-Pecan Frosting, 213

Going Nuts for Banana Bread, 86
Just Peekin' Pie, 140
Nuts about Chocolate Cake, 43
State Fair Pear Pie, 113
Toasted Coconut Pecan Cake, 50–51
Toasted Coconut Pecan Frosting, 208
Wetzel's Pretzel Pie, 102–3

O

oats
   Little Oaties, 25
omega-3 fatty acids, 4
omega-3 oils, 6
Oops, I Dropped My Cake, 62
orange
   Citrus Orange Cake, 48–49
   Fluffy Orange Frosting, 207
   Orange Chocolate Chip Pudding, 175
   Orange Creamsicle Cake, 57
   Orange Creamsicle Smoothie, 193
   Orange You Glad It Has Chocolate Chips Cake, 79
organic ingredients, 10–11

P

"P" Is for Pumpkin Cake, 67
papaya
   Taste of the Tropics, A, 137
parchment paper, 16
partially hydrogenated oil, 7
Patriotic Cream Pie, 132
peaches
   Award-Winning Peach Crumb Pie, 107
   Confetti Fruit Pie, 114
peanut butter
   Brownies, Peanut Butter Twist, 34
   cakes
      Mocha Goober Cake, 45
      Peanut Butter Kandy Kake, 82–83
      Peanut Butter Surprise, 72–73
   candies
      Peanut Butter Balls, 186
   cheesecakes
      Inside-Out Peanut Butter Cup Cheesecake, 156–57
      Peanut Butter Chocolate Chip Cheesecake, 161
      Peanut Butter Cup Cheesecake, 158
   Cookies, Mom's Warm Peanut Butter, 26
   Frosting, Creamy Peanut Butter, 206
   pies
      Chocolate Peanut Butter Boston Cream Pie, 100
      Peanut Butter Boston Cream Pie, 94–95
      Tantalizing Truffle Pie, 142
      That's One Nutty Banana!, 124–25
      You Got Your Chocolate in My Peanut Butter
         Cream Pie, 121
   Pudding, Peanut Butter and No Jelly, 171
   Tart, I'm Nuts for Peanut Butter, 138–39
peanuts
   Raisin and Peanut Clusters, 189
   Wetzel's Pretzel Pie, 102–3
Pear Pie, State Fair, 113
pecans
   German Chocolate Coconut-Pecan Frosting, 213
   Going Nuts for Banana Bread, 86
   Just Peekin' Pie, 140
   Nuts about Chocolate Cake, 43
   Toasted Coconut Pecan Cake, 50–51
   Toasted Coconut Pecan Frosting, 208
peppermint
   Chocolate-Covered Mint, 60
   Fluffy Mint Frosting, 213

Hint of Mint Cream Pie, A, 120
Mint Madness, 75
Minty Chocolate Chip Cheesecake, 152–53
Peppermint Patty Cream Pie, 119
pie crusts
   Standard Vegan Double Pie Crust, 217
   Standard Vegan Single Pie Crust, 216
   Tart Crust, 218
pie weights, 17
pies
   See also tarts
   apple
      All-American Apple Crumb Pie, 106
      Apple Dumplings, 141
      Fall Harvest Pie, 112
      Festive Apple Cranberry Pie, 109
      Mom's Apple Crisp, 105
      Newfangled Mince Pie, 111
   banana
      Midnight Monkey Cream Pie, 126
      Monkey's Choice Cream Pie, 123
      That's One Nutty Banana!, 124–25
   blueberry
      Beats Singin' the Blues Pie, 115
      Patriotic Cream Pie, 132
   Cherry Crumb Pie, Washington's, 110
   chocolate
      Black and White Cream Pie, 122
      Chocolate Caramel Boston Cream Pie, 98–99
      Chocolate Peanut Butter Boston Cream Pie, 100
      Chocolate Raspberry Boston Cream Pie, 91
      Funny Cake, 117
      I Love Chocolate Cream Pie, 104
      Tantalizing Truffle Pie, 142
      Traditional Boston Cream Pie, 96–97
      Wetzel's Pretzel Pie, 102–3
      You Got Your Chocolate in My Peanut Butter
         Cream Pie, 121
   coconut
      Island Breezes Cream Pie, 118
      Piña Colada Cream Pie, 131
   cranberry
      Fall Harvest Pie, 112
      Festive Apple Cranberry Pie, 109
   cream
      Berry Chip Cream Pie, 127
      Black and White Cream Pie, 122
      Chocolate Caramel Boston Cream Pie, 98–99
      Chocolate Peanut Butter Boston Cream Pie, 100
      Chocolate Raspberry Boston Cream Pie, 91
      Hint of Mint Cream Pie, A, 120
      I Love Chocolate Cream Pie, 104
      Island Breezes Cream Pie, 118
      Midnight Monkey Cream Pie, 126
      Monkey's Choice Cream Pie, 123
      Patriotic Cream Pie, 132
      Peanut Butter Boston Cream Pie, 94–95
      Peppermint Patty Cream Pie, 119
      Piña Colada Cream Pie, 131
      Pucker-Up Cream Pie, 128
      Strawberry Surprise Cream Pie, 130
      Traditional Boston Cream Pie, 92–93
      Triple-Chocolate Boston Cream Pie, 96–97
   Fruit Pie, Confetti, 114
   lemon
      Pucker-Up Cream Pie, 128
   Mince Pie, Newfangled, 111
   Peach Crumb Pie, Award-Winning, 107
   peanut butter
      Chocolate Peanut Butter Boston Cream Pie, 100

Peanut Butter Boston Cream Pie, 94–95
Tantalizing Truffle Pie, 142
You Got Your Chocolate in My Peanut Butter
Cream Pie, 121
Pear Pie, State Fair, 113
pecan
Just Peekin' Pie, 140
Pumpkin Pie, 116
Raisin Crumb Pie, Rave Review, 108
raspberry
Berry Chip Cream Pie, 127
Chocolate Raspberry Boston Cream Pie, 91
strawberry
Clouds of Strawberry Pie, 129
Strawberry Surprise Cream Pie, 130
Piña Colada Cream Pie, 131
pineapples
Banana Split Cake, 63
Caribbean Cruise Smoothie, 197
Oops, I Dropped My Cake, 62
Piña Colada Cream Pie, 131
Taste of the Tropics, A, 137
Pink Passion Smoothie, 196
polyunsaturated fats, 6
potatoes
Boston Cream-Filled Donuts, 184–85
Coconut Cream Eggs, 187
Fasnachts, 180–81
Jelly-Filled Donuts, 182–83
Raised Sugar Cake, 80
pound cakes
Just Loafing Around, 44
Lemon Loaf, 36
Pucker-Up Cream Pie, 128
puddings, 168
Bahama Mama Pudding, 172
Berry Best Pudding, The, 173
Chocolate Lover's Pudding, 169
Creamy Rice Pudding, 174
Guiltless Pudding, 170
Orange Chocolate Chip Pudding, 175
Peanut Butter and No Jelly Pudding, 171
Strawberry Fields Pudding, 177
Tangy Lemon Pudding, 176
pumpkin
Fruit 'n' Nut Bread, 87
"P" Is for Pumpkin Cake, 67
Peanut Butter Balls, 186
Pumpkin Pie, 116
Pumpkin Pie Cheesecake, 154–55
Pumpkin Whipped Topping, 205

Q
Queen of Tarts, The, 134

R
Raised Sugar Cake, 80
raisins
Creamy Rice Pudding, 174
Guiltless Pudding, 170
Newfangled Mince Pie, 111
Raisin and Peanut Clusters, 189
Rave Review Raisin Crumb Pie, 108
Rootin' Tootin' Raisin Spice Cake, 84
Ten-Carat Gold Cake, 78
raspberries
Berry Best Pudding, The, 173
Berry Chip Cream Pie, 127
Berry Delicious Smoothie, 196
Chocolate Raspberry Boston Cream Pie, 91

Chocolate Raspberry Celebration Loaf, 40–41
Confetti Fruit Pie, 114
Jelly-Filled Donuts, 182–83
Light Raspberry Frosting, 207
Mellow Yellow Cake, 47
Queen of Tarts, The, 134
Raspberry Sauce, 37
Swirled Raspberry Cheesecake, 149
Swirly Berry Brownies, 31
Tangy Tasty Tart, 135
Rave Review Raisin Crumb Pie, 108
recipes
nutritional comparisons of, 6–7
veganizing, 9–16
Red Baron Smoothie, 197
rice flour, 12, 15
Rich Hot Cocoa, 198
Richer than Fort Knox Cake, 68–69
Rootin' Tootin' Raisin Spice Cake, 84

S
saturated fats, 6–7
sauces
Caramel Sauce, 32
Raspberry Sauce, 37
sea salt, 12
smoothies
Ain't No Chocolate Here Smoothie, 192
Bananas in Pajamas Smoothie, 194
Berry Delicious Smoothie, 196
Caribbean Cruise Smoothie, 197
Green (I Swear to God It's Good!) Smoothie, 195
Orange Creamsicle Smoothie, 193
Pink Passion Smoothie, 196
Red Baron Smoothie, 197
Snappy Ginger Cookies, 23
Snickerdoodles, 27
soy butter spread, 12
soy cream cheese, 12–13
Soy Cream Cheese Glaze, 211
soy milk, 9, 10, 13
spelt flour, 13
Spock, Benjamin, 18
springform pan, 13
Standard Chocolate Frosting, 205
Standard Vegan Double Pie Crust, 217
Standard Vegan Single Pie Crust, 216
staple ingredients, 11–14
State Fair Pear Pie, 113
stevia, 13
stick blender, 16
strawberries
Clouds of Strawberry Pie, 129
Fruity Artistry, 136
Long on Flavor Shortcake, 64
Pink Passion Smoothie, 196
Queen of Tarts, The, 134
Strawberry Fields Pudding, 177
Strawberry Surprise Cream Pie, 130
Tropical Fruit Cake, 58
sucanat, 13, 16
sweet potatoes
Fall Harvest Pie, 112
Swirled Raspberry Cheesecake, 149
Swirly Berry Brownies, 31
Syrup, Vegan Chocolate, 203

T
tahini, 13
Tangy Lemon Pudding, 176

Tangy Tasty Tart, 135
Tantalizing Truffle Pie, 142
Tart Crust, 218
tarts, 133
   See also pies
   Fruity Artistry, 136
   I'm Nuts for Peanut Butter Tart, 138–39
   Queen of Tarts, The, 134
   Tangy Tasty Tart, 135
   Taste of the Tropics, A, 137
Taste of the Tropics, A, 137
temperature conversion table, 219
Ten-Carat Gold Cake, 78
That's One Nutty Banana!, 124–25
Three Cheers for Cherry Cheesecake, 148
Toasted Coconut Pecan Cake, 50–51
Toasted Coconut Pecan Frosting, 208
tofu, 13–14
   candies
      Coconut Cream Eggs, 187
   cheesecakes
      Black Forest Cheesecake, 162–63
      Caramel Apple Streusel Cheesecake, 144–45
      Chocolate-Covered Cherry Cheesecake, 164–65
      Chocolate Tuxedo Cheesecake, 166
      Coconut Dream Cheesecake, 159
      I Dream of Lemon Cream Cheesecake, 150–51
      Inside-Out Peanut Butter Cup Cheesecake, 156–57
      Minty Chocolate Chip Cheesecake, 152–53
      New York-Style Cheesecake, 146–47
      Peanut Butter Chocolate Chip Cheesecake, 161
      Peanut Butter Cup Cheesecake, 158
      Pumpkin Pie Cheesecake, 154–55
      Swirled Raspberry Cheesecake, 149
      Three Cheers for Cherry Cheesecake, 148
      Tropical Chocolate Chip Cheesecake, 160
   Donuts, Boston Cream-Filled, 184–85
   frostings/toppings
      Chocolate Cream Cheese Frosting, 203
      Chocolate Decorative Topping, 212
      Coconut Cream Cheese Frosting, 209
      Coffee Frosting, 206
      Cream Cheese Frosting, 210
      Creamy Peanut Butter Frosting, 206
      Fluffy Mint Frosting, 213
      Fluffy Orange Frosting, 207
      Light Raspberry Frosting, 207
      Maple Cocoa Frosting, 211
      Mega-Coconut Cream Cheese Frosting, 210
      Pumpkin Whipped Topping, 205
      Vanilla Tofu Whipped Topping, 204
      Whipped Cherry Topping, 202
      Whipped Chocolate Frosting, 202
      Whipped Coconut Cream Frosting, 209
      Whipped Cream Cheese Frosting, 212
      Whipped Lemon Frosting, 208
   pies
      Berry Chip Cream Pie, 127
      Black and White Cream Pie, 122
      Chocolate Caramel Boston Cream Pie, 98–99
      Chocolate Peanut Butter Boston Cream Pie, 100
      Chocolate Raspberry Boston Cream Pie, 91
      Clouds of Strawberry Pie, 129
      Hint of Mint Cream Pie, A, 120
      I Love Chocolate Cream Pie, 104
      Island Breezes Cream Pie, 118
      Midnight Monkey Cream Pie, 126
      Monkey's Choice Cream Pie, 123
      Patriotic Cream Pie, 132
      Peanut Butter Boston Cream Pie, 94–95

Peppermint Patty Cream Pie, 119
Piña Colada Cream Pie, 131
Pucker-Up Cream Pie, 128
Strawberry Surprise Cream Pie, 130
Tantalizing Truffle Pie, 142
That's One Nutty Banana!, 124–25
Traditional Boston Cream Pie, 92–93
Triple-Chocolate Boston Cream Pie, 96–97
You Got Your Chocolate in My Peanut Butter
   Cream Pie, 121
   puddings, 168
      Bahama Mama Pudding, 172
      Berry Best Pudding, The, 173
      Chocolate Lover's Pudding, 169
      Creamy Rice Pudding, 174
      Guiltless Pudding, 170
      Orange Chocolate Chip Pudding, 175
      Peanut Butter and No Jelly Pudding, 171
      Strawberry Fields Pudding, 177
      Tangy Lemon Pudding, 176
   tarts
      Fruity Artistry, 136
      I'm Nuts for Peanut Butter Tart, 138–39
      Queen of Tarts, The, 134
      Tangy Tasty Tart, 135
      Taste of the Tropics, A, 137
Tofutti Cream Cheese, 16
toppings
   See also frostings
   Caramel Ice Cream Topping, 215
   Cherry Topping, 201
   Chocolate Decorative Topping, 212
   Chocolate Glaze Topping, 90
   Fudge Ice Cream Topping, 214
   Pumpkin Whipped Topping, 205
   Soy Cream Cheese Glaze, 211
   Vanilla Glaze, 204
   Vanilla Tofu Whipped Topping, 204
   Whipped Cherry Topping, 202
Traditional Boston Cream Pie, 92–93
trans fatty acids, 7
Triple Cherry Treat, 77
Triple-Chocolate Boston Cream Pie, 96–97
Tropical Chocolate Chip Cheesecake, 160
Tropical Fruit Cake, 58
Tropical Mango Cake, 52
TVP (textured vegetable protein)
   Newfangled Mince Pie, 111

U

unsaturated fats, 6

V

Vanilla Glaze, 204
Vanilla Spritz Cookies, 22
Vanilla Tofu Whipped Topping, 204
Vegan Chocolate Syrup, 203
vegans, famous, 18–20
vegetable shortenings, 14

W

walnuts
   State Fair Pear Pie, 113
Washington's Cherry Crumb Pie, 110
Wetzel's Pretzel Pie, 102–3
Whipped Cherry Topping, 202
Whipped Chocolate Frosting, 202
Whipped Coconut Cream Frosting, 209
Whipped Cream Cheese Frosting, 212
Whipped Lemon Frosting, 208

White on White Tropical Cake, 70

X

xantham gum, 5, 10, 14, 16

Y

You Can't Catch Me I'm the Gingerbread . . .. Cake, 53

You Got Your Chocolate in My Peanut Butter Cream Pie, 121

Z

zucchini, 5
    Cherry, Cherry Not Contrary Cake, 38–39
    Nuts about Chocolate Cake, 43